The Unfinished History of European Integration

The Unfinished History of European Integration

Second, Revised Edition

Koen van Zon
Matthew Broad
Aleksandra Komornicka
Paul Reef
Alessandra Schimmel
Jorrit Steehouder

Routledge
Taylor & Francis Group

LONDON AND NEW YORK

Revised edition of *The Unfinished History of European Integration*. Wim van Meurs, Robin de Bruin, Carla Hoetink, Karin van Leeuwen, Carlos Reijnen, Liesbeth van de Grift. Amsterdam University Press, 2018 (ISBN 978 94 6298 814 9); a translation of the original publication *Europa in alle staten. Zestig jaar geschiedenis van de Europese integratie*. Wim van Meurs, Robin de Bruin, Carla Hoetink, Karin van Leeuwen, Carlos Reijnen, Liesbeth van de Grift. Uitgeverij Vantilt, 2013 (ISBN 978 94 6004 126 6).

First published in 2024 by Amsterdam University Press Ltd.

Published 2025 by Routledge
4 Park Square, Milton Park, Abingdon, Oxon OX14 4RN
605 Third Avenue, New York, NY 10158

Routledge is an imprint of the Taylor & Francis Group, an informa business

© The authors / Taylor & Francis Group 2024

ISBN: 9789048566143 (pbk)
ISBN: 9781003707943 (ebk)
NUR 330

Cover design: Mijke Wondergem, Baarn
Maps interior: Bert Heesen

Every effort has been made to obtain permission to use all copyrighted illustrations reproduced in this book. Nonetheless, whosoever believes to have rights to this material is advised to contact the publisher.

For Product Safety Concerns and Information please contact our EU representative:
GPSR@taylorandfrancis.com
Taylor & Francis Verlag GmbH, Kaufingerstraße 24, 80331 München, Germany

Table of Contents

Foreword

Over the past few months, my thoughts have often returned to a now famous speech that French President François Mitterrand delivered to the European Parliament on 17 January 1995. It was the year before his death. Mitterrand appeared fragile, but spoke passionately about the importance of European cooperation and the vital responsibility of his generation. Having witnessed in the 1920s and 1930s how the poison of resentment and revanchism infected the minds of many Europeans, his generation sought to pass on its experience to the next generation. 'Le nationalisme, c'est la guerre', nationalism is war, was the powerful and now very timely slogan for which his speech ultimately became famous.

That day in the European Parliament, Mitterrand pronounced his political testament and made an urgent appeal to his audience: do not forget this continent's past and what it achieved after the First and Second World War on the long, winding path to European integration in all its forms, to an 'ever closer union' – as can also be read about in this handbook. The coming together of different nations based on fundamental freedoms, to prevent them from ever again going as horribly wrong as they did in the previous century, remains a unique feature in Europe's conflict-ridden history.

This central notion has been the driving force behind European integration ever since: we still debate the direction our continent should take, but we do so not on the battlefield but at the conference table, in our national parliaments and in European institutions. We have exchanged naturally recurring conflicts between nation states over power, influence, and territory for a set of values that should provide every European with a solid foundation of peace, security, and prosperity: democracy, human rights, freedom of religion, individualism, albeit always embedded in an idea of solidarity. These values – call it a European spirit – originated on our continent. Just read the work of Erasmus, and you will find all those elements there.

This way of thinking and living characterizes Europe. Everywhere, European societies can be recognized by a combination of (constitutionally codified) freedoms, by democratic decision-making, and the rule of law, functioning to a greater or lesser extent, which serves to protect citizens against arbitrariness and the law of the jungle. Welfare states have been established everywhere to ensure that everyone can count on a reliable safety net in case of illness, misfortune, unemployment, or old age. Each European country differs in this regard, but on no other continent has that combination of achievements, that common roof over our houses as the unsurpassed Václav Havel aptly described it, been as visible as on our European continent in the past seventy years.

With each generation – I feel this more strongly myself now I have grandchildren – the weight of history increasingly compels us to venture to understand it, imbue it with meaning and place it in the context of our own time. All the more so now that the European project finds itself at a crossroads. The invasion of Ukraine by Russia – with the annexation of Crimea in 2014 as its prelude – marks a watershed in recent history and once again puts the question how Europe can guarantee its security at the heart of public debate. It has been a brutal awakening and has made the raison d'être of the Union visible once more, just like it made clear that the responsibility for security on our continent can no longer be left to the Americans. Europe will have to take a leading, autonomous role here.

The history of the European project shows that division on major issues – such as migration, or the enormous challenge that climate change poses – leads to powerlessness and thereby puts the security and stability of member states at risk. The history of the European project also proves that it is an illusion to think that we can manage by ourselves. Even large countries such as Germany and France will hardly ever be able to do so.

Is 'ever closer union' a realistic prospect in our time? I think it is. Provided that the European nation states join forces and do not allow themselves to be paralysed by division, whether fuelled from outside or stirred up from within their own borders. Each generation anew faces the task of resisting the temptation to want to shut itself off from others or to maintain the pretence that it could withdraw from world politics behind literal or figurative walls. The European Union remains a voluntary, institutionally embedded alliance of countries and citizens born out of the desire to build a sustainable basis for peace and security on the ruins of two world wars. That mission still stands strong as ever, and is perhaps even more urgent than it has been for a long time.

Frans Timmermans,
Parliamentary leader of the GroenLinks-PvdA group
Executive Vice-President of the EU Commission, 2019–2023
First Vice-President of the EU Commission, 2014–2019

Acknowledgements

This book has been over a decade in the making. Its origins lie in the decision of colleagues from the Radboud University Nijmegen and the University of Amsterdam to embark on an ambitious project: to write a history of European integration for university students from various academic backgrounds. They found that works on the European Union designed principally for politics students tended to discuss history in only a cursory manner. For their part, they felt that history handbooks ended *in medias res*, usually with the signing of the Treaty of Maastricht. Moreover, the authors wanted to convey to such students that the literature they read in their studies is itself expressive of thinking that has evolved with the history of European integration.

When this book appeared in the Dutch language, published as *Europa in alle Staten* (Nijmegen: Vantilt, 2013), it was the first truly interdisciplinary handbook of European integration with a historical focus. To meet the demand of international European studies programmes, the original was updated and translated into the English language as *The Unfinished History of European Integration* (Amsterdam: Amsterdam University Press, 2018). A German language version followed, titled *Die Unvollendete: Eine Geschichte der Europäische Union* (Bonn: Dietz Verlag, 2018).

In the years since, several other volumes on the history of European integration have emerged. Each in their own way has served to deepen and broaden our understanding of the EU, past and present. They provide much-needed companions for various readerships. It remains the case, however, that relatively few of the volumes out there provide a comprehensive yet concise introduction to EU history to students, be they enrolled in history, political science, law, public administration, or European studies degrees. Scarce are the number of books that introduce students of history to the theory of European integration and, at the same time, students of the contemporary integration process to its history and historical thinking.

True to the English-language title, the original authors decided that much had happened since 2018 – both in Europe's own development and in accompanying scholarship on European integration – to merit revision. They also felt that it was up to a new generation of scholars, each of whom have used the book in their own teaching, to bring the book up to date with the latest insights from European integration scholarship. By handing over the manuscript to this new generation, the original authors made manifest their commitment to academic teaching and the time-honoured tradition where students eventually take over from their teachers. As this new generation, we are deeply indebted to their incredible generosity and grateful of their trust in our ability to do their original project justice. Our inestimable thanks therefore go out to Wim van Meurs, Robin de Bruin, Liesbeth van de Grift, Carla Hoetink, Karin van Leeuwen, and Carlos Reijnen. We can only hope to live up to the standards that they have set.

While paying homage to the original idea of the book – which has lost none of its relevance – this version is a fundamental revision of the English language version. For a start, it brings the story of European integration up to the modern day. It also includes references to new scholarly approaches and discussions that have entered the profession since 2018. Unlike the original book, which bundled the chronological chapters with a discussion of the theory and historiography of the respective period, this version presents a continuous narrative of six chronological chapters. The theory and historiography of European integration are now discussed in standalone chapters.

Over the years and different versions of this book, numerous colleagues have provided their expert comments, written reviews of it, and shared their experiences of teaching it. We thank them for their contributions and the solid basis they have provided for this book. For their very helpful comments on this revised edition, we particularly want to acknowledge Theresa Kuhn, Joris Melman, and Tijs Sikma. We further want to thank Amsterdam University Press – especially Jan-Peter Wissink, Evelien Witte-Van der Veer, Jasmijn Boonacker, and Floor Appelman – for their commitment to this project and their efforts to make this revised edition possible. Thanks, too, to Brian Heffernan for the language editing.

As Frans Timmermans conveys in the foreword to this edition, the big questions that European integration has sparked over the decades feel more prescient and urgent than ever. This latest attempt to understand the unfinished history of European integration therefore feels very timely.

Leiden, Maastricht, Nijmegen, and Utrecht
April 2024

Introduction

Today's European Union (EU) is at a crossroads. On the one hand, the EU can easily be read as a remarkable success story. From its original six members, it has grown into a global force comprising 27 countries and some 450 million Europeans, with an external border that stretches from the Atlantic Ocean to the Baltic and Black Seas. In the process, the EU has emerged as a major promoter of peace and democratization, enlargement having become a key instrument to push for political reforms in, and guarantee the stability of, the countries surrounding it. Yet this influence is not simply restricted to the EU's local neighbourhood. On the contrary, through a complex web of association and cooperation agreements, the EU has become one of the world's primary centres of economic gravity. The sheer size and reach of its internal market mean that the EU now helps to determine standards by which countries trade and cooperate. These standards in fact transcend the realm of trade to include human rights, consumer law, data privacy, and environmental protection – the so-called 'Brussels effect'. Combined with the significance of the euro as a leading reserve currency, this growing economic clout has thus translated into greater strategic influence. The EU's collective voice is heard in a range of important forums such as the United Nations (UN) and international climate conferences. Alongside this, the EU has become one of the single largest global donors of humanitarian aid. And in recent years, it has shown itself to be an ever more critical security actor as well.

At the same time, the EU faces an increasingly complex set of challenges. If anything, Brexit revealed a yearning among some voters to move away from, rather than towards, the EU. The British referendum of 2016 also served as a reminder that questions over the EU's apparent lack of democratic legitimacy have not faded. In fact, political parties sceptical of the EU are now a mainstream feature of national and European politics. Criticism of the pace, range, and depth of cooperation within the EU's existing structures has become widespread. Others go still further and openly question the EU's very existence, calling for completely new and much looser forms of collaboration among sovereign governments. The deteriorating status of democracy and the rule of law in Europe has only complicated this picture. Hungary and Poland stand among those EU countries accused (notably by the European Parliament) of eroding civil rights, weakening judicial independence, and curtailing the independence of the media. If the EU has sometimes struggled to devise an adequate response to this threat, the consequences of this trend have become ever more profound: with the invasion of Ukraine once again bringing war to its doorstep, the EU is surely much less able to stand up for democracy abroad if it is unable to consolidate democracy at home. Internal divisions in other areas also undermine the EU's effectiveness. Matters such as the 2007–2008 financial crisis, the ensuing eurozone crisis, and, more recently, the uptick in migration, have at times exposed a serious lack of cohesion across the bloc. The irony of this is obvious. For at precisely the time when the EU itself is contested more than ever before, the scale and cross-border nature of some of the most pressing questions faced by political leaders – issues such as pandemics, technology, and artificial intelligence, the climate crisis, immigration, terrorism, trade disputes, and geopolitical instability – seem to make the European level the best forum for addressing them.

No one can truly hope to understand today's EU and how we got to this stage in its development without revisiting the past. Our aim as authors is to do precisely that. Over the course of eight chapters – six tracing the chronological evolution of the EU followed by two chapters discussing the theory and historiography of European integration – we provide a wide-ranging account that serves as a companion to newcomers to the topic of the EU: its institutions, politics, and history. At the same time, this book has much to offer those who have a more seasoned interest in the antecedents of contemporary European politics. After all, current debates about its size, shape, and influence serve as a reminder that the EU is not a 'finished' project: its future political, economic, and legal shape are all up in the air. Uncertain though the EU's current situation may seem, this book shows that hope and fear, ambitions and criticisms, have been constant throughout its existence. History to this end serves as an important tool in making sense of this 'unfinished' story. Hindsight, certainly, is the advantage of historians, who can reflect on strategic choices made in the past – including routes not taken – and their unintended consequences. In much the same way, history can signpost how similar issues today might have been dealt with in the past. History can, moreover, unpack previous divergences to better understand contemporary grievances. And, ultimately, a reading of the EU's past helps to capture its true complexity to better appreciate why it and its constituent parts act and behave in the way they do. A survey book of this type can therefore be an important companion for students and scholars of subjects such as political science, law, economics, and international relations.

Four questions

This book identifies four questions that have long been at the heart of European integration. On the face of it, they are deceptively simple and can be summarized in four words: *what, why, who,* and *how*. Yet, how they have been answered throughout history tells us much about the major issues facing the EU at critical moments in its recent and more remote past. The four questions run as a thread throughout this book, a reminder that the core questions of European integration have resurfaced time and again and that most of them have no definitive answer – indeed, they are unfinished. These questions are not mutually exclusive either. Historically, answers to one question have always had implications for others. Ideas of *what* the EU should do have, for instance, inevitably been tied up with questions about its membership – the *who* of European integration – as well as debates over *how* it should function.

What is Europe?

The first question is: what is Europe? This is arguably the broadest of the four questions. It is also one that first requires some conceptual explanation, since the European Union as we know it today was technically only founded as part of the Maastricht Treaty of 1992. But, of course, the EU's history is rooted in several earlier organizations. Formally the EU was born as the European Coal and Steel Community (ECSC) founded in 1952, which as the name suggests was restricted to cooperation in two specific fields. By contrast, the European Economic Community (EEC), which emerged in 1957 alongside the European Atomic Energy Community (Euratom), reflected the wider ambitions of policymakers. But the ECSC did not simply cease to exist; these three legally separate bodies instead formed the European Communities. And even as both 'European Communities' and 'EEC' remained part of official European parlance for a long time afterwards, the Merger Treaty of 1965 consolidated their executives into a single European Commission, with the singular European Community (EC) becoming the name often used to describe the immediate ancestor of today's EU.

This book refers both to the EEC and EC, their use demarcated by the timing of the Merger Treaty. But the reason for including this etymological background serves another purpose. From the very outset of European integration, observers have debated what is colloquially known as 'the nature of the beast' – in other words: what kind of cooperation do European countries want? The different names by which the EU has been referred to over the years helps in part to highlight some of the debates over this point. Are governments striving for a looser community? Are they in search of merely economic cooperation? Or is it something still bigger: a full union? From the interwar years, and especially after the Second World War, advocates of European unity debated various blueprints, ranging from functional cooperation to confederation and federation. The EEC of the 1950s, characteristically, displayed traits of all, but was essentially neither. Ever since, inevitably, much attention has centred on what it *should be*.

At the same time, it is true to say that the EEC/EC/EU has only ever represented one part of a geographically much larger 'Europe'. At its origins, indeed, the EU was a narrow grouping of just six states, half of whom were small by most standards. Conversely, when the Treaty of Rome was signed in 1957, France, Belgium and the Netherlands were also still colonial empires, encompassing territories in Africa, Asia and South America. While historians have argued that the EU's birth was a response to the decline of empire, thus characterizing its formation as the 'management of decline', others have argued that the EU was from the start an imperial project of sorts. Whatever the answer, it is clear that the EU has never been a neatly delineated entity in geographical or cultural terms, and that the question who belonged to it, where its borders lay, and what 'Europe' it represented have always been subject to debate.

Although EU membership had been available to other states from the beginning, formal enlargement only commenced in the 1970s. Each new wave of enlargement brought with it new questions about the EU's political, economic and cultural identity and how far this represents 'Europe' as a whole. The enlargements of the 1980s to include Greece, Spain and Portugal – each once governed by a dictator – established the EU's self-fashioned identity as a promoter of democracy, which it confirmed once more with the 'big bang' enlargement into eastern Europe of 2004–2007 – and might well confirm again in the future. Until 2004, though, the 'Europe' of the EU was distinctly western, northern, and southern – not central or eastern. Enlargement has therefore forced existing EU member states to determine a set of cultural, political, and economic values that together determine what it is to be European. But is Europe really, as is often claimed, a coherent community based on solidarity and shared values and norms? Or is it simply a collection of disparate national interests that are continuously being debated and negotiated? Recently, the issue of democratic backsliding has made this dilemma painfully topical.

Why the EU?

A second, related question is: why the EU? Historically speaking, the EU's immediate forebears – the ECSC, EEC, and the EC – were relatively late additions to Europe's institutional landscape. Moreover, they often replicated the work of other organizations already in existence, such as the United Nations Economic Commission for Europe (UNECE). This not just raises the question *why* the founders of the EU felt its creation was necessary, but also *why* the EU, both historically and today, has often been treated as synonymous with 'Europe'. As it has expanded its sphere of action, the EU has eclipsed, enveloped, or encroached upon the work of other European, and in some cases global, organizations. One example is the Council of Europe, which has seen its importance slowly dwindle as the EU has grown to position itself as a promoter of democracy and human rights – even if the Council of Europe has a significantly larger membership.

This progressive widening and deepening of the EU also begs the question as to why not only national governments ('states') but also non-state actors such as business groups and trade unions have pushed for further and deeper integration in the first place. As much as critics of the EU want to portray it as an insatiable and unstoppable behemoth, it has been the political will of the member states that has either driven integration forward or held it back. The gradual development of new policies, the enlargement process, and the reform of institutions have therefore served national political purposes. Yet as the title of Andrew Moravcsik's influential 1998 book *The Choice for Europe* suggests, understanding European integration is all about understanding its underlying choices and what pressures have shaped them. These pressures never came exclusively from within member states or solely from national governments.

Enquiring into the *why* of the EU is therefore enquiring into what has been driving it. In many ways, the metaphor of the carrot and the stick has been instrumental in this regard. The EU's main carrot has, of course, long been the common or internal market and the economic benefits it has yielded. In fact, the idea of 'integration through market' was to pursue unity through a seemingly technical matter of low politics that would benefit all its participants. Understanding the EU through market integration also helps to understand why the EU's institutional architecture looks like it does and why its decision-making works the way it does. Attempts to move beyond market integration have, as we shall see, often been a bitterly fought battle.

Who made the EU?

Connected to this is the third question: who made the EU? As with many histories, that of the EU is all too often recounted as one of 'great men' such as Jean Monnet, Robert Schuman, and Jacques Delors. In addition to writing out female pioneers of early European integration and the EU specifically – figures including Ursula Hirschmann, Louise Weiss, and Marga Klompé – this narrative is rather simplistic and binary. It pits a benevolent EU against defiant member states and their leaders such as Charles de Gaulle's France in the 1960s and Margaret Thatcher's Britain in the 1980s. Such accounts overlook that such conflicts have always been an inherent part of European integration and that characterizations of progress or setback, winners or losers, do not do justice to the contingent nature of integration and the multitude of perspectives that characterize it.

The question of who makes the EU has also been a constant within its institutions. Members of the European Parliament have for example always had a vested interest in strengthening the representation of citizens – through policies as well as through strengthening its democratic legitimacy. Ironically, the more the EU of the 1980s sought to lay claim to building a 'people's Europe' through European elections, the more vocal critics of European integration and its democratic legitimacy became. Here, again, looms the pitfall of a binary narrative that sets 'European saints' against Eurosceptics. The increasing politicization of both EU politics and the EU itself has seen the EU become a permanently contested subject in national political debates.

This progressive politicization of EU politics also illustrates that as European integration has progressed, it has continued to draw in new groups that have sought to voice their interests. The private interests of corporations and industry have always been well represented in the making of the EU, but this has not necessarily been the case for their counterparts in the labour movement. At the same time, the field has become more crowded. Since the 1970s in particular, new organizations representing public interests such as consumers, the environment, and human rights have established themselves in Brussels and played a role in cultivating new EU policy fields. This diversification of actors involved in EU policymaking allows for a more pluralistic understanding of its past that casts it not just as a project of political elites imposed from above, but also as one shaped from below by a variety of societal actors.

How does the EU function?

The fourth and last question is: how does the EU function? On the face of it, the EU might seem to be the stuff of complex policymaking mechanisms and procedures with daunting names such as trilogues, qualified majority voting, and the Passerelle Clause. By contrast, simplified representations of the functioning of the EU, for instance in organizational charts – including the ones in this book – are inevitably reductive. This is because such a schematic display of institutional relations does not do justice to the complexity, informality, and messiness of decision-making within and between institutions. Such charts are, after all, two-dimensional, and do not show how European governance is layered, involving not just European institutions but authorities at national, regional, and local levels, as well as interaction with other international organizations.

The question of how the EU functions goes to the heart of what the EU does and should do, which has been a source of continuous debate throughout its history. At its core, the making of the common market revolved around so-called negative integration: the progressive removal of barriers to trade. Doing so required little budget and therefore eschewed disputes about funds or their allocation. For a long time, the bulk of the EU's budget was instead dedicated to the Common Agricultural Policy (CAP). With negative integration being the primary instrument in the EU's past, forms of positive integration – industrial policy, cohesion policy, and especially social policy – have typically been less developed. As the EU has enlarged and expanded, it has not just built the world's largest internal market, but has also become a global regulatory and geopolitical power. The Maastricht Treaty acknowledged this with the creation of a foreign and security policy, but that has hardly made the EU into a unitary actor in these fields. Likewise, the question of European defence has been on and off the table ever since the failed initiative for a European Defence Community (EDC) in the early 1950s – of which Emmanuel Macron's vision of a European Political Community is merely the latest illustration.

The EU's long history has also seen the progressive development of a corpus of law that not just prescribes the rules and functioning of the internal market, but also the functioning of its institutions and the rights of its citizens. The European Court of Justice (ECJ) in Luxembourg, through a series of landmark rulings, has gradually expanded its effect and access, to include private individuals. The Court is emblematic, moreover, of the layered nature of European integration, since national courts can refer cases to Luxembourg, and Luxembourg in turn can pass judgement on member states as well as private actors.

Structure of the book

With these four questions as guidance, this book – as already mentioned – encompasses eight chapters. Six of them cover the chronological development of the EU and the broader process of European integration from the interwar period to the present. The final two chapters of the book then delve into the historiography and theory of the EU. These last two chapters connect the historical process of European integration as it unfolded with the ways in which academics have subsequently studied those processes, the aim being to help students and readers navigate the relevant literature and better comprehend our four guiding questions. This book therefore connects not just with historical scholarship, but with other disciplines such as political science, law, public administration, and sociology. For those interested in delving into this scholarship, each of the chapters provide a list for further reading.

As the opening chronological chapter, CHAPTER 1 extends the 'traditional' history of European integration backwards and examines how Europe was conceptualized from the aftermath of the First World War to the launch of the Schuman Plan in 1950. It aims to capture the many idealistic plans and visions for European unity that existed in those early years and to incorporate them into the history of European integration. It shows how visionary ideas for European unity were influenced by international developments such as the devastation of the First World War, the Great Depression, the (path to the) Second World War, and the period of economic reconstruction that followed it. As such, it explains *what* kind of Europe these plans envisaged, as well as *why* European integration took such an explicitly economic turn.

CHAPTER 2 starts with the creation of the ECSC, which marked a momentous turn on the road of European integration, steering it from a broader and European-wide approach towards a 'little western Europe'. It analyses how Europe travelled down this road of predominantly economic integration by highlighting the many ideas and blueprints for European integration that were discussed as part of the creation of, for instance, the OEEC and the Council of Europe. As such, it shows how debates over *what* Europe was and *who* belonged to it gave rise to the first supranational European institutions.

CHAPTER 3 then examines the construction of the EEC/EC between 1958 and 1969. It explores the institutions that were created by the Treaty of Rome and how these institutions went about constructing the Community in practice through the introduction of various common policies. Thereafter, it delves into the series of challenges which the EEC/EC faced in the 1960s, before concluding with a discussion of future plans for the Community proposed at The Hague summit of 1969. In so doing, the chapter explains *how* the EEC/EC emerged against a sometimes inauspicious backdrop and *who* the main actors were in this process.

Continuing this story, CHAPTER 4 examines the period from 1969 to 1986 in the context of the economic crisis, which disrupted the stable era of postwar economic growth. It explores new initiatives, such as plans for the Economic and Monetary Union (EMU) and a common foreign policy, as well as the first two rounds of enlargement, and efforts to democratize the EC. The chapter concludes with a section on the creation of the Single European Act (SEA) signed in 1986. It explains *why* European integration emerged as the most viable solution to the crisis and *who* the key proponents behind it were.

The SEA was the first new Community treaty in nearly 30 years. Its signing in turn ushered in a period of intense treaty making that was to last some two decades. CHAPTER 5 explores this era, starting with the Maastricht Treaty signed in 1992 and ending with the Lisbon Treaty signed in 2007. The European Community – restyled the European Union – changed dramatically between these two dates, as did the world within which it operated. Even before the end of the Cold War, the Maastricht Treaty had been intended as a way of increasing the range of policies discussed at the European level and altering the underlying decision-making structure.

The 'big bang' enlargement of 2004–2007 accelerated these discussions, leading to a sustained debate over how a bigger Union should function and who should make its policies. As the chapter will explain, these debates took place against growing public awareness of, and mounting discontent with, the EU.

As for the last of our chronological contributions, CHAPTER 6 discusses the period from the conclusion of the Lisbon Treaty up to early 2024. During this time, the EU encountered various internal and external crises. The chapter examines how the EU responded to these. The eurozone debt crisis ultimately deepened monetary and economic integration, along with a much strengthened European Central Bank. However, the EU's response of austerity measures and budget constraints exacerbated economic and social disparities between different EU countries and regions, contributing to rising Euroscepticism. Exacerbating this, the so-called migration crisis and Brexit sparked debates about possible European *dis*integration. Particularly after the Russian invasion of Ukraine in 2014, it became evident that a new era of geopolitical tensions had commenced. This raised further questions about *how* the EU should function, particularly in terms of foreign and security policy. In the early 2020s, the COVID-19 pandemic, the climate crisis, and, notably, a further Russian invasion of Ukraine in 2022, placed the EU at a crossroads. These crises prompted the exploration of new directions: strategic autonomy and the development of a geopolitical strategy as well as a shift from austerity to increased economic intervention and stimulus. If anything, the vicissitudes of the most recent past of the EU underscore its unfinished nature.

The final two chapters depart from this chronological structure to discuss instead how scholars have viewed and studied the EU and its history as part of the broader process of European integration. CHAPTER 7 deals with the main theories and theorists of European integration. By placing both in the historical context, it will show how each period has had its own ways of thinking about the EU. The so-called grand theories of European integration that emerged from the 1950s onward were often forward-looking, asking *what* the EEC/EC was, *who* moved it forward, and *why*. In the years since the Maastricht Treaty, theories of European integration have become diversified. They have engaged more with the question *how* the EU system functions and have broadened out the question regarding *who* shapes it, showing that the EU has become an integral part of our economic, legal, and political reality.

Lastly, CHAPTER 8 is devised as a guide to the vast historiography of European integration. First, it reflects on the importance of historical approaches in learning more about the current European Union and in unearthing myths, trials and errors, and breaks and continuities throughout its history. Second, it discusses the classic narratives of European integration history as a starting point for examining contemporary contributions. Third, it looks at recent scholarship, guided by the questions formulated above: *what* is Europe and the EEC/EC/EU, *why* the EEC/EC/EU, and *who* has made the EU.

1919	Establishment of the League of Nations
1923	Richard Coudenhove-Kalergi: Pan-Europa
1924	Dawes Plan
1925	Locarno Treaties
1929	Young Plan
1930	Briand Memorandum
1932	Ouchy Convention
1940	Funk Plan
1941	Ventotene Manifesto
	Signing of Atlantic Charter
1944	Conference of Bretton Woods
1947	Announcement of the Marshall Plan
1948	Creation of the Organization for European Economic Cooperation
	Congress of The Hague, founding of European Movement
1949	Establishment of the Council of Europe
	Creation of North Atlantic Treaty Organization

1.   Many roads to Europe, 1919–1950

On 9 May 1950, French Foreign Minister Robert Schuman outlined a proposal that would lead to the creation of the European Coal and Steel Community (ECSC). Since these early ideas for supranational European integration, more than seven decades have elapsed. Visions of European unity and of European integration, however, date back much further in history, to the 1920s and 1930s – and even before that. The present-day focus on the outcomes of integration and on processes of institution-building, as well as the problems, successes, and failures of European integration, thwarts thorough evaluation of these ideas, practices, and their 'visionary thinkers' at the heart of European cooperation before the founding of the ECSC. Not all these ideas produced equally lasting institutions or mechanisms of cooperation, yet they marked the turns taken on the road towards European integration (or, in many cases, the roads not taken). Such institution-focused accounts of European integration must not allow either the daring or the European idealism of these initial years to be forgotten.

This chapter therefore extends the traditional chronology of European integration backwards and delves into the debates about what Europe should be that were held before the proposal for the ECSC in 1950, as well as the international developments that propelled European cooperation forward. Indeed, European integration, in which national governments subjected themselves to a supranational higher authority as begun with the ECSC, was strongly influenced by the experience of that war and by the pressure of international developments. Striking similarities exist between the proposals of Europe's 'visionary thinkers' during the interwar period and subsequent, post-1945, initiatives for European integration. The combination of economic integration and the promotion of prosperity, on the one hand, and peace in Europe on the other, is but one example. Other recurring elements include the importance of broader western and transatlantic multilateralism, the conviction that European institutions might create a sense of a shared European destiny, as well as the perceived need for European unity to give Europe weight in world politics.

Caution is advisable, however, when evaluating these 'visionary thinkers' of the Europe before that of integration. There is no simple teleological development from nineteenth-century Europe or interwar Europe to post-1945 Europe. Indeed, *many roads* have led from the Europe before 1950 to early European institutions, but not *all roads* did. There were many idealistic plans that never materialized into concrete institutions. However, some of the turns taken in these early years influence European integration up to the present. Ultimately, this chapter grapples with the question 'What is Europe', which occupied the minds of many politicians, intellectuals, and policymakers in the period from 1919 to 1950.

Ideas of unity and cooperation before the Second World War

Talk of cooperation and unity in (part of) Europe during past centuries was seldom based on any grand design. Throughout most of the nineteenth century, European powers achieved stability through a system of conference diplomacy that commenced after the defeat of Napoleon and the subsequent **Congress of Vienna** in 1814–1815. This 'Congress System' worked because there was a clear power hierarchy between bigger and smaller European powers. Occasionally, countries made plans for peaceful, economic integration – literally the fusion of parts into a greater whole. International cooperation and integration occurred along economic lines, for example with postal services (General Postal Union, 1874), river navigation (Central Commission for the Navigation of the Rhine, 1815), and telegraph services (International Telegraph Union, 1864). Building on the absence of war and the new diplomatic system after the Congress of Vienna, the nineteenth century witnessed a steadfast growth of international organizations. For some, they reflected the rise of modern capitalism and new technologies and were meant to promote prosperity. For others, such forms of international organization paved a path towards European political cooperation. No hard and fast dividing line can be drawn between these 'functional' and 'idealist' plans, however.

The 'Congress System' waned towards the end of the nineteenth century and was ultimately pronounced dead with the outbreak of the First World War. After the end of First World War in 1918, the **League of Nations** symbolized the hope for a better world. Established at the initiative of United States President Woodrow Wilson, the League was the first institutionalized form of global organization that was supposed to foster peace among the nations of the world. Through the creation of the League, Wilson advanced a **liberal internationalism** that advocated democracy, self-determination, collective security, and a commitment to capitalism and free trade. These ideals were reflected in the League's tasks, which were to strive for international disarmament, and to prepare former German colonies and Ottoman lands for self-determination through the League's Mandates Section.

The institutional architecture of the League was innovative and provided a blueprint for many later international organizations – most importantly the United Nations (UN) created in 1945. The League was an intergovernmental organization with an Assembly, Council, and a Secretariat. The Assembly was made up of representatives of the member states and convened annually in Geneva. It was responsible for electing the Council and it directed the general course of the organization. The Council functioned as an executive body of the organization and consisted of several permanent and non-permanent members. These permanent members were the winners of the First World War, minus the US and the Soviet Union: France, Italy, the United Kingdom, and Japan.

Lastly, there was the Secretariat, which was made up of civil servants, whose allegiance was to the League rather than to their respective member states. The Secretariat was a crucial part of the organization. Consisting of multiple subsections (such as the Economic and Financial Organization, EFO), it was responsible for administrative work, such as gathering statistics and taking initiatives in proposing innovative solutions to difficult international challenges (for example the shrinkage of world trade). The League Secretariat was an important site for international civil servants to acquaint themselves with the expertise and techniques of modern international organizations. Among them was Jean Monnet, who worked as a Deputy Secretary-General of the League Secretariat, and after the Second World War went on to become one of the 'founding fathers' of the ECSC.

In accordance with its liberal internationalist basis, several other organizations were created under the umbrella of the League. A Permanent Court of International Justice upheld the new rules-based international order and could settle disputes between countries. The International Labour Organization (ILO) concerned itself with safeguarding international labour rights and social policies for workers. Its existence reflected the widespread desire to improve social conditions after four years of bloodshed. International cooperation through the League was thwarted, however, by the draconian conditions for peace that the United Kingdom and France set for Germany. As the main culprit of the war, Germany had to make enormous reparations, imposed in the **Treaty of Versailles.**

The financial and economic burden of these reparations characterized much of the international diplomacy throughout the interwar period and, as we shall see, had important repercussions for the prospects of European unity too. As the famous British economist John Maynard Keynes observed fittingly in his book *The Economic Consequences of the Peace* (1919), the

Versailles Treaty made no provisions for 'the economic rehabilitation of Europe'. Having incurred large debts to the United States, France and the United Kingdom partly relied on reparations paid by Germany to finance their own war debts. France, for example, followed a policy of deficit spending for most of the 1920s by taking out loans, based on the anticipation of forthcoming German reparations. When Germany failed to meet these obligations in 1923, French and Belgian forces occupied the heartland of the German economy: the Ruhr. This situation heightened diplomatic tensions in Europe, brought Franco-German relations to a boiling point, and increased fears of another war.

For some visionary thinkers these prospects of another armed clash were a call to action. The Austro-Japanese count **Richard Nicolaus Coudenhove-Kalergi**, a fervent anti-communist, had initially been an enthusiastic advocate of the League of Nations. Yet he gradually became disappointed in this organization because he thought it suffered from utopian overstretch and did little for his dream of a unified European continent. In response to the sense of crisis in Europe, he published his famous book *Pan-Europa* and founded the **Pan-European Movement** in 1923. In his book, Coudenhove-Kalergi proposed a plan for the political and economic unification of Europe. Protagonists of European unity such as Coudenhove-Kalergi considered the unity of Europe as a second-best option, made necessary because the League of Nations was not functioning well. Coudenhove-Kalergi's plan was based on ideas about peace among the nations of Europe as well as socio-economic peace between capital and labour.

From Coudenhove-Kalergi's point of view, the European tendency towards *Kleinstaaterei* (territorial fragmentation) was at odds with the increased size of the four global power blocs of the future ('Pan-America', the British Empire, the Soviet Union, and the Far East). Compared to the size of these empires, a fragmented Europe could not hold its own, despite its colonies in Africa, South America, and Southeast Asia. The European continent, together with these colonies, would have to form one large economic entity. Coudenhove-Kalergi's ideas for European unity were thus informed by a feeling of European decline and had a strong imperial undertone. The joint European exploitation of the African continent by a merging of the two continents (at the time commonly referred to as 'Eurafrica', and especially present in French discourse) was seen as a means for Europe to maintain its standing in the world. However, for countries relying strongly on economic free trade beyond the European world, the idea of setting up tariff walls around the borders of Pan-Europe was not attractive. The Dutch, for example, had extensive trade relations

with the Dutch East Indies and the extra-European world, especially the
United States. For similar reasons, Coudenhove-Kalergi did not envision
the British Commonwealth as part of a Pan-European world. Clearly, there
were competing visions for a strong continental European organization
on the one hand, and for open trade relations with the rest of the world
on the other.

According to Coudenhove-Kalergi, an integrated and strongly regulated
economy was a constitutive part of Pan-Europe. Its agriculture and industry
would be protected from cheap imported products and ultimately become
self-sufficient. The assumption that larger economic entities would lead
to better coordination of economic production and more mass production
constituted the core of Coudenhove-Kalergi's reasoning. European economic
unity would lead to economic rationalization, increased production, and
lower prices. Consequently, prosperity would grow and spread. European
unity would thus pacify the 'class struggle' between the propertied class
and the workers, and communism would therefore lose its appeal. After all,
poverty was the breeding ground for communism.

Coudenhove-Kalergi's Pan-European Movement attracted many influential followers from all ranks of society. Intellectuals and writers such as
Thomas Mann, Paul Valéry, and Stefan Zweig supported the movement,
as did Salvador de Madariaga (who also headed the Disarmament Section
of the League's Secretariat) and José Ortega y Gasset. The Pan-European
Movement was also successful in gathering supporters among Europe's
political elites. Among its members it counted influential political leaders
such as French Prime Minister Édouard Herriot, French politician Aristide
Briand (who later also supported the Pan-European Movement as a prime
minister) and Czechoslovak President Tomáš Masaryk. Louis Loucheur, a
French industrialist-turned-politician who occupied numerous ministerial
posts in France throughout the 1920s, wholeheartedly supported the Pan-
European ideal because he considered the creation of a European customs
union beneficial to European industries. Support for Coudenhove-Kalergi's
European ideals and for his movement was not universal, but the fact that
there were many supporters across Europe shows the extent to which these
idealistic ideas of European unity permeated the minds of European politicians and policymakers.

Throughout the latter half of the 1920s, such idealism even seemed
to have a chance in the real world, as the economic situation in Europe
improved somewhat. This was partly due to US involvement in European
economic affairs with the so-called **Dawes Plan** in 1924, named after later US
Vice President Charles G. Dawes. Whereas the US pursued a foreign policy

of isolation by not joining the League of Nations in 1919, it was financially and economically deeply entangled with Europe, mostly through the settlement of war debts. Despite its policy of political isolation, the US could not stay entirely aloof from European affairs. After France and Belgium occupied the Ruhr in 1923, the US government sought to formulate a response to both Europe's diplomatic crisis and the staggering rates of inflation in Germany that had thrown many Germans into poverty. The Dawes Plan restructured German reparations (for example by changing the duration of payments) and stabilized the German currency. Most of the necessary funding to back up the Dawes Plan was raised on American capital markets, through Wall Street bonds. German reparations were effectively commercialized through the sale of these bonds to American investors – most of them wealthy businessmen. In doing so, the United States inserted itself as the linchpin into a system of European lending and spending.

The Dawes Plan had a stabilizing influence on Franco-German relations and European economic relations. The latter half of the 1920s witnessed several significant moments of political rapprochement, starting when the Ruhr occupation ended in 1925. Moreover, German Foreign Minister Gustav Stresemann (from 1923 to 1929) and his French counterpart Aristide Briand (from 1925 to 1932) were personally on good terms. Both were inspired by Coudenhove-Kalergi's ideas. The **Locarno Treaties** of 1925 recognized the borders of the Versailles Treaty, which helped normalize relations between Germany and the rest of Europe, after which Germany joined the League of Nations in 1926. It was a momentous event that earned Briand, Stresemann, and the UK's Minister of Foreign Affairs, Austen Chamberlain, the 1926 Nobel Peace Prize. In signing the Kellogg-Briand Pact of 1928, states even agreed to abolish war as an instrument to resolve international conflict. In 1929, the US government launched the so-called Young Plan, after the American radio-entrepreneur, industrialist, and diplomat Owen D. Young, as a follow-up to the Dawes Plan. It was a prolongation of the American position as a stabilizer of European economic (and thus social and political) relations by providing further loans to Germany.

This favourable international atmosphere induced Aristide Briand to issue the so-called **Briand Memorandum** in 1930, which contained a plan for European cooperation within the framework of the League of Nations. Briand envisioned an intergovernmental organization much like the League. Institutions of the cooperation envisioned were a European conference with representatives from the national governments, a permanent political committee as an executive body for the conference, and a secretariat.

Although the plan did mention a common market, peace among the great European powers was Briand's priority. When Briand had first presented his plan to the League's General Assembly a year earlier in September 1929, he could still count on the support of Stresemann. Several weeks later, however, Stresemann unexpectedly died, and with him, enthusiasm for the plan dwindled.

In the absence of Stresemann, Germany read the Briand Memorandum as a French attempt to consolidate its own position of power in Europe. The government of the United Kingdom felt the same way and was more focused on political and economic relations within its empire outside Europe (the British Commonwealth of Nations, adopted first in 1926 and formalized in 1931). Economically speaking, the times became unfavourable for the plan too. After the New York stock market crashed in October 1929, a worldwide financial crisis set in, causing a global turn towards policies of economic protectionism. Closing off trade with one another and implementing tariff walls became common practice. Such measures were aimed at preventing the spread of unemployment and socio-economic instability.

Governments responded to the stock market crash and the Great Depression with new economic doctrines. Keynesianism – named after John Maynard Keynes – challenged free market ideology (or *laissez-faire* economics) and held that the state should assume greater responsibility for the socio-economic wellbeing of its citizens. Free market economics did not produce the kind of socio-economic stability that citizens increasingly desired after the First World War. During the Great Depression this newfound role for the state manifested itself on the one hand by the introduction of tariff walls and export restrictions, commonly referred to as **economic nationalism**, and on the other hand by large-scale infrastructural plans commissioned by the government. The most famous example is US President Franklin D. Roosevelt's New Deal, which boosted general employment levels by commissioning the construction of public works such as railroads, electricity networks, and dams. Fascist Italy and national socialist Germany implemented similar policies. Socialists in Belgium (*Plan de Man*) and the Netherlands (*Plan van de Arbeid*) proposed similar, but less rigorous plans. Overall, these new governmental responsibilities added to a growth of government bureaucracies and the professionalization of the state apparatus. Politicians increasingly depended on a state apparatus with technocratic experts who collected and interpreted economic statistics about imports, exports, levels of employment, trade balances, and currency values.

This global turn towards what was effectively a form of state-led capitalism went hand in hand with policies of economic autarky, which coincidentally only increased unemployment and socio-economic instability, because such policies 'exported' unemployment to other countries. An important lesson of the Great Depression was that protecting domestic socio-economic stability also required new modes of international economic governance. Many of the European policymakers who became influential in postwar Europe were driven by this rationale.

The League of Nations was an important platform where the first steps towards such international collaboration were taken, particularly in the offices of its EFO. To fight the economic crisis, the EFO pursued the reduction of trade barriers on a global level. When this proved difficult to achieve, several European countries tried on a smaller scale. In December 1930, Norway, Sweden, Denmark, the Netherlands, Belgium, and Luxembourg signed the **Oslo Convention**. This rather modest trade agreement stipulated that signatory states could not increase existing import tariffs or unilaterally promulgate new duties without prior consultation. The Oslo countries wanted to set a good example in trade policy for the major European powers. As the United Kingdom and other countries refused to join, their objective shifted to the expansion of trade among members of the convention instead.

In July 1932, three Oslo countries (the Netherlands, Belgium, and Luxembourg) concluded the more ambitious **Ouchy Convention**. Their goal was the gradual reduction of tariffs among the signatories. Existing import duties would not be raised, nor would new ones be introduced. The agreement, intended as the first step towards a customs union in Europe, was open to accession by the Oslo states and other countries on an equal footing. Yet, after the United Kingdom rejected this convention, too, and allowed its imperial trade interests to prevail over continental trade, hopes for liberalizing European trade faded.

Over the course of the 1930s Europe was carved up into multiple trade blocs. In central Europe, for example, there was the *Mitteleuropäischer Wirtschaftstagung* (Central European Economic Conference) set up by Hungarian economist Elemér Hantos, aimed at a more integrated economy in central Europe's former Habsburg lands. One of the motives for creating such economic frameworks and trade blocs had been to seek insulation from the volatile German market, but over the course of the 1930s the economic pull of the German market paralysed these trade blocs. A conflict arose within Hantos' *Wirtschaftstagung* over German inclusion in the bloc (Hantos opposed it). Similarly, cooperation between the Oslo states suffered because its members could not agree on taking a common stance against Germany's growing aggressiveness. In other words: it was hard to align the economic interests of maintaining trade relations with Germany with some of the Oslo states' political desire to sanction Germany.

A major (and ultimately final) attempt to mitigate the effects of the Great Depression and to end the wave of economic nationalism was made in 1933, when the League organized the World Monetary and Economic Conference in London. However, the conference failed early after US President Roosevelt terminated dollar-convertibility for gold, ending the conference's hopes for currency stabilization. It signalled the end of the so-called 'Gold Standard', which had fixed the values of currencies to a fixed amount of gold (representing value and thus stability in international finance). From 1933 onwards, economic nationalism was thus no longer limited to protecting one's own domestic market against products from abroad, but governments now also engaged in currency wars. One by one, governments proceeded to devalue their own currencies vis-à-vis those of their trading partners, which made their own exports cheaper. Some even 'dumped', selling their products onto the markets of their trading partners at rock-bottom prices to ruin the competition. Such 'beggar thy neighbour' policies ultimately exported employment to other countries.

The Oslo and Ouchy Conventions (as well as the wider attempts at bringing down trade barriers) can be seen as attempts to cushion countries' economies against these shocks from the international economy. At the time, the idea that domestic economic stability *and* international free trade could only be achieved through durable (European) economic cooperation took root and was uncontested by most financial experts. Tragically, attempts to transform such ideas into new practices and institutions were short on political capital and suffered from unfavourable economic conditions. Belgian Prime Minister Paul van Zeeland, who was intimately involved in such efforts, concluded in 1938 that 'nobody wanted to commit himself to advance in any direction, before being certain that the path had been taken, or that at any rate it had been mapped out, by several others'. It was precisely this idea, of international economic cooperation, combined with the haunting memory of the economic warfare of the 1930s and its social and economic effects, that drove ideas for economic integration in western Europe during and after the Second World War.

Hitler's New Order and the federalist Europe of the resistance

In the end, plans and initiatives for cooperation and unity in Europe before the Second World War broke down in part because of a lack of political will and unfavourable economic conditions. European cooperation in and of itself had often been a second option, after worldwide cooperation for the sake of peace and free trade through the League of Nations failed. European cooperation was thus always entangled in broader forms of multilateralism. Yet, important turns in the European project had been taken in the interwar period. It was clear that economic cooperation would become a central part of any such scheme, a notion that was only strengthened during the Second World War.

Adolf Hitler's **Nazi Germany** wanted nothing to do with either the League of Nations, or Coudenhove-Kalergi's *Pan-Europa*. According to the Nazis, it was not peoples but governments that created these artificial institutions. They saw Coudenhove-Kalergi's *Pan-Europa* as an overture to cosmopolitanism and global capitalism. By contrast, the Nazis pursued a Europe under German leadership that would be independent of imports from the rest of the world. Despite their objections to *Pan-Europa,* the Nazi leaders championed a European vision of their own. Albert Speer – Nazi Germany's Minister of Armaments and War Production and a key economic figure in Hitler's Third Reich during the Second World War – wanted to create an organization like the later ECSC by integrating the industries of occupied countries, albeit mostly to facilitate the production of arms for the German war effort.

As the dominant power on the European continent, Nazi Germany propagated European economic cooperation in a *Großraumwirtschaft* (bloc economy). On 25 July 1940, Nazi Germany's minister for Economic Affairs Walther Funk presented a financial plan for a multilateral clearing of assets and debts in territories under German rule. When trade between two countries was out of balance, the assets and shortages would no longer be calculated bilaterally but rather multilaterally among all the participating countries. This would downsize the currency restrictions for mutual trade between these countries, which would simplify trade with one another. In Nazi Germany, many farther-reaching plans were considered, such as a customs union with free movement of capital, but these plans were not a priority for the political leadership.

National socialism was primarily geared towards the military conquest of territory for the German *Herrenvolk* (master race) in Poland and (from June 1941 onwards) in the Soviet Union. The national socialist plans for an economic *Großraum* in western and central Europe were a facade for economic exploitation by Nazi Germany. Nevertheless, some institutions in Nazi Germany as well as a few authorities in the occupied territories believed in a new economic Europe under German leadership. Among these 'believers' were many non-Nazis as well. To them, these plans constituted the first step towards economic unification on the European continent. Many hoped that the Hitler regime would be pushed aside by more moderate forces in the German army after the passage of time, so that the fall of the Nazis would not be followed by the collapse of Germany. Such a collapse, in their mind, would open the door to a Soviet invasion of Europe.

Hitler's New Order and the occupation of much of the European continent by Nazi forces constituted a frame of reference for many others in conceptualizing their ideas for European unity. Examples of such circles were the various underground European resistance networks or European policymakers living in exile in London. German continental hegemony compelled the organized **German resistance** against Hitler to develop a vision for Europe. There had to be a plan for the occupied territories once Hitler was pushed aside. Carl Goerdeler, a leading figure in the German resistance, hoped for a unification of the European people against Soviet communism. In 1941, he foresaw a future European league of states under German leadership. Even though he was still thinking of a separate German *Wehrmacht* at that moment, he had become a proponent for creating a European army a year later.

The leaders of the Kreisau Circle, a Christian resistance network, wanted to turn the economic exploitation of the national socialists into economic cooperation in Europe by establishing a European federation that would break the spell of nationalism. In its plans for the future of Europe, the Kreisau Circle developed a blueprint for a European community (with European legislative institutions and a constitution). Much like in the EU many years later, the plan emphasized the principle of subsidiarity: decisions should be taken at the lowest competent administrative level. Furthermore, the Kreisau Circle spoke out in favour of a world organization that would be stronger than the League of Nations. Other networks, such as the Freiburg Circle, also developed plans for the future of Europe. Among the members of this group were influential economists such as Walter Eucken, an economics professor at the University of Freiburg. As the founding father of a new branch of economic liberalism called ordoliberalism, Eucken and the Freiburg Circle laid out their plans for the socio-economic basis of a future Europe. According to ordoliberal principles, the state was to act as an *Ordnungsmacht* (ordering power), by creating an environment in which free market competition was curbed by a state that prevented the abuse of economic power and economic cartels. This would give citizens the freedom and security for self-development and enable them to build meaningful social relations. The ideas advocated by Eucken would later become influential in laying the foundations for the postwar German social market economy.

Beyond Germany, in the ranks of the resistance against national socialism and fascism, a federalist European ideal also developed during the war. A key document in this regard is the **Ventotene Manifesto.** It was written in 1941 by socialists Altiero Spinelli and Ernesto Rossi, who had been imprisoned by the fascist regime of Italy on the secluded island of Ventotene. The manifest was widely shared within the Italian resistance and outlined a socialist federation of Europe, though its interpretation of socialism was by no means dogmatic like in the Soviet Union. The goal of the European federation was mostly to establish peaceful relations on the European continent.

According to the federalist European ideal, which was omnipresent among European resistance networks, the German conquest of the European continent proved that European countries could not defend themselves individually, and that national sovereignty in Europe had become a chimera. They believed that the era of *Kleinstaaterei* was at an end, both militarily and economically. Despite fundamental differences, on such issues as respect for human dignity and democratic values, their federalist ideal had a few similarities with the national socialist idea of Europe. Both for the Nazis and the organized European resistance (including the German resistance), 'Europe' had undertones of a socio-economic 'third way' between the capitalist free-market economy of the United States and the centrally planned economy of the communist Soviet Union.

Similar ideas arose in London, where the European governments-in-exile pondered the creation of regional European groupings. Here too, the idea of federalism was strong, although the policymakers engaged in making plans for after the war often preferred schemes of cooperation in which states retained their sovereignty, instead of subjecting them to some kind of supranational political federation. Some of those present in London, such as the Polish government, were very active in formulating postwar strategies along the lines of (con)federations, motivated by geopolitical ideas of creating a bulwark against future German or Russian aggression. Others, such as governments of the Netherlands, Belgium, and Luxembourg, could not envision such political or military cooperation with countries in central and eastern Europe, and opted for cooperation along more 'functional' economic lines. Between 1943 and 1944, these three countries – also building on the experience of Ouchy – signed agreements for a monetary union and a customs union. This later transpired into the founding of the Benelux.

Neither the exiled governments nor the resistance networks laid out the ideological roadmap for the postwar period, however. In August 1941, US President Roosevelt and Prime Minister Winston Churchill of the United Kingdom signed the **Atlantic Charter.** The Atlantic Charter emphasized the importance of a free and open world economy, international economic cooperation, and the increase of social welfare after the war. Anglo-American financial experts, including Keynes, were already working on new financial institutions designed to promote global currency convertibility and free trade. This culminated in the creation of the World Bank and the International Monetary Fund (IMF) at the **Conference of Bretton Woods** in New Hampshire in 1944. Such global schemes were at odds with the ideas held by the European exiles in London, who hoped for a more gradual approach towards free trade, possibly by limiting themselves to a regional European framework first – though this had to be firmly embedded in transatlantic and global structures such as the IMF. During the war, European cooperation became increasingly entangled in transatlantic and western instances of financial and economic multilateralism – a trend that only continued after the war.

European reconstruction, the Cold War, and the German question

After the cannons in Europe fell silent in May 1945, the emerging Cold War and the German question became important catalysts for the integration of western Europe. At the heart of this German question stood the age-old opposition between France and Germany, and how to re-establish Germany as an independent state in Europe while also preventing a resurgence of German domination on the continent. Also on the agenda were the issues of European economic reconstruction and the ambition to reinvigorate the promise of higher levels of prosperity and of increasing the standard of living, which had been omnipresent after the First World War. European governments wanted to prevent a return to the social and political instability of the interwar period which stemmed from the widespread unemployment and poverty caused by the Great Depression, still fresh in the collective memory. Added to this mix were the ideological, economic, and geopolitical tensions of the Cold War.

At the Yalta Conference in February 1945, Soviet leader Joseph Stalin, Roosevelt, and Churchill met to discuss the contours of postwar Europe. There, and at the Potsdam Conference in July, Europe was divided into eastern and western spheres of influence. Germany was carved up into four zones of occupation. The United States, the Soviet Union, the United Kingdom, and France each governed their own zone under the overarching structure of the Allied Control Council (ACC). However, the four occupying powers had wildly different opinions on how Germany should be governed and to what extent they should aid Germany on her path to economic recovery. This eventually became a bone of contention and not just increased the Cold War antagonisms between the Soviet Union and the United States, but also caused friction between the western allies.

Towards the end of the war there were plans in the United States to de-industrialize Germany as a punishment, encapsulated in the so-called Morgenthau Plan, named after Henry Morgenthau Jr., the US Secretary of the Treasury. Germany, which from the nineteenth century onwards had been the industrial core of Europe, was to be divided and become primarily agricultural. The plan was designed to prevent Germany from ever being able to produce tanks, airplanes and explosives, whereby it could once again become a threat. Such plans, however, quickly proved impracticable, as it turned out that western Europe had much to gain from rebuilding Germany economically. In fact, it was not long after the end of the war that the US abandoned the Morgenthau Plan and replaced it by a policy of aiding German economic reconstruction. In what became known as the *Rede der Hoffnung* (Speech of Hope) in Stuttgart in 1946, Secretary of State James Byrnes marked this restatement of US policy on Germany when he told the German people: 'The American people want to help the German people to win their way back to an honourable place among the free and peace-loving nations of the world.' By contrast, the Soviet Union followed a policy of economic extraction in its zone of occupation, dismantling German industrial equipment and transporting it to the Soviet Union.

Economic integration of the western occupation zones of Germany into a western European framework became a significant objective in the larger aim of European economic reconstruction. This was especially so for countries like the Netherlands, which profited tremendously from exports to the German market. Already in 1946, the Dutch government had undertaken a study that concluded that German economic recovery was indispensable for Dutch economic recovery. France remained wary of German economic reconstruction, because fears of a resurgence of German power loomed large in postwar France. The puzzle for postwar Europe and the crux of the German question was thus to profit economically from rebuilding western Germany without risking a renewed threat from Germany as a dominant economic and political power at the heart of Europe. Integration prevented the creation of a reunited and neutral Germany, which over time might have ended up siding with the Soviet Union.

As the US and countries such as the Netherlands increasingly saw western Germany as a common partner rather than an enemy, the mutual fears between the communist East and the democratic and capitalist West increased, resulting in the Cold War. On 12 March 1947, American President Harry S. Truman gave an historic address to the American Congress, in which he promised aid to all countries that felt threatened by communist expansion. The so-called **Truman Doctrine** was translated into the policy of containment, with the objective of blocking further expansion of communism throughout the world, including western European colonies, where the pursuit of independence was rising markedly.

In addition to geopolitics, the Cold War had a strong economic dimension. The fact that the United States and the Soviet Union wanted to acquire as much worldwide economic influence as possible contributed to the Cold War. Moreover, the West and the East were determined to maximize their economic power as a precondition for military power as well as to demonstrate the superiority of their respective ideologies. The postwar economic order of the western world had already been established at Bretton Woods during the Second World War. From that point on, the currencies of the various participating countries had fixed exchange rates vis-à-vis the American dollar, and the IMF regulated international payments. The dollar was itself convertible to gold and therefore inflation-proof. Simultaneously, based on the principles enshrined in the Atlantic Charter, global trade liberalization was pursued through conventions such as the General Agreement on Tariffs and Trade (GATT) in 1947. The driving force behind such efforts was the United States.

For European countries, however, it was difficult to participate in global free trade and currency convertibility because this involved the opening of their (ravaged) economies to international competition from – among others – the United States, which had come out of the war much stronger. In that sense, postwar European economic reconstruction was not just about increasing the standard of living, combatting unemployment, and preventing Europe from falling prey to communism; it was also about helping Europe to make the transition to the global system of economic governance agreed at Bretton Woods, and thus embedding it in the wider web of western multilateralism.

In the immediate postwar period, the history of the interwar years repeated itself. Western European economies were heavily closed off to one another because of tariff barriers and other protectionist measures that governments put in place after the end of the war. A web of bilateral (instead of multilateral) trade relations emerged in postwar Europe, and this hampered the growth of trade and production (and thus economic recovery). The most urgent foreign trade problem for western Europe was its shortage of hard currency in the form of gold and US dollars (the so-called 'dollar gap'), caused by an increased demand for imports from the United States (food, fuel, fibre, industrial machinery), after Germany was eliminated as a supplier. Initial assistance to Europe had come through the United Nations Relief and Rehabilitation Administration (UNRRA) and stop-gap aid to specific European countries, such as France. Mostly it was the United States that was footing the bill for this. But by 1947, in view of the rising influence of communism in Europe, it was clear that this stop-gap aid was not solving Europe's long-term economic problems, which required it to move beyond the bilateral fabric of its economic relations.

In June 1947, the US Secretary of State George C. Marshall ended the situation of stasis and delivered a famous speech at Harvard University, in which he declared that the US government would assist in European economic reconstruction. However, Europeans themselves had to come up with a plan on how this aid should best be used. In return, the US government insisted on European economic integration, which it saw as a precondition for efficiency in production and, therefore, for rising prosperity. American aid, in that sense, was an act of enlightened self-interest, because a strong, economically integrated Europe would be a durable partner in the Cold War while simultaneously offering American business owners increased opportunities to export to Europe. Over the summer of 1947, European countries crafted a response to Marshall's speech at the **Conference for European Economic Cooperation** (CEEC) by measuring their total request for aid, and seeing how they could cooperate to bring down the dollar gap as much as possible. In April 1948, the US Congress sanctioned the aid package to western Europe. Though the aid was also offered to eastern Europe, Stalin pressured his satellites not to join the economic reconstruction programme, thereby confirming the gap that had grown between East and West since the end of the Second World War.

Officially the plan was called the European Recovery Program, but it was widely known as the **Marshall Plan**. Owing to a sophisticated financial mechanism, no US dollars crossed the Atlantic. Europeans paid for their imports by depositing national currencies into a so-called counterpart account, which was used for national reconstruction. The exporter from the United States was compensated for its exports by the

US government in dollars. The European countries thus repaid their national debts and paid for reconstruction projects with money from the counterpart account.

The occupied territories of western Germany were not represented at the CEEC. At the meeting in Paris in July 1947, the Benelux countries (Belgium, the Netherlands, and Luxembourg) acted in unison for the economic benefit of western Germany. Intense controversy arose between the Benelux countries and France over the inclusion of these German territories in the Marshall Plan. The French took the position that a recovery of German industry constituted a threat to European security, and they preferred to maintain production restrictions for Germany. The Benelux delegation successfully insisted on including Germany in the Marshall Plan, also because their position was closely aligned with that of the US government, which started advocating the economic rehabilitation of Germany from 1946 onwards.

Ultimately, the European conference that crafted a response to Marshall's speech in June 1947 transformed into the most important institution for postwar European economic cooperation. In April 1948, the sixteen European recipients of Marshall Plan funds established the **Organization for European Economic Cooperation** (OEEC). As an intergovernmental organization, it was primarily responsible for administering and dividing Marshall Plan funds. Beginning in the autumn of 1948, for instance, it evaluated proposals for the use of Marshall Plan dollars from the various European countries. Subsequently, the OEEC presented these proposals to the US Congress for approval. The total aid between 1948 and 1952 amounted to more than 12.4 billion US dollars, distributed across sixteen European countries. At the same time, financial support from the United States forced the western European countries to cooperate. Washington saw the OEEC as the primary platform for European economic integration, and State Department officials hoped that the United Kingdom would play a leading role in this process.

An important element in the OEEC's work was the creation of multilateral payments schemes in which currencies could be exchanged more freely within Europe. As one observer at the time noted, the OEEC was in fact the institution that helped Europe 'grow into its Bretton Woods coat', as it facilitated a gradual transition to the global order of currency convertibility agreed at Bretton Woods. The initiative of the OEEC to cancel claims and debts in a multilateral western European payments framework constituted the first step towards the **European Payments Union** (EPU), created in July 1950. The EPU made currencies convertible: no restrictions on currencies applied for reciprocal trade, ensuring that trade was not hampered by deficits or surpluses in the balance of trade between two countries. Crucially, West Germany was included in the EPU, marking the beginning of its economic reintegration into a western European market framework – two years before the ECSC started operating.

The financial and economic integration that gained traction within the OEEC was preceded by action on a smaller scale. This ultimately drew on the ideas for international economic cooperation that had existed in the interwar years. The spirit of cooperation between the Ouchy countries, which had been revitalized during the period of exile in London with the agreements for a Benelux monetary and customs union, led the way. In practice the Benelux did not work too well because of the participating countries' diverging interests. Despite this, the Benelux has often been seen as preparing the way for European economic integration. If not in practice, then at least in spirit, because the Benelux spoke to the imagination of advocates of European unity (American policymakers, for example). As such, it became a framework of reference upon which further initiatives for European integration were grafted.

In sum, after the Second World War ended in 1945, western Europe feared a renewed threat from Germany as well as communism from the East. In the minds of policymakers, the best remedy for communism was more prosperity for their own citizens, but a vibrant West German economy was indispensable to generate this kind of welfare. It was this economic rationale of a politics of productivity that drove the Marshall Plan and the work within the OEEC. Through multilateral intra-European payment schemes, western Europe achieved currency convertibility, after which an increase in intra-European trade and European production quickly followed. With the help of American aid and the creation of the OEEC, western Europe struck a new socio-economic balance not only between labour and capital, but also between the domestic and the international economy. The economic integration of Europe – including West Germany – thus offered a solution to the ills of the 1930s and was driven largely by a deeper quest for socio-economic stability.

Intergovernmental and federalist routes to Europe

The first steps in European integration took off on the back of European economic reconstruction, German economic recovery, and the emerging Cold War. Above all, they harked back to ideas about international economic governance that had emerged in the 1930s. As with the Marshall Plan and the OEEC, this 'functional' economic cooperation among the nation states in western Europe produced remarkable results only three years after the end of the Second World War. Alongside these functional initiatives, European political idealism also emerged, with its two currents of **intergovernmentalism** (or unionism) and **federalism**. In the case of intergovernmentalism, international cooperation between states was based on conferences and compromises between states retaining full sovereignty over all aspects of their policies. Conversely, European federalism pursued a federal European state with a supranational government and parliament. In supranational organizations, national states transferred certain competences to institutions above the nation states. Federalists such as Altiero Spinelli wanted to integrate the European nations through a directly elected constituent assembly. Spinelli was not primarily concerned with the question what competences states would transfer to a supranational authority, but he aspired to a quick political unification through democratic means. Federalists such as Spinelli were critical of functional approaches to European integration because they allowed states to retain sovereignty and did not take away the breeding ground for the kind of nationalism that had been the root cause of two devastating wars. In a federation, the constraining influences of national governments would be avoided. This kind of idealism, fuelled by the many wartime ideas for European unity from resistance movements, witnessed its peak in the years directly following the Second World War.

After the war had ended, resistance movements across Europe were instrumental in founding different federalist movements for European unity. In Italy, Spinelli founded the Movimento Federalista Europeo as early as in 1943. Similar movements were founded in other European countries. In December 1946, the Dutch social democrat Hendrik Brugmans brought the different European federalist movements together in one common organization: the Union of European Federalists (UEF). It was the peak of the postwar federalist movement, which could count on widespread public support. Referendums organized in different municipalities showed overwhelming support for the creation of a federal Europe. This kind of political idealism was not limited to the federalist movement. Former Belgian Prime Minister Paul van Zeeland and Polish diplomat Józef Retinger (who had advocated European unity among the exile governments in London) created the European League for Economic Cooperation (ELEC) in 1946. There were also many direct links with the interwar movements for European unity. For example, Coudenhove-Kalergi was still active in postwar Europe, trying to foster support for a united Europe by bringing together parliamentarians from different European countries in the European Parliamentary Union.

In May 1948, these movements for European unity joined forces in the European Movement (EM) and came together in The Hague at the **Congress of Europe**. Gathered there were prominent people from dozens of European countries, as well as Canada and the US. They came from labour movements, trade unions, churches, youth organizations, intellectual circles, business communities, and politics. Among them were many prominent political leaders, and without doubt the most prominent was Churchill. As Britain's wartime prime minister, Churchill had been an ambivalent advocate of a united Europe. In a famous speech in Zürich in September 1946, he advocated for Franco-German reconciliation as an initial step towards creating a United States of Europe. Yet, in his view, the UK – with its Commonwealth – should initially stay aloof. He opposed supranational structures and certainly did not want the UK to become part of a federal European state.

The foremost question at the Congress of Europe was whether the European countries would be willing to accept the principle of a common authority for common interests. Despite the lip service that political leaders paid to federalism, this pivotal question remained unanswered. While the European Movement was an important trans-European outlet for ideas and helped to pass on the interwar idealism for European unity to the postwar period, it is difficult to ascribe concrete institutional outcomes in terms of European integration to this idealistic movement. The most durable legacy of the Congress was the creation of the **Council of Europe**, an organization that promoted peace through protecting human rights. The international study commission for this Council of Europe, consisting of delegations from the United Kingdom, France, Belgium, the Netherlands, and Luxembourg, tackled the question of whether this future organization should hold supranational authority. Owing to British disapproval, power was placed in the hands of an intergovernmental Committee of Ministers. Additionally, the British kept the parliamentary assembly, set up as counterpart to the Committee of Ministers, from acquiring any real competences. The Council of Europe was established in Strasbourg on 5 May 1949. Initially, ten countries took part: the five countries mentioned above, as well as Italy, Ireland, Norway, Sweden, and Denmark.

The Council of Europe had a Committee of Ministers and a Consultative Assembly. It was in fact the first veritable pan-European assembly, proving that dreams of a democratic assembly of states were no illusion. Initially, some federalists hoped that the Strasbourg assembly would become the nucleus for European political unity, but such hopes evaporated quickly. The Committee of Ministers showed a lack of ambition in terms of further European unification, and the Assembly had no real powers. The Council of Europe was responsible for supervising observance of the **European Convention for the Protection of Human Rights and Fundamental Freedoms** (ECHR), which stipulated the rights of individuals and citizens in the contracting states. The Convention was drawn up in 1950, following the example set by the United Nations' Universal Declaration of Human Rights in 1948. The Council of Europe expanded quickly in terms of member states. From 1959 on, citizens who believed their rights as set forth in the ECHR had been violated, could appeal to the **European Court of Human Rights**, headquartered in Strasbourg.

Functionalist routes to Europe

In the end, the Council of Europe hardly lived up to federalist aspirations. Federalism proved to be an unachievable ideal because nation states opposed relinquishing sovereignty to far-reaching supranational European structures. After the creation of the Council of Europe, states made attempts to integrate Europe by way of the so-called functionalist route. **Functionalism** is about incremental integration, and it is about policies instead of politics. This meant that a form of technocratic administration by experts without a strong political or national allegiance dominated the process of integration, instead of politicians, who were subject to short-sightedness and the whims of the electorate. According to the functionalists, Europe could not be created all at once or by following one single plan. Rather, they sought out a supranational shared destiny in a crucial 'sector', such as heavy industry, agriculture, or the military apparatus. In doing this, they expected that the foundation could be laid for an increasingly closer union of nations. This method was called 'sectoral integration'. In practice, functionalists were just as attached to supranational political institutions as federalists, because such entities would aid in the formation of a European spirit among politicians.

The Frenchman **Jean Monnet** is seen as the driving force behind this functionalist method and is widely regarded as the founding father of postwar European integration. Yet at the end of the Second World War, he was above all concerned with the interests of French industry. As a high-ranking official, he developed a plan for French economic and industrial modernization, the so-called Monnet Plan, which was adopted by the provisional French government under the leadership of Charles de Gaulle. The French government (but not Monnet) wanted to keep West Germany small to prevent it from once again constituting a military threat as well as to provide room for French economic growth. For this development and modernization, France required access to German coal and for that purpose it demanded assurances.

The Saarland, traditionally important for Germany's coal and steel industry, had been under French occupation and administration since 1945. Additionally, France also wanted the Ruhr region (in the British occupation zone) as well as the Rhineland to come under French or international administration. The Americans, however, did not want to detach these territories from Germany, for fear that it would drive the Germans into the hands of Stalin, just as the Treaty of Versailles had driven them into the arms of Hitler. Instead, in 1949, the International Authority for the Ruhr (IAR) was created as a precondition of the western allies for establishing the Federal Republic of Germany (FRG, West Germany) in the western occupation zones. Even before that, the western zones of occupation had been merged in the so-called 'Trizone', and cooperation with the Soviet Union over the future of Germany through the ACC had ended. This IAR – an international entity that in effect controlled the West German economy by way of the Ruhr region – was a thorn in the side of the young West German state.

The French strategy failed, but Monnet had a clear eye for the American desire for European cooperation. At the time, the Americans were increasingly frustrated because of British foot-dragging over the liberalization of intra-European trade and payments within the OEEC. Moreover, the British were obstructing European integration through the OEEC by strongly opposing American plans for a more supranational leadership in the OEEC. Monnet saw an opportunity in the absence of British leadership for European unity. For the sake of French economic interests, he elaborated a plan in which French management of German raw materials was worked into a comprehensive peace plan. Prompted by Monnet, **Robert Schuman**, the French minister for Foreign Affairs, made an appeal for Franco-German reconciliation on 9 May 1950. Only Adenauer had been consulted in making the plan, but other European countries had not.

In his declaration, Schuman argued that France had been championing a united Europe for more than twenty years (ever since the Briand Plan), but that plan had failed because it was launched at an unfavourable moment and because war had broken out once again. Now the age-old opposition between France and Germany was finally set to disappear. The countries were to be brought closer to each other by the creation of a supranational High Authority for coal and steel. It transferred the control of coal and steel production to a supranational body. This entity would hinder dumping and other forms of unfair competition resulting from government protectionism. In 1950, coal still constituted the most important industrial source of energy, and steel was essential for the arms industry. Given the installation of a High Authority for coal and steel, a war between France and West Germany became not only unthinkable, but materially impossible, according to Schuman. Participation was open to all European countries that wanted to join.

The **Schuman Plan** was in essence a peace project, which combined a functionalist approach with supranational elements. Even the day of its declaration – one day after the fifth anniversary of the capitulation of Nazi Germany – recalled that intention. Without joint control and solidarity in coal and steel production, the nations of Europe would be headed for a new war. In addition, Schuman's declaration was a combination of various objectives. It was about bringing about the socio-economic stability and prosperity that had been the goal of European economic reconstruction. Yet it was also permeated with the spirit of European colonialism. Schuman announced that this new European community was also more capable of focusing on what he deemed another essential task: the joint European development of the African continent, which was at that time largely under French administration. Here, the reformist nature of Europe went hand in hand with imperial conservatism.

Other countries joined the nascent community for their own reasons. The Netherlands, for example, was interested in participation with an eye towards a future without its most important overseas territory, Indonesia, which had become independent in 1949. Decolonization obliged the Netherlands to undertake economic reorientation through industrialization, among other things. Because of its recent past, West Germany could not count on much international prestige. For Bonn, participating in the plan was a strategy to regain international stature. On top of that, the United States exerted pressure on West Germany to participate in the project.

Conclusion

A flood of ideas and initiatives for European unity emerged in the aftermath of the First World War and during the Great Depression. Many shared characteristics of economic cooperation and a desire for lasting and durable peace. This peace, according to the lessons of the Great Depression, had to be based on socio-economic stability, which required sound international economic governance that ensured currency stability and free trade, and that would end practices of economic nationalism. During the Second World War, these principles gave rise to a new global architecture of economic governance with the financial multilateralism of the IMF and the World Bank.

Not long after the war the first steps in so-called 'functional' European economic cooperation transpired within the framework of western Europe's postwar economic recovery and the broader field of transatlantic and western financial-economic multilateralism. The German economy was included in this western world through the EPU, and ultimately the ECSC, serving as the linchpin of broader European economic recovery in the context of the Cold War.

Throughout the interwar years, the US occasionally aided in pacifying European relations through the Dawes and Young Plans. After the war, this responsibility became much more apparent with the Marshall Plan, though its reliance on the instrument of economic aid remained the same. The OEEC became the primary platform for European economic integration. In the end, the British blocked American-inspired attempts to make the OEEC into a supranational institution. In their search for reliable European partners, the US government increasingly turned to France. French leadership in Europe emerged with the ECSC, which preferred supranational integration, and was backed strongly by the US government. The ECSC itself would become a blueprint for further European integration, with its sectoral approach and institutional set-up. Nonetheless, it would also inherit the dualism between intergovernmentalism and supranationalism that had characterized the debates on Europe from the 1920s to the late 1940s, and which still carries on in today's EU.

Further reading

- Clavin, Patricia. *Securing the World Economy: The Reinvention of the League of Nations, 1920–1946*. Oxford: Oxford University Press, 2013.
- Fischer, Conan. *A Vision of Europe: Franco-German Relations during the Great Depression, 1929–1932*. Oxford: Oxford University Press, 2017.
- Gillingham, John. *Coal, Steel, and the Rebirth of Europe, 1945–1955: The Germans and French from Ruhr Conflict to Economic Community*. Cambridge: Cambridge University Press, 1991.

- Hansen, Peo, and Stefan Jonsson. *Eurafrica: The Untold History of European Integration and Colonialism*. London: Bloomsbury, 2014.
- Milward, Alan. *The Reconstruction of Western Europe, 1945–51*. London: Methuen & Co., 1984.
- Palm, Trineke. 'Interwar Blueprints of Europe: Emotions, Experience and Expectation.' *Politics and Governance* 6, no. 4 (2018): 135–43.
- Patel, Kiran Klaus. *Project Europe: A History*. Cambridge: Cambridge University Press, 2020.
- Patel, Kiran Klaus. *The New Deal: A Global History*. Princeton: Princeton University Press, 2016.
- Segers, Mathieu. *The Origins of European Integration: The Pre-History of Today's European Union, 1937–1951*. Cambridge: Cambridge University Press, 2023.
- Steehouder, Jorrit. 'In the Name of Social Stability: The European Payments Union.' In *European Integration Outside-In*, edited by Mathieu Segers and Steven Van Hecke, 209–33. Vol. 1 of *The Cambridge History of the European Union*. Cambridge: Cambridge University Press, 2023.

1950
Schuman Declaration
Pleven Plan for a European Defence Community

1951
Signing of the Treaty of Paris for the establishment of the European Coal and Steel Community

1952
Beyen Plan
Plan for European Political Community presented

1954
Creation of the Western European Union
French Parliament rejects Treaty for the European Defence Community

1955
Benelux Memorandum
Conference of Messina
West Germany joins NATO

1956
Spaak Report
Plan for European Free Trade Area

1957
Signing of the Treaties of Rome
European Economic Community and Euratom

2. Europe in the making, 1950–1958

When on 9 May 1950, Robert Schuman proposed to German Chancellor Konrad Adenauer to eliminate the 'age-old opposition of France and Germany' by pooling their coal and steel production, he did not believe that Europe was 'to be made all at once, or according to a single plan'. Rather, he wanted to work towards 'concrete achievements', which could then serve as stepping stones for further integration. As the two major continental European powers, France and Germany were to take a logical first step. 'Europe', as Schuman understood it, was to be created gradually, following sectoral paths and functionalist logic. Gradualism had long been present within the Organization for European Economic Cooperation (OEEC) too, where the idea of economic integration had been institutionalized. Contrary to the OEEC's cumbersome and intergovernmental cooperation, however, Schuman desired a functionalism that would ultimately lead to a fully-fledged European federation. Due to the intergovernmental nature of the OEEC and British unwillingness to go beyond this, the OEEC could not evolve into such a polity. By way of Schuman's declaration, France seized the initiative and assumed a leading role in European integration. Schuman outlined a form of supranational integration in which nations transferred part of their sovereignty to a higher body. The subsequent integration that took shape within the European Coal and Steel Community (ECSC) thus outlined a radically different approach to European integration than the one that European states had pursued up to 1950 through the OEEC.

The creation of the ECSC was a momentous turn on the road of European integration. It marked a departure from a broader and European-wide approach towards a 'little western Europe'. This chapter analyses how Europe travelled down this road of integration over the course of the 1950s, touching upon the questions of *what* Europe is, *why* it came into existence, as well as *how* it functioned. It shows that while the OEEC would ultimately be side-tracked as the main platform for European integration, it did not lose all its relevance, for it remained a site where (rivalling) conceptions of European integration were presented and debated even after the Schuman Plan was launched.

The 1950s were characterized by intense debates over the shape and nature of European integration. How should 'Europe' function and what should it be for? Should it be an intergovernmental economic organization like the OEEC, with its difficulties in reaching agreement, or a smaller and more specialized European unity through the supranational ECSC? This chapter focusses on these rivalling ideas, blueprints, actors, and negotiations that characterized the debates about European integration in the 1950s. Gradually, closer cooperation between a Europe of the Six ultimately led to more market integration and the signing of the Rome Treaties in March 1957, which established the European Economic Community (EEC) that was launched in January 1958.

Creating the European Coal and Steel Community

Initial reactions to Schuman's speech were positive, though the proposal came as a surprise. The Schuman Plan (as it came to be known) had been drafted by Jean Monnet in the utmost secrecy, with only an inner circle of trusted people involved. Building on his extensive American network, Monnet also sought support from Dean Acheson, the US Secretary of State, who wholeheartedly endorsed Monnet's plan. After growing frustration on the part of the US Department of State with the slow pace of European integration through the OEEC, it was ready to support other initiatives to further its policy aims of European economic integration. After Schuman won support for his proposal from the French cabinet in early May 1950, the governments of the United Kingdom, Italy, and the Benelux countries were informed – but only a day before Schuman made his announcement to the world. The West German Chancellor Konrad Adenauer was the only one who had been consulted on the details of the plan. Two days before his speech, Adenauer pledged his support to Schuman, setting the stage for Schuman's speech. Adenauer immediately grasped the political significance of Schuman's plan and saw in this an opportunity for Franco-German reconciliation as well as for *Westbindung*. Adenauer sought to align his country with the democratic states of western Europe and North America by joining international organizations (such as the OEEC) and treaties.

Other reactions to the Schuman Plan varied from lukewarm support to mild criticism and open hostility. Part of the reason Monnet had crafted the plan in secrecy was because he realized that the element of supranationalism and the transfer of national sovereignty to a European organization it entailed was highly sensitive. He did not want this to leak and be discussed in the press before Schuman had made the plan public. After it was out in the world, criticism was most vivid in the communist press across Europe, which mostly lamented the American support for the plan. Communists across Europe had equated American involvement in European economic reconstruction and unification with 'American imperialism' ever since the Marshall Plan. For them, the Schuman Plan was yet further proof of Washington's influence in western Europe and its aim of overthrowing socialism and communism. On the other hand, industrialists and figures from the political right criticized the Schuman Plan because they feared it would limit the freedom of enterprise. The subjugation of the coal and steel industries to a higher authority that could enforce certain production levels was something that they associated with a Soviet-style planned economy and totalitarianism, and they resented this *dirigiste* nature of the Schuman Plan.

Besides these harsh and ideological criticisms driven by the Cold War, there were other concerns too, especially in the Netherlands, which shunned the supranational elements of the plan. Nevertheless, its economic interest in embedding the German economy more firmly into a European framework meant the Dutch had little choice but to become involved in negotiations over the Schuman Plan. Negotiations commenced in Paris in June. As a precondition, Schuman insisted that all parties agreed to the principle of supranationalism. France, West Germany, Italy, Belgium, the Netherlands (reluctantly), and Luxembourg all accepted, but the United Kingdom declined and refrained from joining a continental organization based on the principle of supranationalism. The British effectively withdrew from the process of European integration.

The main bone of contention during the negotiations were the institutional design of the new organization, as well as its competences. The Dutch government was the most critical voice where it came to supranationalism, though it felt that the Schuman Plan was a necessary price to pay for embedding West Germany in a European economic framework. In coordination with their Benelux partners, the Dutch argued that the High Authority should be balanced with an intergovernmental decision-making body in the form of a Council of Ministers. Ultimately, their critique reflected a fear among the smaller European powers of being subjugated to a Europe dominated by France and West Germany. For that matter, the British decision to stay aloof from continental European integration was a bitter disappointment for the Dutch, Belgian, and Luxembourg governments. They had hoped that the United Kingdom, which traditionally acted as a counterweight to France and Germany, would participate in the new organization. On the other hand, Monnet, head of the French delegation during the negotiations, grudgingly agreed to the creation of the Council of Ministers, which thwarted his own hopes for a fully supranational continental organization.

France, West Germany, Italy, Belgium, the Netherlands, and Luxembourg subsequently established the ECSC, the first supranational community, based on a treaty that would be valid for 50 years. This **Treaty of Paris** was signed on 18 April 1951, and after ratification by the national parliaments, it went into effect when the ECSC was established in July 1952. The creation of the ECSC made the existence of the International Authority for the Ruhr (IAR), which had controlled West Germany's coal and steel production up to this point, redundant and it was abolished. The central mission of the ECSC was to ensure the permanent supply of coal and steel, which was important for the reconstruction of Europe after the Second World War. The participating countries saw this as a contribution to the 'workings of peace', as the preamble of the Treaty of Paris stipulated. This can be understood in two ways. First, the ECSC marked the reconciliation of the two European archenemies France and Germany. Second, because it would facilitate a social peace between labour and capital. Postwar European economic recovery had been undergirded by the economic logic of a politics of productivity (CHAPTER 1), which entailed that increased industrial output would take away an important seedbed for the kind of social and political discontent that had fuelled the Second World War.

The institutions which were set up to govern the new organization started operating in August 1952, when the High Authority, the supranational body of the ECSC, met for the first time. The Council of Ministers, the intergovernmental body of the ECSC, met first in September. The approval of this Council was required for important decisions by the High Authority, and it could also give the High Authority guidelines concerning issues that potentially touched upon various national policies. Additionally, the Common Assembly, the parliament of the ECSC, also convened for the first time in September.

The **High Authority** consisted of nine members, to avoid any appearance that members of the High Authority were representatives of their member states. Instead, they were expected to act as supranational European government ministers. The largest member states (France, West Germany, and Italy) each had two representatives, and the three Benelux countries counted one each. Eight of these officials were appointed through negotiations between the member states, after which they appointed the ninth by majority: the president of the High Authority. Members had to swear an oath that they would represent the interests of the Community as a whole and as such give no priority to the interests of their member state. Monnet, adamant on the principle of collegiality, ensured that the High Authority functioned as a

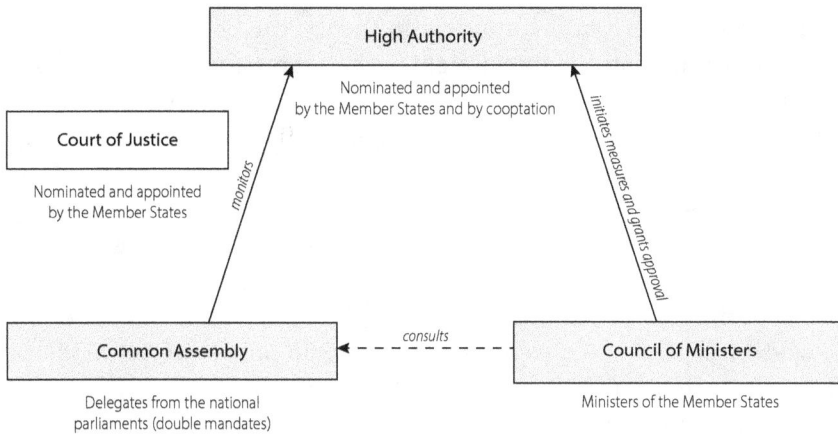

European institutions: Treaty of Paris (1951/1952)

bloc and only took decisions by mutual consent. Initially, the members of the High Authority had a mandate of six years, but this was later reduced to four years.

The primary responsibility of the High Authority was to guard the execution of the Treaty of Paris and to ensure the functioning of the common market for coal and steel. In doing so it had three legal instruments. First, it could provide non-binding advisory *opinions* to member states and to individual parties. Second, it could make *recommendations* that were only binding regarding the objectives, but which left the member states with the freedom on how to implement these objectives. In essence, the High Authority of the ECSC acted in cooperation with the member states and the big coal and steel industries. The third instrument in the High Authority's toolbox was its most powerful. Its so-called *decisions* were binding to all member states and thus had a supranational character. For example, it could act whenever it felt that the objective of maximizing the output of the coal and steel industries was at stake, or whenever shortages of coal and steel emerged. The High Authority had several policy options at its disposal for this: price intervention and production quotas. Another important task of the ECSC was to prevent the concentration of production power and cartelization (in particular, the traditionally strong German coal syndicates had to be broken up). The High Authority thus stood above national governments in areas strongly demarcated by the ECSC Treaty.

At the insistence of the Benelux, the Treaty of Paris also created a **Council of Ministers.** Individual ministers advocated the interests of their member states in the Council. In theory, the Council constituted an intergovernmental counterweight to the supranational High Authority. In this line of reasoning, political and democratic responsibility for decision-making lay with the Council of Ministers. Initially, every state delegated one member of its cabinet to the Council. Except for the very first President (Chancellor Adenauer), these delegates were mostly ministers of Economic Affairs or of Industry and Trade. The presidency was carried out in rotation for a period lasting three months according to the alphabetical order of the participating states. In practice, the powers of the Council were limited, as it could only issue 'opinions' to the High Authority. The supranational character of the ECSC was robust in the areas where it had competence, leaving no room for influencing by the Council. If compared to later stages of European integration, the ECSC was in fact the Community with the strongest supranational element (CHAPTER 3).

A third institutional pillar of the ECSC was the so-called **Common Assembly**, usually called 'the Assembly'. This forerunner to what we now know as the European Parliament would convene annually in Strasbourg, or in extraordinary sessions upon request of the Council. The 78 members of the Assembly were members of the national parliaments delegated by their home parliament. Their simultaneous membership in the national parliament and the Assembly was called the 'double mandate'. The delegates were representatives of the peoples of the member states. The main political families represented in the Assembly were Christian democrats, social democrats, and liberals, though representatives of smaller parties could also be found there. Compared to the national parliaments, the Common Assembly had few legislative powers. However, it did have the power to review the annual report of the High Authority and exercise democratic control, for example by adopting a motion of censure that would depose the High Authority. The Assembly was established primarily at the insistence of the West German delegation led by Walter Hallstein. He considered the Assembly crucial in controlling the High Authority, and also viewed it as the appropriate body to develop a public debate on matters of common European concern.

Besides the High Authority, Council, and Assembly, there was also the **Consultative Committee**, consisting of employers, employees, and businesspeople, the members of which were appointed by the Council. The goal in involving these stakeholders was to create consensus for the policy that was to be executed so that 'social peace' between labour and capital would be maintained. After all, the decisions to pool coal and steel production also entailed a certain level of harmonization in terms of labour policy, and the duty to provide for those who would lose jobs because of shifts in production. Moreover, it was important to involve these stakeholders because labour unions were particularly strong among workers in the coal and steel industries. The power of the Common Assembly was limited, because it could only offer advice upon the request of the High Authority. Finally, there was the **Court of Justice**, to which member states or Community institutions could have recourse for the adjudication of disputes concerning decisions and recommendations of the High Authority. Businesses and organizations could do so too in certain cases. The Court consisted of seven judges and two advocates general.

This institutional set-up was a mere paper reality, however, until the ECSC started operations with the High Authority's inaugural session in August 1952. Its president, Monnet, wanted the High Authority to embody the ideal of European unity. He was therefore a strong advocate for the principle of collegiality, which dictated that the nine members would act as a collective and seek to reach decisions by consensus. It reflected Monnet's belief in the power of deliberation, and in reaching optimal solutions to technical problems in this way. Reality was different, however, as decisions the High Authority took were often political, and required a majority decision through voting. Likewise, Monnet's ideal of the High Authority as a small, non-hierarchical organization soon faded as the Luxembourg-based bureaucracy grew in size. In policy terms, too, the High Authority struggled to deliver on its commitments. By most accounts, it failed to deliver on one of Monnet's principal aims, namely the breaking up of cartels in the steel sector, particularly in the Ruhr. All in all, however, the ECSC did prove successful as a model for supranational decision-making. This hinged not just on the High Authority, but also on the other institutions, including the Common Assembly, despite its humble beginnings. Its members, who started out as delegates from their respective national parliaments, soon came to regard themselves as members of a veritable European Parliament and gradually extended their prerogatives accordingly (CHAPTER 3). Thus, soon after its beginning, the institutions of the ECSC showed a tendency to develop beyond the confines of the treaty.

A failed attempt at a constitution for Europe

Monnet and Schuman's intention had been for the Schuman Plan to evolve into a federal union; the functional community of coal and steel was seen as the trunk upon which other projects of European unity could be grafted. This did not take long. Driven by the successful creation of the ECSC, as well as international pressure from the Cold War, European integration was also pursued in the military and political domain. Ideas for this had already floated since the early 1940s, when Monnet had proposed the creation of an Allied Union between France and the United Kingdom through merging their militaries. This ambitious proposal was launched at a moment when the survival of France was at stake and British troops were trapped at Dunkirk, which seemed to offer a window of opportunity. But this opportunity past after some hesitation on the part of political leaders as well as the defeat of French forces and the German capture of Paris in late June 1940.

In postwar Europe, new pressures arising from the Cold War precipitated a revival of such ideas. Despite the Truman Doctrine (CHAPTER 1) of March 1947, the United States reduced its troop strength in Europe, creating a sense of vulnerability in western Europe. After the communists seized power in Czechoslovakia in February 1948, western European governments feared they would fall prey to a communist takeover from the East. Various western European countries pursued military cooperation, which, they hoped, would also strengthen ties with the United States. This pursuit culminated in the Brussels Pact that France, the United Kingdom, Belgium, the Netherlands and Luxembourg concluded in March 1948. It was formally a military alliance against a possible renewed threat from West Germany. However, it was also created as a western defence against the Soviet Union. A year later, the **North Atlantic Treaty Organization** (NATO) was established, forging a shared military destiny between the United States, Canada, and European countries against the Soviet Union and its eastern bloc of communist states: an attack on one of the countries was viewed as an attack on all of them.

The German question (CHAPTER 1) was not only connected to European economic reconstruction but increasingly also played a role in aspects of European defence. After the establishment of the Federal Republic of Germany (FRG, West Germany) in 1949, the German Democratic Republic (GDR, East Germany) was established in that same year. During the summer of 1950, the outbreak of the Korean War put the question of western rearmament on the policy agenda. The United States wanted to shore up western defence and insisted upon **German rearmament**. A rearmed West Germany would make western Europe less vulnerable to an attack from the Soviet Union.

The potential rearmament of West Germany only five years after the end of the Second World War not only stirred concerns among its European partners, but also created tensions in the young West German state itself. Chancellor Adenauer wanted there to be no doubt that West Germany was tied to the West. This position contrasted with Kurt Schumacher, his socialist political rival, who prioritized a *Wiedervereinigung* (reunification) of Germany. In his view, Adenauer's *Westbindung* thwarted the possibilities of a *Wiedervereinigung*. In 1952, Stalin offered both Germanies the possibility of reunification, provided that this reunited Germany would be neutral in the Cold War. Despite their fierce anti-communism, West German socialists were more susceptible to this offer than Adenauer's Christian democrats. Under Adenauer's leadership, however, West Germany resisted this seductive appeal from Moscow, which was only designed to sow division in the young West German state.

Adenauer's European partners felt no immediate enthusiasm for an autonomous West German army under German commanders and struggled with the issue of German rearmament. Monnet therefore crafted another proposal; yet another plan of his that did not bear his name. In November 1950, French Prime Minister René Pleven announced a plan for a **European Defence Community** (EDC). Through the Pleven Plan, West German troops would become part of a European army, thus expressing reconciliation with the joint pursuit of peace and defence in western Europe. The army would be under orders from a joint European command. Just like the Schuman Plan, it was a proposal for a functional community, which could be set up alongside the ECSC. It would have a similar (and partly shared) institutional structure. Moreover, the reasoning underpinning the plan was very similar to the ECSC: by embedding West Germany firmly into a European supranational institutional structure, both economically and militarily, it was allowed to reclaim its place within the European family of nations, something which Adenauer understood very well.

There were many hurdles to overcome in establishing the EDC. West Germany initially had little influence on the plan and felt degraded as a result, whereas other potential participants were afraid of too much West German power. At first, the US government was not happy about the plan. The US saw it as a French attempt to delay the rearmament of West Germany. Moreover, the Americans preferred to structure this rearmament in the context of NATO. Through his many influential American connections, Monnet lobbied the US government about the need to integrate West Germany into western Europe and convinced it of the plan's value. After Monnet succeeded in this, bringing the US government in on the plan, the EDC Treaty was signed in Paris on 27 May 1952. In accordance with the usual procedures, the EDC awaited ratification by the parliaments of the member states to come into effect. The signing of the EDC Treaty did not complete Europe's institutional architecture, however.

In September 1952, the foreign ministers of the Six met for the first time in the ECSC Council of Ministers. They agreed that political leadership of the EDC should be in the hands of a **European Political Community** (EPC), with a directly elected parliament that controlled a supranational executive branch. After all, creating common European defence structures entailed the transfer of an essential state capacity (the monopoly of violence) to the European level. This required additional institutions that ensured democratic legitimation and control. Thus, the foreign ministers swiftly adopted a resolution that called on the brand-new Assembly of the ECSC to draw up a **European Constitution**. While the ECSC was primarily designed for the management of coal and steel, the importance of its institutions clearly lay also in discussing other ideas for European unity. Suddenly it seemed like a European federal state with a democratic parliament had come within arm's reach. The members of the Assembly of the ECSC constituted a dedicated Ad Hoc Assembly for the occasion, to which a few members of the Consultative Assembly of the Council of Europe were delegated as well. A Constitutional Committee, consisting of 26 members, was formed to draw up the statute of the EPC, which would effectively amount to a European constitution. The results of the Constitutional Committee were discussed in January 1953, after which the draft version of the statutes for the EPC was transferred to the ministers.

West European politicians remained deeply suspicious that the EDC would give the US an excuse to withdraw its troops from Western Europe, which would imply a strong rise in defence costs for Western European countries themselves. The death of Stalin in 1953 and an armistice in the Korean War in the same year inaugurated a moment of thaw in East-West relations. After the Americans ratcheted up their military presence in Europe, the urgency for the EDC dwindled. With it, the plans for the EPC were also shelved, because they hinged on ratification of the EDC Treaty. Ultimately, the EDC was rejected by the French parliament in August 1954, when a majority voted against the Treaty. For European federalists, this rejection was a major disappointment. All other member states had already ratified the Treaty, except for Italy. It signified the definitive end for the EPC and the EDC, and halted European political and military integration for the foreseeable future.

The question of West German rearmament remained unresolved. In 1955, West Germany entered NATO by way of the **Western European Union**

(WEU, a 1954 successor to the Brussels Pact). The countries in the Eastern bloc formed the Warsaw Pact a few days after this accession. As a joint European voice in NATO, the WEU never weighed very heavily, because the participants were afraid that if they acted jointly, they would alienate the United States.

The market as a method of integration

The failure of the EDC and EPC was perceived as the first major crisis of European integration. At the same time, it unlocked opportunities to pursue European integration through new avenues, this time through the market. A preference for economic integration had become increasingly visible over the course of the 1950s. As it turned out, the OEEC remained an important platform for European economic integration throughout the first half of the 1950s. The European Payments Union (EPU, CHAPTER 1), created in September 1950, provided a multilateral clearing house for international payments resulting from intra-European trade. The smooth functioning of international payments was an essential precondition for any kind of economic integration.

Furthermore, building on this newly established clearing house for international payments, the sixteen OEEC members worked towards further trade liberalization. In September 1950, in the shadow of signing the EPU agreement, the OEEC also agreed to a so-called **Code of Liberalization**. This agreement obliged countries to reduce trade restrictions for intra-European trade. It was carried out according to principles that ensured a gradual process, allowing countries initially to shield certain industries from trade liberalization. Between 1950 and 1958, intra-European trade increased more than twofold – a spectacular achievement that can be largely attributed to the successes of the EPU. West Germany profited from this in particular and emerged as an important creditor in intra-European trade, leading to a recovery of its productive capacity and unprecedented economic growth. As such, the work undertaken by the OEEC – which ultimately reflected global developments in the International Monetary Fund (IMF) and the General Agreement on Tariffs and Trade (GATT) – helped build the preconditions for a period of long and stable economic growth in western Europe, commonly referred to as the *trente glorieuses* (glorious thirty), which lasted until the 1970s (CHAPTER 4).

The success of the EPU and the generally favourable atmosphere for European economic integration prompted others within the OEEC to launch initiatives. Averell Harriman, a key American diplomat who oversaw the implementation of the Marshall Plan in Europe, dubbed this phase in European economic relations a 'rebirth of initiative'. This statement not only referred to the many plans for European cooperation launched by the Europeans, but it also alluded to the fact that increasingly European countries were able to do without American economic aid. In July 1950, when it was clear that an agreement on the EPU would be reached, and shortly after the Schuman Plan negotiations had started in Paris, three proposals for further European economic integration saw the light of day. All three outlined a preference for more **market integration**. The first proposal was by the liberal Dutch Minister of Foreign Affairs Dirk Stikker, who had been appointed chairman of the Council of the OEEC. On behalf of the Dutch government, he presented a plan for sectoral integration of the European economies, or put differently, an industry-by-industry approach to trade liberalization. The aim of the so-called Stikker Plan was to increase the production and productivity of European industries. This would lead to economic specialization as well as increased levels of employment.

Stikker anticipated that such industry-by-industry liberalization would prompt industrial adjustments that could lead to a corresponding rise in unemployment. Such negative social effects were to be countered by the creation of a European Integration Fund, backed by credits from the participating countries. The Fund could assist the participating countries in modernizing their industries or provide them with the means for investments in other industrial sectors, so that the overall result of the sectoral integration would not harm the precarious postwar balance between labour and capital. These proposals show how European economic integration had to navigate (and partially incorporate) the political priorities of national welfare states. However, Stikker's proposal for intergovernmental sectoral integration was effectively overtaken by the reality of the supranational Schuman Plan before he even launched it in the OEEC.

A second plan, in conjunction with the Stikker Plan, was by the Italian Christian democrat Minister of the Budget Giuseppe Pella. The Pella Plan proposed creating an intra-European preferential trade zone, which was soon discarded by the other members of the OEEC. A third proposal was by French Minister of Finance Maurice Petsche. The Petsche Plan shared some characteristics with the Stikker Plan, most notably in its proposal for the creation of a European Investment Bank. This Bank would cushion the negative effects of trade liberalization that would inevitably emerge in the shape of rising unemployment. It was also hoped that overall European competitiveness vis-à-vis the rest of the world would increase because of these large (infrastructural) investments. In a way, ideas like those of Stikker and Petsche harked back to Franklin D. Roosevelt's New Deal policies (CHAPTER 1), which had been embraced by many countries during the interwar period to fight off unemployment. This time, however, the ideas had a distinctly European rather than a national scope and they were launched in conjunction with trade liberalization, instead of creating restrictions in international trade.

Market integration is often referred to as negative integration because the focus is on the removal of obstacles to trade, such as tariff walls, import restrictions, or even borders (as with the Schengen Agreement, CHAPTER 5). During the first steps in this process, European policymakers and statesmen realized that negative integration also required forms of what is called positive integration. There was a strong awareness within the OEEC that the abrupt elimination of import restrictions would hit some countries harder than others in terms of increased unemployment due to international competition. A European Investment Bank or a European Integration Fund would help industries in the harder-hit countries to modernize, or to create substitute industries. Above all, positive integration was about safeguarding welfare systems, and softening the blow of international economic competition by increasing Europe's economic resilience.

In the early 1950s, the OEEC thus remained a very vibrant and relevant platform where new ideas for European integration were launched. The choice for this platform was not coincidental, since the ECSC was not yet institutionalized, and the Americans had supported European cooperation through the OEEC with the Marshall Plan since the late 1940s. Moreover, the OEEC was home to the kind of (economic) expertise that was required for developing ideas about further economic integration. In the case of the Dutch government, working through the OEEC also made sense because the Dutch preferred an intergovernmental form of economic cooperation that included the UK rather than supranational integration without the UK. This fell short of American ambitions for European integration, however, since the US backed the supranational integration of the Schuman Plan. Ironically for the Dutch, it was the British government that was most hostile within the OEEC to further European economic integration. It considered the Stikker, Pella, and Petsche proposals to be beyond the scope of the original treaty provisions of the OEEC and therefore blocked them.

Despite these failures, thinking along the lines of sectoral market integration continued – not just within the OEEC, but also in the Council of Europe, especially its Consultative Assembly. Several other proposals emerged, outlining very specific and focused forms of sectoral integration. Like the EDC and the EPC, these were also partly spurred on by the external pressures of the Korean War. The first was the **Green Pool** (CHAPTER 3), which was developed by French Minister of Agriculture Pierre Pflimlin over the summer of 1950. The Korean War caused sharp price increases in agricultural products and a decline of world trade. Pflimlin wanted to improve European agricultural output and proposed to stabilize the prices of European agricultural products. Additionally, this also benefitted the French agricultural sector, which could increase its exports on this broader common market for agriculture. The idea of a Green Pool fitted neatly with plans that had been floated within the OEEC, the Council of Europe, as well as the European Movement to integrate Europe's agricultural market. Pflimlin wanted to open this common market for agriculture to more countries than just the Six. Working together with his Dutch counterpart Sicco Mansholt, Pflimlin further developed the plan and discussed it within the Committee of Ministers of the Council of Europe. In 1952, the British government rejected it because of its supranational architecture, and the British did the same when the idea was relaunched through the OEEC in 1954.

In September 1952, the French Minister of Health and Population Paul Ribeyre aired another ambitious proposal, this time to create a European Public Health Community (the so-called **White Pool**). It aimed at the creation of a European common market between the OEEC members for medicines and medical equipment, while simultaneously harmonizing medical research. The White Pool was discussed between the ECSC members, the United Kingdom, Turkey, and Switzerland, but was vehemently opposed by the medical industry itself, primarily for its supranational nature. In addition to the plans for agriculture, coal and steel, and medical industries, another plan emerged to integrate the European transport sector by creating a **European Transport Community**. First launched by French member of parliament Édouard Bonnefous in August 1950 within the Common Assembly of the Council of Europe, the ideas for a European Transport Community were relayed to a newly established European Conference of Ministers of Transport (ECMT) that was part of the OEEC. The intergovernmental character of this conference, and the opposition of European countries to giving up sovereignty in key industries, ensured this initiative did not produce any permanent institutions.

While some of these 'pools' were intended to incorporate just the member states of the ECSC countries and others possibly also alluded to wider cooperation within the OEEC, they were all perfectly compatible with the ECSC and could coexist alongside it. They fitted neatly within the functionalist principles upon which Monnet had built the ECSC and were exactly what he and Schuman had in mind for European integration: a gradual process that would proceed step by step. The early 1950s thus witnessed a storm of ideas for further European integration. Many of them never materialized into concrete action or institutions, but some of them had successful afterlives. For example, the European Green Pool was important in the creation of the Common Agricultural Policy (CAP), and the Petsche's and Stikker's ideas were ultimately incorporated into the creation of a European Investment Bank (CHAPTER 3). The White Pool had a very long afterlife, resurfacing during the COVID-19 pandemic in the 2020s when the EU initiated joint procedures for the purchase of vaccines and medical equipment during times of extreme scarcity. It is important to capture the spirit of these faded ideas because they are exemplary for the direction that the project of European integration was taking in these years. A strong preference emerged for functional integration, in different sectors of the economy, and towards market integration, and there was also a strong desire to maintain socio-economic stability. Such practices of cooperation relied heavily on technocratic expertise and were sustained by sizeable bureaucracies and institutions, with clear-cut procedures.

Social market Europe?

The period of sustained economic growth and international trade that began in western Europe in the 1940s, emerged as a compromise between two economic doctrines: that of the planned economy and that of economic liberalism. This compromise was also visible in the earliest institutions for European cooperation and integration, such as the OEEC and the ECSC, and it related directly to the international force field of the Cold War. The compromise that is visible in these early European institutions must be situated between two rival (and more radical) economic blocs, both representing the extreme ends of these economic doctrines. On the one hand there was the planned economy of the Soviet Union, and on the other the free trade empire of the United States.

After Stalin barred central and eastern Europe from choosing its own political and economic future through joining the OEEC, ideas to create a cooperative economic framework were floated behind the Iron Curtain too. In January 1949, five states from central and eastern Europe (Poland, Hungary, Czechoslovakia, Bulgaria, and Romania) and the Soviet Union founded the **Council for Mutual Economic Assistance** (CMEA, or Comecon). Essentially, this was the communist response to the creation of the OEEC. Together with the Warsaw Pact – the defensive pact of central and eastern Europe, which was modelled on the institutional structure of NATO – Comecon constituted another Europe, relying on centralized planning and dominated by the Soviet Union.

By contrast, more moderate forms of planning undergirded western economic structures such as the OEEC and the ECSC. Within the OEEC, national governments undertook a collective action of planning for economic reconstruction aided by US financial assistance, and with regard for their national welfare priorities. At the same time, and in parallel to this planned resurrection of the European economy, the OEEC was all about free trade and economic liberalism. This hybrid form between economic liberalism and planning, 'embedded liberalism', adopted to cushion the negative effects of the free market, was characteristic of postwar western European economic recovery. The goal was to soften the social costs of trade liberalization by adopting a gradual approach. Western Europe's embryonic welfare states would suffer too much from international competition rising from fast-track trade liberalization or currency convertibility. In other words, free trade and the principles of the free market should not have a negative impact on socio-economic stability. Stikker's plans for a European Investment Fund, and Pella's European Investment Bank, can be evaluated in this light.

Within the ECSC, this 'embedded liberalism' manifested itself in the goal of preventing cartelization of the coal and steel industries. Market forces could operate freely up to a certain point, at which the High Authority would intervene under conditions prescribed by the ECSC Treaty. This was the case, for example, whenever the aim of maximizing coal and steel production was at stake, or that of improving the 'living and working condition of the labour force in each of the industries under its jurisdiction'. This provision left the High Authority with ample room to act in the field of social policy. It could, for example, finance the retraining of workers in the coal and steel industries who lost their jobs, or seek alternative employment for those whose jobs were threatened. Additionally, the ECSC had an impressive track record in the field of social housing policy. The ECSC helped overcome the lack of housing that prevented adequate recruitment of personnel in the coal and steel industries by issuing loans at low interest rates and developing new building methods.

The general assumption among western Europe's postwar policymaking elite was that social issues (working hours, wages, security of employment) would eventually all be resolved naturally once production was stimulated to the extent that economic growth would pick up – hence the emphasis on increasing production through trade liberalization. The notion of a 'social Europe', with a focus on citizens, was not fully developed in the 1950s and would only become more relevant in the 1970s, when international economic crises put pressure on western Europe's welfare states and the idea that social conflict could be resolved through increased production (CHAPTER 4).

The European relaunch

By around 1954, after the failure of the EDC and EPC, market integration seemed the most viable option for European integration. Considering the failures of political and military integration, many policymakers had lost their appetite for any form of supranational European federation. Frustrated by the political resistance against the creation of a federal European union, Monnet decided to give the process of integration another push. Together with Paul-Henri Spaak, who had taken over from Paul van Zeeland as Belgian minister of Foreign Affairs in 1954, he tried to restart European integration. Early in 1955, Monnet and Spaak worked out a plan to establish a community for atomic energy, then the energy source of the future. It was yet another functional community, like the ECSC. The plan was designed especially to appeal to the French government, which wanted to develop nuclear energy (and ultimately nuclear weapons too) so that it would be less dependent on the US and UK – the only nuclear powers in NATO. Monnet had hoped for support from the West German government, like with the Schuman Plan, but was disappointed. In West Germany, there was now more appetite for a broader type of market integration, instead of the sectoral integration Monnet had pursued with the ECSC. Ludwig Erhard, the German minister of Finance, was an outspoken critic of the 'planned' or 'interventionist' nature of the ECSC. In his view, the market should be allowed to function unrestricted and as free as possible. Social provisions by the state had to be kept to a minimum, for they limited the freedom of the market.

Luckily, ideas for a broader type of market integration were in no short supply. Just over two years prior, at the end of 1952, the Dutch Minister for Foreign Affairs Johan Willem Beyen fashioned what became known as the **Beyen Plan.** In a memorandum which he shared with his European counterparts, the pro-European Beyen argued for the creation of a European common market through a customs union, based on supranational decision-making. It was designed to make economic warfare as had been waged in the 1930s impossible once and for all and signalled a radical overhaul of the previous Dutch European policy of Stikker that had been characterized by an intergovernmental sectoral approach.

According to Beyen, a lax form of economic cooperation based on the intergovernmentalism of the OEEC would not be able to withstand the selfishness of national states, which would try to solve their own economic problems at the expense of their trading partners if necessary. Whereas France, specifically, did not want a customs union on account of the weak competitive strength of its own economy, the Netherlands considered the Beyen Plan to be the most attractive component of the agenda for European integration. Supranationalism was suddenly attractive, if it enabled and served the creation of an integrated common market from which the Dutch economy could profit. Initially, the Dutch government tied the Beyen Plan firmly to the negotiations over the EPC (thus complicating these even further), because it did not want to go along with political integration without any flanking economic initiatives. The creation of a customs union and subsequently a fully developed common market constituted crucial preconditions for the economic survival and modernization of the Netherlands.

However, the timing of the Beyen Plan was not right, because Beyen's European counterparts were not ready for such far-reaching plans. The Beyen Plan was shelved alongside the ideas for the EPC. Yet they did not remain forgotten for long. As soon as June 1955, when Monnet and Spaak were looking to restart European integration, an opportunity presented itself to discuss the plan further at Messina in Italy, where the foreign ministers of the ECSC met to discuss progress in the ECSC. Ahead of the conference, Spaak and Beyen created the so-called **Benelux Memorandum,** which postulated three directions for further European integration. First, it called for the expansion of competences for the High Authority of the ECSC (such as in transportation). Second, it called for the creation of a European community for atomic energy built on supranational principles. This was what Monnet had wanted, but what the West German government had deemed too much of a sectoral approach. Hence the third element of the memorandum: the step-by-step creation of a European common market, based on the Beyen Plan.

The Benelux Memorandum served as input for the assembled ministers for Foreign Affairs of the ECSC member states at the Messina Conference in June 1955. They appointed Spaak to create an intergovernmental committee to investigate the possibilities for the step-by-step creation of a common market. Under Spaak's leadership, this so-called **Spaak Committee** initiated a series of Intergovernmental Conferences between the Six. Initially, the British also took part in these discussions, but they withdrew in October 1955, when it became clear that the talks were aimed at the creation of a customs union. The UK government did not want to go any further than a free trade zone based on the OEEC.

In April 1956, Spaak finished his 'Brussels Report on the General Common Market', leaving no questions about its intentions and recommendations. More commonly known as the **Spaak Report**, it recommended the so-called horizontal integration of the European economy, amounting to the gradual reduction of trade barriers, thus creating a customs union. The Spaak Report suggested creating a separate community for atomic energy. In May, at the Venice Conference, the foreign ministers agreed that the Spaak Report would be the starting point of discussion to prepare for the creation of a European common market. The final phase of negotiations that led to the creation of the European Economic Community (EEC) as well as a European Atomic Energy Community (**Euratom**), started in Brussel with yet another Intergovernmental Conference in June 1956.

During the negotiations that took place in Brussels, the negotiators avoided talks concerning ambitious new supranational objectives. The rejection of the EDC represented a real trauma, and no one dared to endanger these new negotiations in any way. All in all, the negotiations were long and strenuous, marked by sharp differences. The French were interested above all in the community for atomic energy and had to take the customs union as part of the bargain. West Germany and the three Benelux countries wanted to create a common market that leaned more towards economic liberalism, while France and Italy opted for market mechanisms that would allow for more protectionism. France especially questioned whether its agricultural sector was competitive enough to survive in such a European customs union. The French demand for 'social harmonization' in Europe – the accommodation of generous French policy on overtime, leave, and equal pay for women and men – ran into robust German resistance. Moreover, agreeing on the elimination of obstacles to intra-European trade was a painstaking process, touching upon each member state's desire to maintain high levels of employment. Additionally, agreement had to be reached on common external tariffs against trading partners that were not part of the Six. For countries relying also on extra-European trade, this was inherently more difficult than for others.

In the end, external pressures infused the negotiations with a new sense of urgency. International tensions due to the Suez Crisis in November 1956 (when France and the UK recaptured the Suez Canal from Egypt) and the crushing of the Hungarian uprising by Soviet troops in Budapest that same month, increased the willingness to compromise on the part of both Adenauer and the French Prime Minister Guy Mollet. American resistance to the Anglo-French military intervention in Suez convinced France that its interests did not run parallel to those of the United States. It also had an enormous impact on British foreign policy (CHAPTER 3).

The French therefore focused their gaze on the European continent. For West Germany, the Suez Crisis was also an international development that increased its willingness for European integration. West Germany had no confidence in lasting protection from the United States and saw European integration as a safeguard against the communist bloc, which began right at the eastern border of West Germany. In the new harmonious relations between France and West Germany, a new supranational authority was no longer taboo. At the request of the Netherlands and France, earlier ideas about integration in the agricultural sector, such as the Green Pool, were incorporated into the common market. However, much of this was left to be worked out in subsequent negotiations, and the common market that was adopted in the Rome Treaties was essentially an open-ended product.

A controversial issue in the concluding phase of the negotiations concerning the EEC Treaty was the association of **overseas territories**, an affiliation desired by France and Belgium, as it meant their colonies would receive money from a European fund to bring about development in Africa. Other member states were not very enthusiastic about paying for France's colonial ventures, in particular, which had dominated by a complicated and bloody war of decolonization in Algeria. The laborious final negotiations were conducted by government leaders and ministers for Foreign Affairs in February 1957. After an informal bilateral meeting between Mollet and Adenauer, a breakthrough was reached – an example of the Franco-German 'engine' that would continue to fuel the process of integration. In March 1957, the Six signed the Treaties of Rome, establishing both the EEC and Euratom.

The United Kingdom and the Free Trade Area

While momentous steps were being taken in European integration based on Franco-German reconciliation and cooperation, the third great power of western Europe withdrew from the process of European integration. It had initially hoped to accommodate European cooperation as much as possible through the OEEC, strictly based on intergovernmentalism. When the Schuman Plan was launched, this prospect was lost. After the British government pulled out of the negotiations over the Spaak Report in the wake of the Conference of Messina, it was essentially left with two policy options. The first was to stay aloof from continental European integration and let it run its course. The second was the development of an alternative to the Europe of the Six. The British government chose the second option.

The United Kingdom was not alone in its opposition to supranational European integration, nor in developing an alternative. In conjunction with the creation of the OEEC in April 1948, Denmark, Sweden, Norway, and Iceland had set up a Scandinavian Joint Committee for Economic Coopera-tion, which eventually proposed plans for the creation of a Nordic customs union. In January 1950, a joint British-Scandinavian customs union under the name of Uniscan was established. However, this customs union became little more than a talking shop shortly after its formation. Most of the ideas for customs unions between Scandinavian countries, which were discussed in more detail in 1953 and 1954, eventually amounted to nothing because the economic interests of its prospective member states varied widely. Encouraged by the progress in the discussions over a European common market that were ongoing between the Six, the idea for a Nordic common market nevertheless remained on the table. The fundamental difference with the project of the Six was that it relied strictly on intergovernmentalism.

Meanwhile, the British government also explored alternatives to the proposal of a European common market. In July 1956, after pulling out from the negotiations over the Spaak Report, it launched a so-called 'Plan G' for a **Free Trade Area** (FTA) at the Council of Ministers of the OEEC. The idea was to establish a larger free trade zone that included the whole OEEC. The proposal created friction between the United Kingdom and the parties negotiating the EEC. Until the signing of the Treaties of Rome in March 1957, negotiations on the creation of an FTA based on the British plan ran parallel to the negotiations on the EEC and Euratom. After the creation of the EEC and Euratom, membership of both the FTA and the EEC became untenable for the Six. Embodying a common market with a common external tariff, the Six had to take a joint position each time in the OEEC when discussing the FTA proposal. At a stretch, the proposed intergovernmental free trade zone could be seen as a complement to the EEC. Yet many regarded it as a divide-and-conquer tactic by the British to torpedo the EEC customs union – potentially a much more powerful trading bloc than the individual member states separately. The British plan ran into resistance from Adenauer and especially from Charles de Gaulle, who vetoed the FTA in November 1958. The British FTA lived on in the European Free Trade Area (EFTA), created in 1960 when the British were joined by the Nordic countries (CHAPTER 3). EFTA was composed of seven member states (the United Kingdom, Denmark, Norway, Sweden, Portugal, Austria, and Switzerland); there was now a Europe of the Six and a Europe of the Seven.

By 1958, European integration had produced three communities that existed alongside each other and shared a similar institutional layout. The ECSC was joined by Euratom and the EEC, which was to evolve step by step into a customs union. A solution to the problem of a common external tariff was found by allowing for certain differences between countries. The external tariffs (for trade with non-EEC countries) of a trading country like the Netherlands were generally low compared to those of France, which shielded its own economy from foreign competition with import duties. As a trading country, the Netherlands benefited from low common external tariffs and it wanted to head rapidly towards a customs union. As agreed in the EEC Treaty, this customs union subsequently needed to be developed further into a fully-fledged common market with free cross-border movement of goods, as well as services, capital, and labour. The customs union was to be complete by 31 December 1969, allowing for a twelve-year period after the signing of the EEC Treaty. The common market thus remained a work in progress. It was this pressure of a ticking clock that kept the wheels of European integration turning time and again over the course of the next decade (CHAPTER 3).

In terms of institutions, the EEC and Euratom were each dressed up with their own executive bodies, which were comparable to the High Authority of the ECSC. The Assembly was expanded from 78 to 142 members and from that point on also included the two new communities in its parliamentary oversight. While the ECSC Treaty only mentioned the competence to exercise oversight by the Assembly, this competence was expanded in the EEC Treaty and the Euratom Treaty to 'the powers of deliberation and control'. These were explicitly advisory powers, but nevertheless served as an important prelude to the legislative powers that the **European Parliament** would later obtain.

Despite the many similarities between Communities, the EEC and Euratom had a different nature than the ECSC. In the two new Communities, the Council had a much more central role in the decision-making process. From the very beginning it was clear that the member states would promote their national interests, and that they would be supported in this by the Committee of Permanent Representatives to the European Communities, the so-called COREPER (*Comité des représentants permanents*) (CHAPTER 3).

Just like the ECSC, Euratom was a sectoral community, concentrating on a demarcated economic sector. At the end of the 1950s, it had become clear that the primary interest of member states was not in these kinds of communities, but in the much broader EEC. As a result of the growing appetite for more horizontal integration over the course of the 1950s, the sectoral approach was eventually side-tracked. The Commission of the EEC was less supranational than the High Authority of the ECSC because it had less autonomy to intervene in the functioning of the common market. Instead, the EEC required more political cooperation between the member states, which entailed much more intergovernmental bargaining. The High Authority of the ECSC had to adhere strictly to the letter of the Treaty, while the Commission of the EEC could develop its own initiatives and thus expand its power to bring about a political union – even though it was left unresolved as to how the final objective exactly looked. The first president of the EEC Commission, the West German Christian democrat Walter Hallstein, spoke of the EEC as 'the uncompleted federal state' (*der unvollendete Bundesstaat*), thus highlighting his understanding of the new Community as a work in progress.

Conclusion

The period between the launch of the Schuman Plan in 1950 and the signing of the Treaties of Rome in 1957 witnessed intense debate over the scope and shape of European cooperation. Concerning the scope of European cooperation there were numerous proposals and attempts based on a so-called sectoral logic, or industry-by-industry approach. Launched through the OEEC as well as the Council of Europe, and encompassing just the Six member states of the ECSC, as well as wider groupings of states, the sectoral approach, it was hoped, would eventually yield political forms of European integration. However, such forms of political European unity did not transpire and came to an end when the EDC was voted down by the French parliament. Over the course of the 1950s, this sectoral approach gradually lost its appeal, giving way to a more comprehensive type of economic integration: market integration.

This type of integration was not without its risks, as the countries involved quickly realized. It rested on forms of negative integration, such as bringing down trade barriers and reducing other obstacles to intra-European trade. But based on the lessons and experiences of the 1930s (CHAPTER 1), market integration also entailed forms of positive integration in the form of plans to counter the possibly socially destabilizing influences of market integration. For example, in addition to plans for a European Integration Fund or Investment Bank, the ECSC had ambitious housing programmes and focused on occupational retraining.

In addition to the scope of integration, controversy revolved around the shape of cooperation. Should Europe be governed according to supranational or intergovernmental logics? The ECSC was founded on the principles of supranationalism, but these principles met with opposition when it came to key national competences such as defence. After the failure of the EDC, European integration was relaunched as a form of supranational market integration. The United Kingdom decided to stay out of it, offering an alternative to continental 'little western Europe' by creating the EFTA. The first common European institutions reflected these debates and were of mixed design, comprising elements of supranationalism and intergovernmentalism. Tensions between the two, as well as the debate about the scope of European integration, would continue well into the 1960s and 1970s.

Further reading

- Broad, Matthew, and Richard T. Griffiths. *Britain, the Division of Western Europe and the Creation of EFTA, 1955–1963*. Cham: Palgrave Macmillan, 2022.
- Diefendorf, Jeffrey M., Axel Frohn, and Hermann-Josef Rupieper, eds. *American Policy and the Reconstruction of West Germany, 1945–1955*. Cambridge: Cambridge University Press, 1994.
- Eichengreen, Barry. *The European Economy since 1945: Coordinated Capitalism and Beyond*. Cambridge: Cambridge University Press, 2007.
- Gillingham, John. *Coal, Steel, and the Rebirth of Europe, 1945–1955: The Germans and French from Ruhr Conflict to Economic Community*. Cambridge: Cambridge University Press, 1991.

–   Monnet, Jean. *Memoirs*. Garden City, NY: Doubleday & Company, 1978.
–   Ruggie, John G. 'International Regimes, Transactions, and Change: Embedded Liberalism in the Postwar Economic Order.' *International Organization* 36, no. 2 (1982): 379–415.
–   Segers, Mathieu. *The Netherlands and European Integration, 1950 to Present*. Amsterdam: Amsterdam University Press, 2020.
–   Warlouzet, Laurent. 'Competition versus Planning: A Battle that Shaped European Integration.' In *European Integration Inside-Out*, edited by Mathieu Segers and Steven Van Hecke, 234–60. Vol 2 of *The Cambridge History of the European Union*. Cambridge: Cambridge University Press, 2023.

1958	Treaties of Rome enter into force
1960	Establishment of the European Free Trade Area
1961	First membership application of the United Kingdom, Ireland, and Denmark
1962	Membership application of Norway Algeria gains independence from France
1963	Elysée Treaty Yaoundé Convention European Court of Justice Van Gend & Loos ruling
1964	European Court of Justice Costa/ENEL ruling
1965	Merger Treaty Empty Chair Crisis
1966	Luxembourg Compromise
1967	Second membership application of the United Kingdom, Ireland, Denmark, and Norway
1969	Summit of The Hague

3. The Community under construction, 1958–1969

The Treaty of Rome (1957) established the European Economic Community and set out its objectives and institutional framework. It aimed for the realization of a European common market with all its concomitant regulations and conditions, thereby moving beyond the objectives of the European Coal and Steel Community (ECSC). In subsequent years, the institutions of the EEC, the European Commission, the Parliament, and the Court of Justice provided important contributions to the consolidation of this framework. At the same time, the national governments of the member states occasionally expressed hesitation regarding the scope and speed of integration, most notably the French government of Charles de Gaulle. Moreover, the European Economic Community joined an already crowded field of other western European organizations and transnational forums, with which it sometimes overlapped and sometimes competed. The EEC thus had to forge relationships with these other international organizations. And against the background of the Cold War, this broader framework shaped the options for European cooperation. In the period between 1958 and 1969, the European Economic Community was therefore very much under construction.

This chapter examines how the construction of the European Economic Community developed throughout the 1960s. First, it focuses on the European institutions and bureaucracy created by the Treaty of Rome, and how a functioning relationship was established among them in subsequent years. Second, it analyses how the newly established institutions went to work by introducing common policies, in particular the customs union and the Common Agricultural Policy (CAP). Third, it considers the European Economic Community in the wider world: as part of the Atlantic Alliance in the Cold War; as a global trade actor; as embedded in a framework of relationships and associations with (former) colonies of the member states; and as a Community to which other countries sought membership too.

The Treaties of Rome: institutions and bureaucracy

The **Treaty of Rome**, which formed the basis of the newly established European Economic Community, entered into force on 1 January 1958. The ministers of the six member states declared to 'lay the foundations for an ever-closer union among the peoples of Europe' – a cautious reference to the ultimate political goal pursued by Jean Monnet and his followers. In more concrete terms, the EEC Treaty was supposed to further 'a harmonious development of economic activities within the entire Community, a continuous and balanced expansion, an increased stability' and the 'accelerated raising of the standard of living'. The pursuit of prosperity not only served the economic interests of the member states; its objective was the realization of peace and stability as well. Many in western Europe feared that poverty made the population vulnerable to communist propaganda. Against the backdrop of the Cold War, the joint western European pursuit of increased prosperity also served to keep the balance of power in place between the Western capitalist bloc and the Eastern European communist bloc.

The EEC Treaty was quickly seen as *the* Treaty of Rome, whereas a second treaty was also signed in Rome in March 1957. This second treaty established the European Atomic Energy Community, better known as **Euratom**. This new community too was intended to bring more prosperity. As a cheap source of energy, nuclear technology was still seen in the 1950s as one of the greatest promises for the future. It was also an area where energy and security converged: the military power of the atom had already been recognized, in particular in the context of the Cold War. Euratom was supposed to stimulate the nuclear power industry by turning the supply of raw materials and the sales market into a joint task. Monnet – one of the biggest advocates of the atomic community – hoped that this new joint source of energy would encourage the industries involved to increase cooperation step by step, as had also been intended for the ECSC. However, as a result of the quickly increasing supply of cheap oil from the Middle East, it was not atomic energy but oil that became the most important replacement for the dwindling production of coal. Partly because of this, Euratom would play a much smaller role in the integration of Europe than was initially expected.

The Treaties of Rome established the European Economic Community and Euratom alongside the ECSC. They also set out ambitious goals for economic and social integration, which were to be carried out by four core **institutions**: the Council of Ministers, the European Commission, the European Parliamentary Assembly (named the European Parliament from 1962 onwards), and the Court of Justice. The precise functioning of these institutions, however, was yet to be figured out. Although the Treaty of Rome set out a blueprint, in practice, the institutional structure of the EEC that was established from 1958 onwards was often more a reflection of negotiations and compromise between member states and Community bodies than a grand overarching plan.

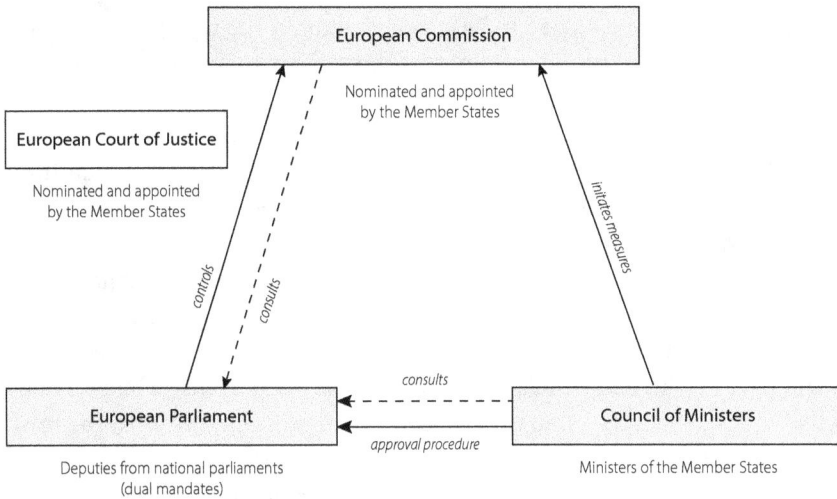

European Institutions: Treaties of Rome (1957/1958)

The Council of the European Economic Community, commonly referred to as the **Council of Ministers**, was the Community's main decision-making body. It consisted of different ministers of the member states, depending on the subject matter under negotiation, and met at least once a month in Brussels. The presidency of the Council rotated among the member states every six months. The Treaty of Rome stipulated that the Council of Ministers was the only body that was able to make laws ('regulations' in European terminology) that applied directly and generally in the member states (that is, without further intervention from the national legislature). Additionally, the determination of rules ('directives') that were to be adopted by member states into their own national legislation was reserved for this Council of Ministers. In addition, only the Council of Ministers acquired the competence to indicate new areas of collaboration. In this way, the member states wanted to ensure that any such step forward could only be made with the approval of all member states.

Initially, the Council of Ministers had to take all decisions unanimously: each member state had a veto on every decision during the phase in which the foundations for European cooperation were being established. The Treaty, however, provided for the increased use of qualified majority voting from January 1966 onwards, which gradually gave the Council of Ministers a different character. The qualified majority requirement included a weighted vote for each of the six member states. On the one hand, the six member states were 'equal' as sovereign states but, on the other hand, West Germany represented many more European citizens than Luxembourg, and that difference also had to be accounted for in the intergovernmental decision-making process. To ensure that the smaller countries were not able to outvote the larger ones, West Germany, France, and Italy each received four votes, the Netherlands and Belgium two each, and Luxembourg one vote. Twelve of the seventeen weighted votes were required for a qualified majority, which means that in certain cases the consent of at least four member states was required.

The Council of Ministers also established a permanent representation in Brussels, or rather, six such representations. On account of the ministers' domestic commitments, the Council could only convene a few times a year. To prepare for these meetings as well as possible, each minister had officials who – under the leadership of a Permanent Representative with the rank of ambassador – resided in Brussels continuously, followed developments in the Commission closely and consulted with officials from the Commission and with one another about new proposals. Above all, these mutual consultations among officials of the six member states proved to be of great importance as a kind of pre-consultation for the meetings of the Council of Ministers. In practice, the majority of the negotiations concerning new regulations and directives took place in this Committee of Permanent Representatives (Comité des représentants permanents, or COREPER). The ministers then only had to express their approval during the meeting of the Council of Ministers. Very soon, the permanent representations developed into mini-bureaucracies, following the various specializations of the Council of Ministers.

The **European Commission** consisted of nine members who represented the interests of the Community. As such, the Commission constituted the supranational component in the Community structure, in contrast to the Council of Ministers' intergovernmental disposition. The members of the Commission were appointed in mutual consultation: the three larger member states (France, West Germany, Italy) appointed two commissioners each for a period of four years; the smaller member states (Belgium, the Netherlands, Luxembourg) one commissioner each. These commissioners were to act independently of their national interests, in order to further the general interest of the Community. The Commission operated based on collective responsibility: all commissioners were equal in the decision-making process, and the Commission was collectively accountable to the European Parliament.

The Commission's most important competency was its 'right of initiative': the power to propose regulations and directives to the Council of Ministers and the Parliament. The idea was that by granting the Commission this prerogative, the EEC's laws and policies would be based more on the general interest of the Community and its citizens, at least more than would result from initiatives of the individual member state governments. Strengthened with this power of initiative, the European Commission was in its early days often considered the driving force behind the Community. The Commission's second most important role was that of 'guardian of the Treaty', tasked with ensuring both the provisions of the Treaty and the decisions taken on the basis of the Treaty. To that end, the Commission had the power to take 'decisions' on its own. These included binding legal acts dealing with specific cases, as well as advisory 'opinions' and 'recommendations'. Finally, the Commission was tasked with ensuring that both the member states and the Community institutions properly applied the arrangements in the Treaty concerning the customs union and the common market. The latter responsibility was shared with the Court of Justice, where both the Commission and member states could appeal in the case of a violation of these arrangements.

The **European Parliament** was one of the oldest common institutions and originated in the Common Assembly of the ECSC. The Treaty of Rome still referred to it as the European Parliamentary Assembly, but in 1962 its members voted to harmonize the name to 'European Parliament', a statement which reflected the institution's political aspirations. It consisted of 142 members who were elected by and from the national parliaments. Having a 'double mandate', they sat in both their national parliament and the European Parliament. To emphasize their Europeanness, Members of the European Parliament (MEPs) grouped themselves by political ideology rather than nationality. Although the Treaty of Rome already expressed the wish that the Parliament should be elected directly by European citizens, prolonged discussions on how to realize this in practice, coupled with resistance from the Council of Ministers, meant that the first direct elections of the European Parliament only took place in 1979 (CHAPTER 4).

The EP's most important task was the democratic monitoring of the activities of the European Commission. On the basis of the Treaty, the EP was only obliged to convene once a year, to discuss the Commission's annual report. In practice, it met more often, and established many parliamentary committees to aid it in its activities. As a consequence, the European Parliament quickly was in session almost permanently. In addition, the European Parliament was required to produce an advisory opinion regarding new legislation that was to be prepared jointly by the Commission and the Council of Ministers. Increasingly, the European Parliament was issuing opinions on *all* new legislative proposals, and also put forward proposals relating to policy areas in which the EEC was not yet active. In doing so, the EP gradually expanded its scope. Despite its limited formal competences as stipulated in the Treaty, the EP was thus able to gain informal power and influence, and to carve out an agenda-setting role for itself beyond its advisory role.

The European Parliament shared its advisory function with the **European Economic and Social Committee** (EESC). This body consisted of 'representatives from all sectors of economic and social life', such as labour unions and employer organizations. Using its expertise, the 101 appointed members of the European Economic and Social Committee were to assist the Council of Ministers in the usually technical problems that had to be settled in relation to regulations. As with the European Parliament, many subcommittees were formed rather quickly in the process, such as those for agriculture and the transport sector.

The **Court of Justice**, lastly, similarly had a longer institutional history, as it was created as part of the ECSC. In the European Economic Community, it consisted of nine judges who were appointed by the governments of the member states for a period of six years. The Court of Justice was tasked with ensuring observance of the law in the interpretation and application of the EEC Treaty. In doing so, it judged cases concerning the legality of Community acts; actions by the Commission against a member state or among member states; or cases brought by individuals or companies.

It would be another year after the Treaties of Rome were signed in 1957 for the new institutions to be set up, mostly because the question as to where they were to be established was still unresolved. Luxembourg and Strasbourg were logical contenders, as the ECSC was based in Luxembourg and the Council of Europe in Strasbourg. Brussels was an option as well: the EEC Treaty was, for the most part, prepared in Brussels (under the leadership of Paul-Henri Spaak). As many member states wished to host the new organizations, they ultimately decided on a compromise whereby the European institutions were spread across three cities. Luxembourg retained the offices of the ECSC, as well as the Court of Justice shared by the ECSC, EEC, and Euratom. In Strasbourg, the European Parliament was to make use of the plenary chamber for the Parliamentary Assembly of the Council of Europe. The EP's offices, however, were located in Luxembourg, but its committee meetings took place in Brussels. The European Commission and the Council of Ministers were to be headquartered in Brussels.

In 1965, this convoluted institutional arrangement was somewhat adapted by the signing of the Treaty of Brussels, commonly known as the **Merger Treaty**. This treaty joined the existing ECSC, Euratom, and EEC into one entity to be set up in 1967: the European Communities (EC). The institutions of the various Communities were merged: the Councils of Ministers of the ECSC, the EEC, and Euratom were combined into one Council of Ministers. The High Authority of the ECSC, the Commission of the EEC, and the Commission of Euratom were subsumed into one Commission of the European Communities. In view of the fact that the Parliament and the Court had been joint institutions from the beginning, their merger was an obvious one. Additionally, this treaty combined the budgets of the three Communities.

The institutional beginnings of the Community were thus rather haphazard. In terms of personnel, the staffing of the old and new European institutions saw a lot of horse-trading, in which positions were exchanged and negotiated among the member states. Since Belgium had received the new European 'capital', West Germany received the honour of providing the first president of the Commission: Walter Hallstein, who had worked with the German Chancellor Konrad Adenauer for a long time. Other member states were allowed to designate the president of the Court or an additional judge. In addition, the young Community brought in a number of veterans of other international organizations. Like the ECSC in the 1950s, the EEC was embedded in a web of international organizations with a network of key actors. Paul-Henri Spaak, for instance, had served as president of the first United Nations General Assembly, before becoming president of the ECSC's Parliamentary Assembly and one of the main architects of the EEC Treaty. The Frenchman Robert Marjolin previously served as secretary-general of the OEEC, and from 1958 became one of France's commissioners. Partly by drawing on these transnational networks of experienced technocrats, the Six ultimately succeeded in having the Community ready to start in January 1958.

Getting to work: the introduction of common policies

As the work of the Community commenced in January 1958, expectations of the EEC Treaty were high. Its objective, to promote a 'harmonious development of economic activities, a continuous and balanced expansion, an increase in stability, an accelerated raising of the standard of living' throughout the Community, was to be realized through the creation of a common market. In concrete terms, the EEC Treaty first of all contained an ambitious roadmap for the establishment of a **customs union**, which was to create a homogeneous economic area vis-à-vis the outside world. Over a transitional period of twelve years, the member states were to gradually abolish border taxes and/or tariffs that were hampering trade with one another. Quotas that fixed the maximum quantities of goods to be traded were to be lifted at the same time. On top of that, national legislation on trade with countries outside the EEC was also to be coordinated, step by step, until a fully-fledged common external tariff would apply.

The formation of a customs union was already a major step, but for the Community, it was only the basis for the eventual formation of a **common market**. Besides a prohibition on internal tariffs and quotas and a common external tariff, the EEC treaty also stated that 'obstacles to the free movement of persons, services and capital' were to be abolished. To achieve this, the EEC Treaty required the harmonization of national legislation ranging from matters such as product standards to the establishment of new businesses. Under the heading of 'the right of establishment', for example, the Treaty prohibited the introduction of new restrictions on the establishment of nationals and companies from another member state and proposed that the existing restrictions on establishment should be gradually phased out during a transitional period. Additionally, and more specifically, it prescribed the outlines of common policies in sensitive areas such as agriculture, transport, and competition.

However, during the Treaty negotiations, the member states had become aware that the new Community-wide competition would not be beneficial in all regards. Whereas on the one hand competition would make sure that products would become cheaper for European consumers, on the other hand free competition could have disadvantageous effects for antiquated companies and structurally weak regions. In order to support the modernization of companies as well as employment opportunities in these regions, the EEC Treaty also provided for a **common social and economic policy**. For instance, the European Social Fund (ESF) was to gather financial resources for retraining employees who would lose their jobs as a consequence of this competitive pressure. However, the ESF lacked financial strength, and the general process in the field of common social policies remained insubstantial. In addition, a European Investment Bank (EIB) was established, which was supposed to extend inexpensive loans for furthering development in regions that lagged behind or for modernizing antiquated companies. Reducing differences in levels of prosperity and development within the EEC was seen as an important condition for further integration.

Important steps also had been taken elsewhere to strengthen the supranational nature of the EEC. In 1963 and 1964, the European Court of Justice put itself on the map with two spectacular rulings. The first followed from a case that the Dutch transport company **Van Gend & Loos** had brought against the Dutch government, on account of the increase in the import tariff on chemical products that the company transported. According to Van Gend & Loos, this increase breached Article 12 of the EEC Treaty, which prohibited member states from introducing new import and export duties, or levies having equivalent effect. The central question in this case, however, was whether a company was allowed to make an appeal directly on the basis of a Treaty provision. International treaties, after all, were arrangements between states, on the basis of which citizens or companies could not lodge appeals. The Court of Justice nonetheless found in its judgement that the EEC Treaty, in provisions such as Article 12, could in fact have direct effect, and therefore could be invoked by citizens and companies. This became known as the principle of direct effect. With this interpretation of the Treaty, the Court went beyond what the member states had foreseen in 1957, thus severely limiting the scope for national policymaking in the areas concerned.

A year later, the Court went a step further in the case of **Costa/ENEL**. On the occasion of a case brought by the lawyer Flaminio Costa against the Italian government regarding the nationalization of the electricity company ENEL, the Court ruled that EEC law also took precedence over subsequent national legislation. Costa believed that the nationalization of the electricity company went against several stipulations of the EEC Treaty. The Italian government argued that a conflict of this sort did not exist because the nationalization law was of a later date than the EEC Treaty and was therefore based on a new decree of the sovereign national legislature. The Court judged in this matter that subsequent national laws were not allowed to contravene the EEC Treaty. It thus established the supremacy of European law over national law, which had immense significance for European integration. Through these and later rulings, the Court of Justice was able to position itself as an authoritative supranational institution, interpreting the treaties as the de facto constitution of the Community. Its role was frequently decisive in expanding the powers and competences of the Community (CHAPTER 4 and 5). European law thus became one of the Community's strongest instruments in furthering integration.

The second main area in which the EEC Treaty stipulated the creation of a common policy was in the field of **agriculture**, which was considered a vital issue as the Treaty of Rome created an agricultural market of 200 million consumers. In the immediate postwar years, food security and the modernization of agriculture became a political priority throughout western Europe. Furthermore, the agricultural sector still employed a major part of the workforce. However, there were massive differences between national, even regional, agricultural structures in western Europe, in terms of size, product type, level of modernization, and government intervention. The formation of a common agricultural policy thus required the reconciliation of national disparities in agricultural systems; different ideas as to how agriculture should be organized within the European economy and on the desired extent of liberalization; and the position and income of farmers, who were increasingly regarded as a socio-economic minority in decline.

Prior to the signing of the EEC Treaty, attempts had already been made to organize agricultural cooperation (CHAPTER 2). France in particular had pursued agricultural cooperation in the early 1950s, hoping to ensure a permanent market for its agricultural products at fixed prices. Such pricing regulations were intended to provide income security to the relatively insecure agricultural sector, which remained a major economic sector in France. The French proposal was to set up a **Green Pool** in the framework of the OEEC, but this plan eventually failed, as no agreement could be reached on the nature of the proposed supranational body. Nevertheless, the experience gained from these discussions proved useful in subsequent negotiations on the agricultural policy in the Treaty of Rome.

The Treaty of Rome assigned five objectives to the **Common Agricultural Policy** (CAP): to increase agricultural productivity; to ensure a fair standard of living for the agricultural community; to stabilize markets; to assure the availability of agricultural supplies in the Six; and to ensure that supplies reached consumers at reasonable prices. What the Treaty did not provide for was the method to be used to implement these objectives. The Commissioner for Agriculture, **Sicco Mansholt**, who had already been involved in the negotiations over the EEC Treaty as the Dutch minister of Agriculture, was tasked with drafting the details of the CAP. Mansholt began his work with an exploratory conference in 1958, to which he invited representatives from national agricultural organizations, agricultural ministers, civil servants, and other experts. Meetings which lasted for days led not only to the first agricultural policy proposals, but also to the establishment of the Comité des Organizations Professionelles Agricoles (COPA, the Committee of Professional Agricultural Organizations). In 1962, COPA merged with the European umbrella organization of agricultural cooperatives COGECA. Headquartered in Brussels, COPA-COGECA developed into the strongest interest group for European farmers and became an important partner in dialogue with the European Commission. Prolonged rounds of negotiations with both farmers' interest groups as well as governments of the member states wishing to safeguard their own national agricultural interests became characteristic of the creation and subsequent development of the Common Agricultural Policy.

Broadly speaking, the CAP continued the policy of regulating and sub-
sidizing that was already being conducted by national governments in the
member states. Community subsidies took the form of **price supports**, and
farmers received a price for their products guaranteed by the Community, so
that their incomes were not dependent on fluctuations in the global market.
During the 1960s, the fixing of these common prices was the most important
point of discussion. The price of grain in particular, which was to constitute
the starting point for the prices of other agricultural goods, formed a major
hurdle because of major price differences among the member states. The
nationally guaranteed grain prices were traditionally much lower in France
than those in West Germany. The West German agricultural organizations
blocked several proposals, until the West German farmers received promises
from the European Commission and the government in Bonn in 1964 that
a transitional period would apply to the West German agricultural sector.

Eventually, the common market in agricultural products entered into
effect in 1967. Common pricing applied to grain, sugar, milk, beef, pork
and several kinds of fruit and vegetable. In many ways, the CAP met the
expectations of a supranational community perfectly. First of all, the CAP
instigated cooperation in all manner of other areas. This was the 'spillover
effect' that Monnet and his followers had hoped for, as the common pricing of agricultural products more or less required that coordination and
cooperation also took place in the monetary area. Second, the CAP gave
the Commission the possibility of playing a leading role in shaping the
process of integration, with the CAP as the central mechanism for instituting
new political and administrative structures in the Community. Its sheer
size reflected this: in the mid-1960s, the Common Agricultural Policy accounted for 95% of the Community budget, 90% of legislation, and 70% of
ministers' meeting time. Third, the European agricultural lobby quickly
grew into a model for other interest groups aiming to organize themselves
at the European level, and to enter into dialogue as social partners with
the European Commission. Examples of this are the umbrella group of the
business organization UNICE (Union des Confédérations de l'Industrie et des
Employeurs d'Europe, Union of Industrial and Employers' Confederations
of Europe), the European consumer group BEUC (Bureau Européen des
Unions de Consommateurs, European Bureau of Consumers' Unions), and
the European Trade Union Confederation (ETUC).

At the same time, the Common Agricultural Policy also had **negative
consequences** from the very beginning. The system of guaranteed prices
not only incentivized production, but increasingly caused *overproduction*.
As a consequence, it did not take long before the first signs of agricultural

surpluses – the notorious 'butter mountains' and 'milk lakes' – appeared. This led not only to artificially high food prices for European consumers but was also considered wasteful and environmentally damaging. The impact of the CAP on the Global South increasingly came into view too: the protectionist character of the CAP made it difficult for products from the Global South to access the European market, and the European food surpluses stood in stark contrast to food shortages and hunger elsewhere in the world. Furthermore, maintaining the system of subsidies required substantial funds: almost the entirety of the Community's overall budget was being spent on the agricultural policy. Famers' incomes, however, remained low, causing widespread discontent among European famers. Attempts to reform the CAP were consistently opposed by the agricultural organizations, which in several instances resulted in large demonstrations. The paradox here is that farmers benefitted greatly from the CAP but were also more dissatisfied with the policy (and with the Community in general) than many other groups.

In 1968, the Commission proposed a radical overhaul of the CAP in the so-called **Mansholt Plan**, also known as the '1980 Agriculture Programme'. Mansholt saw that the European agricultural sector was for the most part still characterized by small and not very profitable family businesses. He furthermore predicted a substantial reduction of the agricultural population by 1980, and the subsequent transformation of smaller family farms into large-scale agricultural enterprises. With the Mansholt Plan, the Commission set out its proposals for the long-term reform and modernization of the agricultural sector to advance productivity and self-sufficiency among European farmers. The plan immediately prompted widespread outrage among farmers and the famers' organizations, resulting in a massive and violent demonstration on the streets of Brussels in March 1971. Under further pressure of the agricultural organizations, Mansholt was forced to limit the scope of his proposals, and the Mansholt Plan was eventually reduced to only three not very radical directives.

Despite the problems of the CAP, the development of the Community in the 1960s gave many reasons for optimism. The customs union provided for in 1957 was set up very rapidly. It was completed in 1968, eighteen months ahead of the schedule foreseen in the EEC Treaty. At the same time, almost all economies in northwest Europe experienced unprecedented growth figures, while unemployment fell to a minimum. The exact effect of Community cooperation on these growth figures is difficult to determine, as many countries that were not part of the Community also experienced significant economic growth. Therefore, the economic boom in Community member states cannot solely be explained in terms of the integration process. However, the stabilizing effect of the Community's economic policies and activities in terms of social peace was highly influential in boosting the legitimacy of the integration project.

The Community in the world: decolonization, challenges, and compromises

The European Economic Community was a European project, but it was also strongly embedded in the wider world. First, it was part of a North Atlantic region that was increasingly defined in terms of the ideological opposition between the superpowers, against the background of the Cold War. Second, the colonial pasts (and presents) of its member states had greatly influenced the integration process in its early stages. In the era of decolonization, the EEC was thus faced with the challenge of dealing with the subsequent political and economic implications of this, and to negotiate future relationships with third states. Third, the 1960s also saw an expansion of European cooperation in the form of association treaties and applications for membership. The development of the European Economic Community in the 1960s thus also played out on the world stage, and was strongly structured by its external relations in the context of the Cold War.

The **colonial dimension** was a key element of early visions of European integration, as feelings of European decline had informed ideas for European unity with a strong imperial undertone (CHAPTER 1). When the Treaty of Rome was signed in 1957, France and Belgium were still colonial powers, and even Italy retained part of Africa, through the UN trusteeship of its former colony Somaliland, which remained under Italian administration until 1960. The Treaty of Rome subsequently also took into account the special relations between the Six and their (former) colonies. Before 1957 these had often had favourable trade agreements with their (former) mother countries, which would be broken by the EEC Treaty. In order to continue these relations as much as possible, the EEC Treaty stipulated the possibility of a five-year association with the EEC. This association meant that the same conditions would apply to trade with these countries that applied to trade among the six member states. In addition, the Treaty declared developmental aid to these associated countries to be a common Community matter. To coordinate this aid, a European Development Fund (EDF) was created.

The five-year association expired in 1963, and many of the countries concerned had in the meantime gained independence. The EEC thereupon concluded the **Yaoundé Convention** with eighteen African countries, which renewed the arrangements concerning the establishment of a free trade zone between them and the EEC, and developmental aid funding from the EDF. In 1969, this agreement was renewed for another five years: Yaoundé II. The association agreements were not uncontested, both in the countries concerned and within the Community itself. Critical voices lamented the lack of influence of the African states themselves, the evident power imbalance between the EEC and the associated states, and the prevalence of European economic interests. The contrast between the Yaoundé arrangements and the EEC association treaties with its NATO allies was also significant. The EEC concluded association treaties with Greece (1961) and Turkey (1963), setting forth the intention to form a customs union in the long term. This was clearly oriented towards far-reaching cooperation and possible accession, whereas the Yaoundé countries were denied the accession perspective, but were associated through development aid. The Yaoundé arrangements were revised in the **Lomé Convention** (1975). Lomé was extended to a large number of states in Africa, the Caribbean and the Pacific Ocean (the 'ACP states'), mostly former British, French, Belgian, and Dutch colonies. The Lomé Convention was renegotiated and renewed three times: in 1979 (Lomé II); 1984 (Lomé III); and 1989 (Lomé IV).

In the meantime, membership of the EEC had changed with the often-overlooked departure of **Algeria** in 1962, the first time a member state left the EEC. Algeria was still part of France's colonial empire when the Treaty of Rome was signed in 1957. The Treaty also treated Algeria as part of the EEC itself, and not as an associated territory. After fighting a bloody war of independence since 1954, Algeria declared its independence from France in 1962. The actual disentanglement of Algeria from the EEC, however, proved a lengthy affair, made all the more difficult by the inclusion of Algeria in the Treaty of Rome. The six member states also held differing opinions as to what the future status of Algeria in relation to the EEC should be, complicated by ongoing economic and labour ties. Only in 1976 did the Community and Algeria agree on a bilateral cooperation agreement.

The EEC also took part in worldwide negotiations on free trade. The General Agreement on Tariffs and Trade (**GATT**) was signed by 23 countries in Geneva on 30 October 1947, with the aim to lower customs tariffs. As such, these were the first large-scale multilateral customs negotiations in history. Between 1947 and 1995, the agreement was updated in a series of renegotiations, or *rounds*, until its role was largely adopted by the World Trade Organization (WTO). The GATT emerged from the United States' determination to maximize western economic power through the global liberalization of trade. Under

President Kennedy, the US was attempting to achieve worldwide free trade, through a series of negotiations between 1963 and 1967 known as the Kennedy Round. To the intense annoyance of the US, the Community, on the contrary, was seeking internal liberalization of trade but external protection of its market, through the common customs tariff and the scheme for associating the (former) colonies. Fears arose that the Community (represented by the European Commission) would further impose protectionist measures which were in conflict with the principles of the GATT. Crucially, the EEC managed to speak with one voice during the negotiations and defend its unanimous position – a first step by which the EEC set about establishing itself as a major player on the world stage. In this way, the Community succeeded in forming an important countervailing power to the US.

The role of the United States in the process of European integration had consistently been of enormous significance, both in steering the integration process and in the Atlantic framework and the OEEC (CHAPTER 1 and 2). The role of the US in western Europe was challenged in multiple ways in the 1960s, which greatly affected the European Community. The French President **Charles de Gaulle** played a crucial role in these challenges. De Gaulle returned as prime minister in June 1958, fewer than six months after the Treaties of Rome came into force. Following a referendum in December 1958, he was elected the first president of the Fifth Republic and was inaugurated in January 1959. Although de Gaulle saw the EEC as a useful means for effecting increased prosperity, he was known to be an opponent of the European idealism of compatriots such as Schuman and Monnet. In the years following 1958, he developed his own vision for the future of Europe, which rested on two main considerations: the defence of the authority of national states within the Community, and the role of the EEC as a third power in Cold War competition.

In de Gaulle's '**grand design**', economic cooperation in the Community would become embedded in a greater plan for a political union, which served as a means to advance French power and leadership. De Gaulle made it clear that in his view European cooperation had to be based at all times on the autonomy of the national states. The united Europe he had in mind was a 'Europe of the states' – an intergovernmental image that he contrasted with the technocratic reality of the EEC, and with the federalist and functionalist ideals of Schuman and Monnet. In the long term, according to de Gaulle, this kind of united Europe would have to constitute a third power bloc in the bipolar world politics dominated by the United States and the Soviet Union. De Gaulle's predecessors had already aimed at a more autonomous European power by pursuing the joint development of a European atomic weapon in the initial plans for Euratom. Partly on account of their close alliance with the US and NATO in this area, however, other European countries had rejected these ambitions.

De Gaulle's plans for a political union clearly implied a leading role for France. After the military defeat of France in the Second World War and the crumbling of its colonial power, a leading role in a Europe that also had military clout was to give the French nation something of its old grandeur back. De Gaulle's plans for Europe were elaborated by a study group under the leadership of the French diplomat Christian Fouchet. In November 1961, it proposed the first so-called **Fouchet Plan**, calling for a political union of the Six. This 'Union of States' had a clear intergovernmental design. Cooperation in this union was oriented towards foreign policy, trade policy, defence, and culture, and would take the shape of regular meetings of government leaders, who would, moreover, have to take decisions unanimously. The Fouchet Plan received criticism above all from the Netherlands and Belgium. These smaller countries turned against the anti-Atlantic tone of the plan and the intergovernmental nature of the union. The Netherlands and Belgium feared that this design would work above all to the advantage of the two dominant member states, France and West Germany. In April 1962, a second Fouchet Plan failed as well, as no agreement could be reached among the member states.

In response to the failure of the Fouchet Plans, France sought further rapprochement with West Germany. Relations between the two countries were long dominated by the idea of Franco-German enmity, exacerbated by the resentments of two world wars. State visits by de Gaulle and his West German counterpart, Chancellor Konrad Adenauer, aimed to ameliorate these resentments. The rapprochement was eventually formally ratified in the **Élysée Treaty**, a treaty of friendship signed by de Gaulle and Adenauer in January 1963. The treaty provided above all for regular meetings and cultural cooperation between the two largest Community member states. Political cooperation was temporarily put aside for the EEC as a whole. Meanwhile, the Franco-German treaty signified a foreshadowing of the 'Franco-German engine' that would prove to be crucial on several occasions during the subsequent history of the European integration process. Franco-German rapprochement was not enough, however, to defuse a mounting crisis within the Community, which played out in the context of the issue of enlargement of the EEC, and in particular of the first British application to join the Community.

The **United Kingdom** had been observing the advances made in European integration since the early 1950s, but remained outside of this venture altogether (CHAPTER 2). Historical ties with its former empire and the Commonwealth, a strong 'special relationship' with the United States, and self-identification as an 'island nation' prompted a more global and Atlantic – and less European – perspective, upon which the UK's postwar foreign policy was founded. The postwar reality, however, was at odds with this conception of Britain's role in the world. Starting with the independence of India in 1947, a wave of nationalist sentiment surged throughout the British Empire, precipitating the independence of numerous countries in the following decades, and a diminishing importance of the Commonwealth in terms of UK foreign policy. The Suez Crisis of 1956, although it was a serious political breach between the US and the UK, ultimately strengthened the UK's adherence to American leadership in the global politics of the Cold War. Nevertheless, the UK government saw the advantages of free trade in Europe, and therefore presented proposals in 1957 for a competing, more intergovernmental free trade zone through the already existing OEEC. This free trade zone between participating countries clearly did not go as far as the common market, as it did not provide for a common external tariff, for example, much less for the further harmonization of social and economic policy (CHAPTER 2).

The Dutch government, which viewed the United Kingdom as an important trading partner, supported the British intention that the EEC in its entirety would be part of this new free trade zone. However, at the end of 1958, Charles de Gaulle abruptly called off negotiations over this new organization, after consultations with the German Chancellor Konrad Adenauer. De Gaulle feared that the free trade zone would primarily benefit the United Kingdom, because this country could preserve its favourable agreements with its former dominions and at the same time acquire free access to the European market. The French president gave even more weight to the fact that, due to mutual competition, this intergovernmental free trade zone would dismantle early EEC cooperation before it even had a chance to flourish. Following de Gaulle's example, the other Community member states chose not to take part in the British initiative. The remaining OEEC countries (Denmark, Portugal, Austria, Sweden, Norway, and Switzerland) joined in the British plans, and established the **European Free Trade Association** (EFTA) in 1960.

Not long thereafter, the UK government noticed that the Community member states had the wind in their sails economically speaking, whereas the UK's own economic growth was falling behind. In addition, the plans of the Six for further political cooperation prompted British fears of political marginalization in Europe. Reflecting on the country's economic and political interests, the Conservative Prime Minister Harold Macmillan decided to alter the country's European policy. Consequently, **the UK applied for membership** of the European Economic Community in August 1961. In addition to the UK, Ireland and Denmark quickly put forward their own applications for membership, as the United Kingdom was an important trade partner for both of them. In 1962, Norway followed suit, and submitted its accession request as well.

From the moment the negotiations between the UK and the Community commenced in November 1961, it was clear that it would be a laborious process. The UK government, still resting on its imperial laurels and failing to come to terms with its diminished role on the world stage, demanded all sorts of exceptions to existing EEC agreements, and behaved as if a new Treaty of Rome could be concluded among the seven states. The Community member states worked on the basis of the opposite principle: the Community's existence was a reality, and if the United Kingdom wished to join, it simply had to adopt the 'acquis' (the formal term for the set of European legal precepts). The negotiations were further complicated by the fact that the EEC was permanently evolving, so that the acquis and the conditions that the British had to meet changed as well. Above all, the never-ending stream of developments in agricultural policy proved difficult for the British to accept.

Although considerable progress was achieved over the course of the summer of 1962, French concerns over nuclear weapons and the Common Agricultural Policy ultimately caused a breakdown in the negotiations. From the very beginning, France had been hesitant vis-à-vis British accession as long as the Common Agricultural Policy was not consolidated. On account of the strongly divergent structure of the agricultural sector in the United Kingdom, the French feared that this policy would turn out to be a lot less favourable for their own farmers, if the British were also participants at the drawing board. During the negotiations about British accession, France had therefore put very strong demands on the table concerning agricultural policy. The negotiations were abrogated definitively when, after consultations with US President Kennedy, the British Prime Minister Macmillan announced closer cooperation with the US in the area of missile technology. The provision of American nuclear missiles to the United Kingdom was unacceptable to de Gaulle, who was pursuing a more independent 'European' policy in this very area of nuclear armament. De Gaulle primarily regarded the UK as a Trojan horse concealing US interests, and believed the British were in cahoots with the US, which would obstruct French ambitions in Europe.

On 14 January 1963, de Gaulle held a press conference, during which he unilaterally, without conferring with the five other member states, declared his **veto** of the United Kingdom's application for accession. Ireland, Denmark, and Norway subsequently withdrew their accession requests as well. De Gaulle's press conference was a major breaking point in the talks concerning political cooperation among the Six. The other five member states were extraordinarily upset by de Gaulle's self-willed actions, especially the governments of Belgium and the Netherlands, who had always advocated for British membership of the Community. Chancellor Adenauer, on the contrary, sided with his French counterpart. De Gaulle's veto was a major setback for the Community and constituted a starting point for another series of confrontations, culminating in a major crisis in 1965. It was brought about by deteriorated relations between France and the other five member states as well as by several disputed questions in the Common Agricultural Policy.

A proposal for the financing of the Common Agricultural Policy drawn up by Commission President Walter Hallstein marked the beginning of what became known as the **Empty Chair Crisis**. The Commission's plan linked the financing of the agricultural policy to institutional reforms and consisted of several elements: proposals for the financing of the CAP; the creation of the EEC's own financial resources; additional budgetary powers for the European Parliament (to the detriment of the Council of Ministers' powers), and a greater role for the European Commission. Furthermore, the third phase in the transitional period for the establishment of the common market – to begin on 1 January 1966 – was to involve the application of majority voting in the Council of Ministers, rather than unanimous voting. France regarded these plans as an unacceptable renouncement of its sovereignty. De Gaulle also condemned Hallstein for presenting the Commission's plan before the European Parliament in March 1965 without prior consultation of the member states. On 1 July 1965, following France's presidency of the Council in the first six months of 1965, the French foreign minister withdrew the French Permanent Representative and other officials from their positions in Brussels, and announced France's intention not to take its seat in the Council of Ministers until it had its way. This was the Empty Chair Crisis, which effectively paralysed the entire Community, as without a French representative – and thus the possibility of unanimity – the Council of Ministers could not take any decision at all.

The Empty Chair Crisis pointed to the central dilemma: the fundamental opposition between a supranational and a more intergovernmental approach towards European integration. Uncertainty arose as to whether this crisis would mean the end of ten years of successful cooperation. These concerns were intensified even further when de Gaulle elucidated the standpoint of his government in yet another press conference in September 1965. In his view, the crisis was an inevitable consequence of the development of the Community in the direction of a technocratic organization that lacked all democratic legitimacy. In making this statement, the French president cast himself as the defender of national states, in opposition to the supranationally minded technocrat Walter Hallstein, the Commission president, who over the previous years had come to adopt an increasingly autonomous profile.

In the meantime, the other five member states had continued cooperating as best they could so as not to concede too much to French obstruction. In response to de Gaulle's press conference, they decided to attempt reconciliation. The five proposed to devote a separate discussion to the topic of qualified majority voting, in advance of the regular meeting of the Council of Ministers in January 1966. The five added that, in derogation from the norm for meetings of the Council of Ministers, Hallstein, the Commission president criticized by the French, should not be present. Subsequently, pressure from the French voters forced their leaders to consider this proposal. In December 1965, de Gaulle had to substantially adjust his anti-European course, to avoid losing the support of farmers and entrepreneurs during the French presidential election. Once back at the table in January 1966, the Six reached an agreement referred to as the **Luxembourg Compromise**. It recognized that, on the one hand, the introduction of qualified majority voting would go ahead, but on the other hand, each government was allowed to pronounce a veto if it believed that the matter at hand affected a 'vital national interest'. In practice, the requirement of unanimity remained more or less intact. And yet, as an 'agreement to disagree', this curious compromise also signified a victory for supranational cooperation, even if only because the Community had not fallen apart in spite of this profound crisis.

After the Luxembourg Compromise was reached in January 1966, the EEC could get to work again. The completion of the customs union and the common market for agriculture was next on the agenda; it had been somewhat delayed, but not altogether blocked by the crisis. Things were moving with regard to enlargement too: the United Kingdom once again submitted a request to be allowed accession to the Community in May 1967. The poor condition of the British economy was the main motive for the Labour prime minister, Harold Wilson, to take this step. Relations with the Commonwealth had continued to weaken, and trade relations within the European Free Trade Association were developing at a slower pace than expected. Participation in the EEC was thus regarded a way to circumvent these problems, as well as the prospect of playing an active role in the continuously growing Community. Like in 1961, the British application for membership was accompanied by those of Ireland, Denmark, and Norway. Nevertheless, the dominant role of the French in European cooperation had not come to an end. In November 1967, de Gaulle once again announced his veto against the enlargement, on account of the economic problems in the United Kingdom, which was not ready for accession in his view. What was left unsaid was that France still feared for its own position of power, seeing the United Kingdom as a competitor for the leadership of the EEC on the world stage. As a result of its departure from NATO in 1966, France had distanced itself from the United States and it was reluctant to accept the most important ally of the US into the EEC.

The French veto against this second British accession request led to a new crisis among the member states, which coincided with broader stagnation in the integration process. With the completion of the customs union in 1968, the road map that had determined the rhythm of cooperation since 1958 faded away. More distant goals, such as the structural agricultural reforms proposed by Commissioner Mansholt, or the introduction of the common market, proved to be more complicated to realize than hoped. At the same time, the favourable economic climate that had driven cooperation during the first ten years was in decline. A threatening monetary crisis confronted the Six with a problem – deepening cooperation by taking steps in the direction of a common economic and monetary policy seemed inevitable. Otherwise, cooperation in areas that required stable rates of exchange, like common agricultural prices, would be in jeopardy. However, further integration did not appear to be a viable option as long as de Gaulle was in the Élysée Palace.

1968 was the year in which youth protests throughout Europe gave the impression that everything could be different. In the Community member states, this year of protest constituted the prelude to important changes in power, after which a new generation of politicians came onto the European scene. Most importantly, in France, de Gaulle resigned in April 1969, and was succeeded by his fellow party member Georges Pompidou. Pompidou was not only less hostile towards the UK, but his political style was less adversary, more accommodating than that of his predecessor. After taking office, he immediately set upon a course more oriented toward Europe.

The renewed impetus to the integration process was expressed at a summit organized in The Hague in December 1969, at the initiative of President Pompidou. The heads of state and government of the six member states discussed new plans there for further European cooperation. The **summit** of The Hague resulted in a final communiqué that brought together three strands of further cooperation under the heading of 'completion, deepening, enlargement'. The first aim, completion, referred to resolutions in the Treaty of Rome. In The Hague, the European leaders decided to finally settle several subjects that had been on their to-do list since the Empty Chair Crisis. The second aim referred to plans for cooperating in new areas, including monetary and foreign policy. Enlargement was the third aim; it referred to the re-opening of negotiations with the United Kingdom, Ireland, Denmark, and Norway.

Conclusion

Between 1958 and 1969, the European Economic Community was under construction. The Treaty of Rome established the main objective and institutional framework of the EEC: the creation of a European common market, overseen by common institutions. The years after 1958 saw the elaboration of this aim, in which the European Commission, the European Parliament, the Council of Ministers, and the Court of Justice all participated. Beyond the creation of the common institutions, this period also saw the emergence of a supranational bureaucracy, which furthered the consolidation of the EEC. Nevertheless, intergovernmental elements remained, both in the set-up of certain institutions and in ideas for the future direction of European integration. The UK, for instance, held its own views as to how European cooperation should be organized, as became evident in both its proposal for a free trade area and in the negotiations over British EEC membership. The role of France was also of great significance in this period, in challenging US influence in western Europe and proposing another vision for Europe as a 'third power' in the superpower opposition of the Cold War.

Over the course of the 1960s, the European Economic Community also became more strongly embedded in the wider world. Decolonization structured the EEC's external relations, through a series of association treaties with former colonies. The EEC also established itself as an actor in global free trade negotiations, which would expand in the following decades. The period between 1958 and 1969 thus saw both the internal and external consolidation of the European Economic Community. 1969 was marked by an optimistic mood for the future integration of Europe, signalled by the organization of a summit in The Hague to discuss prospective plans. The onset of a global economic crisis in the early 1970s brought uncertainties, but also new initiatives for the integration of Europe.

Further reading

- Brown, Megan. *The Seventh Member State. Algeria, France, and the European Community.* Cambridge, MA: Harvard University Press, 2022.
- Bussière, Éric, Vincent Dujardin, Michel Dumoulin, N. Piers Ludlow, Jan Willem Brouwer, and Pierre Tilly, eds. *The European Commission, 1958–72: History and Memories of an Institution.* Luxembourg: Office for Official Publications of the European Communities, 2007.
- Coppolaro, Lucia. *The Making of a World Trading Power. The European Economic Community (EEC) in the GATT Kennedy Round Negotiations (1963–67).* London: Routledge, 2013.
- Grob-Fitzgibbon, Benjamin. *Continental Drift. Britain and Europe from the End of Empire to the Rise of Euroscepticism.* Cambridge: Cambridge University Press, 2016.
- Kaiser, Wolfram, Brigitte Leucht, and Morten Rasmussen, eds. *The History of the European Union: Origins of a Trans- and Supranational Polity.* London: Routledge, 2008.
- Knudsen, Ann-Christina. *Farmers on Welfare: The Making of Europe's Common Agricultural Policy.* Ithaca: Cornell University Press, 2009.
- Loth, Wilfried, ed. *Crises and Compromises: The European Project 1963–1969.* Baden-Baden: Nomos, 2001.
- Ludlow, N. Piers. *The European Community and the Crises of the 1960s: Negotiating the Gaullist Challenge.* London: Routledge, 2006.

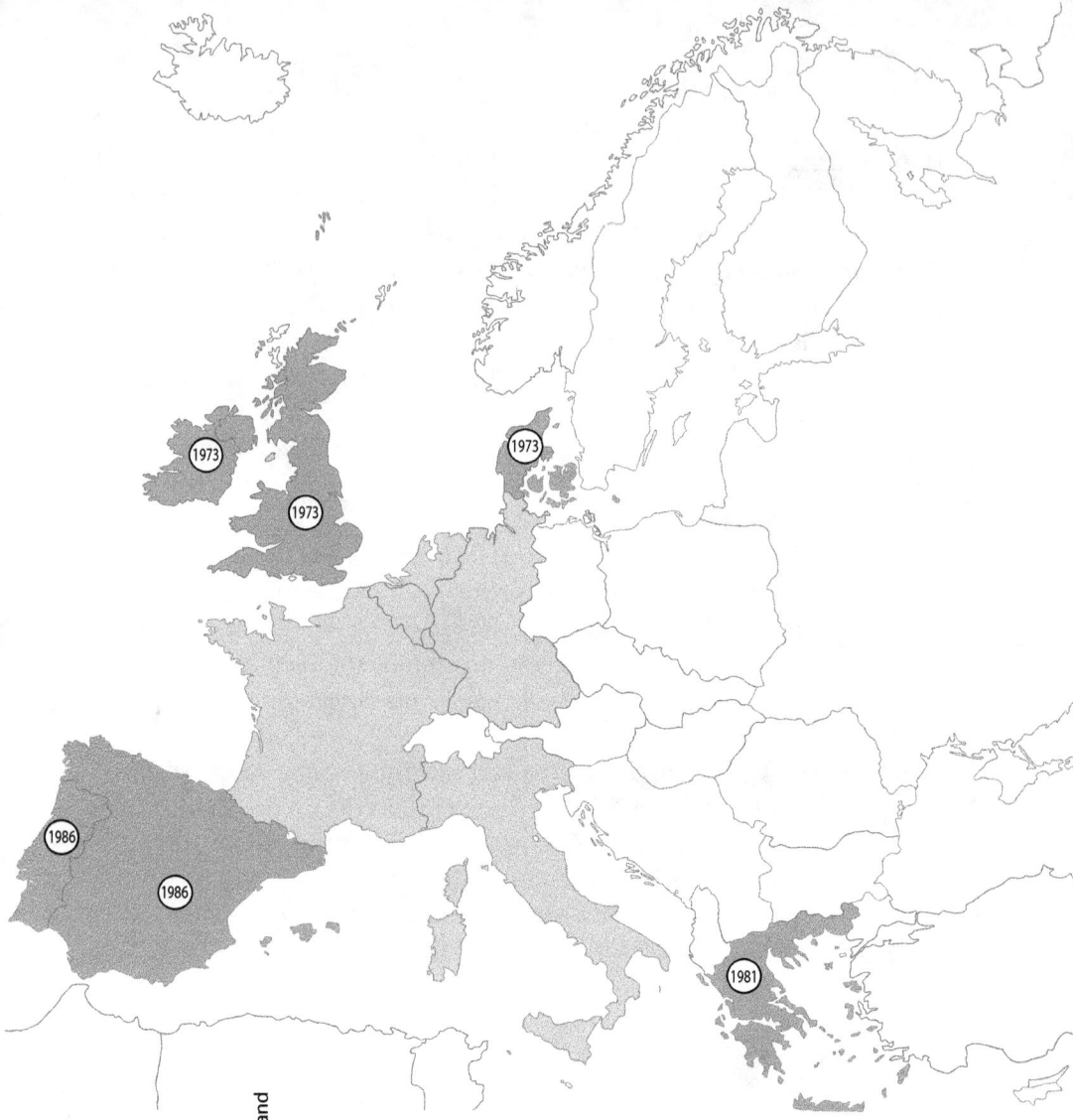

1969 — The Hague Summit

1973 — Accession of the United Kingdom, Denmark, and Ireland

1975 — The Final Act of the Conference on Security and Cooperation in Europe

1979 — Entry into force of the European Monetary System
First direct elections of the European Parliament

1981 — Accession of Greece

1984 — European Council of Fontainebleau: British 'rebate'

1985 — Signing of Schengen I

1986 — Accession of Portugal and Spain

1987 — Entry into force of the Single European Act

4. What is Europe for? 1969–1987

The changes in power in key western European capitals and the commitments made during the summit of The Hague foreshadowed a new impetus for the European project. However, these plans were once again complicated by a crisis. This time, the crisis did not emerge within the institutional framework of the European Community (EC) but from outside. The 1970s brought an end to the unprecedented economic growth that had benefited western European economies since the end of the Second World War.

For many years, scholars presented this crisis and the European response to it as Eurosclerosis. According to this narrative, western European states resorted to national rather than European measures to cure their economies. However, in recent years, historians have challenged this interpretation, arguing that the crisis was pivotal for new European initiatives. This chapter examines how the crisis of the 1970s shaped European integration between 1969 and 1986. After explaining the crisis and the institutional and economic responses, it turns to the realization of the commitments made at the summit of The Hague, namely 'completion, deepening, enlargement'. Following this, the chapter looks at the changes in the fields of European identity and democratization and the drafting of the Single European Act (SEA).

Crisis and responses

The 1970s marked the end of postwar economic growth, also known as the golden age of capitalism. This period, which witnessed the beginning of European integration, gave way to economic malaise and uncertainty. Multiple factors contributed to this change, and European policymakers debated various solutions to overcome the crisis.

First, European economies lost the impetus that the need to rebuild and reconstruct had given them in the postwar years. Different interpretations have been proposed by historians regarding the unprecedented economic growth in Europe during that period (CHAPTER 2). Some argued that it was due to the economic policymaking, support from the United States, or European integration. However, one thing is certain: the effort put into reconstructing European states after the war secured high levels of economic growth and employment. Once the major postwar problems were overcome, the capacity to maintain such results also decreased.

Second, the **Bretton Woods System**, which had underpinned the western monetary arrangements since 1944, collapsed. In this system, European currencies had a fixed exchange rate against the dollar, which in turn was tied to gold (CHAPTER 2). However, due to the prolonged Vietnam War, the United States incurred significant expenses, causing the overvaluation of the dollar. This hurt the European economy as dollar problems quickly spread to Europe. In 1971, the United States declared that dollar convertibility into gold would end, leading to the abandonment of the fixed exchange rates of European currencies. After 1973, western currencies began to float against each other freely. While this development freed the EC members from dependency on the dollar, the floating exchange rate system also undermined trade between them.

Third, the **oil crises** of the 1970s added to economic problems in Europe. Arab nations belonging to the Organization of the Petroleum Exporting Countries (OPEC) imposed an embargo on the sale of oil to countries support-ing Israel in the Yom Kippur War with Egypt in 1973, causing a significant rise in oil prices. Although the embargo was lifted after a few months, the prices of oil continued to increase. Also, the Iranian Revolution in 1979 led to a decrease in oil production, further exacerbating the situation. Consequently, the price of oil per barrel increased from three US dollars in 1971 to its peak at almost 32 US dollars in 1981.

Finally, the oil crises brought the phenomenon of **globalization** to the fore. Technological progress encouraged the expansion of supply chains, financialization, and the rise of multinational corporations. As a result, the common market had to face increasing competition not only from the US but also from rapidly growing Asian economies, most prominently Japan.

The low rates of economic growth, rising inflation, and unemployment characterized the European economies in the 1970s. Finding a response to these challenges was not an easy task. Moreover, it was not clear in advance whether this response should be given at the national, global, or European level, and what type of response it should be.

In the mid-1970s, the phenomenon of stagnation of European economies was called **Eurosclerosis**. The term initially described the inflexibility of the European economic model, characterized by heavy regulation and an expanded welfare system. Over time, the concept also took on political significance, suggesting the inability of European governments to formulate a collective regional response to the crisis. Instead, focusing on concerns such as unemployment and the imperative to maintain social benefits, national leaders often pursued measures that diverged from the larger EC objectives. This was evident in their support for at-risk businesses sectors, as well as in matters related to monetary, regional, and agricultural policies, which often disrupted the functioning of the common market.

However, some of the challenges which emerged in the 1970s proved difficult to tackle at the national level. This was reflected in the long and heated negotiations during the Tokyo Round of the General Agreement on Tariffs and Trade (1974–1979) and in the emergence of a new intergovernmental forum G7 (1976), whose members are the most advanced economies worldwide. The EC members France, West Germany, Italy, and the United Kingdom participated, and since 1981 the G7 summits have also invited the president of the European Commission.

The intergovernmental course also impacted the institutional architecture of the EC. In 1969, the heads of states or of governments of the EC met for the first time since the talks on a political union in 1961 and 1962, at the summit of The Hague. This meeting laid the groundwork for a new intergovernmental form of cooperation, which became customary and led to its institutionalization as the **European Council** in 1974. Although the European Council became responsible for strategic choices in European integration from the mid-1970s onward, it was not until 1986 that this Council was mentioned for the first time in any treaty, and not until the Treaty of Maastricht (1992) that its role in the European governance was formalized. Operating at the highest level of decision-making, the European Council was regularly able to push for cooperation in making wide-ranging compromises whenever talks between member states in the specialized substructures of the **Council of Ministers** had failed. Over the years, the Council of Ministers had been divided into more and more specialist councils, one for virtually every larger policy area. However, it operated without a clear common course and proved rather indecisive. Moreover, it was still being held hostage by the Luxembourg Compromise, which had effectively provided member states with a right to veto and seriously obstructed decision-making (CHAPTER 3).

The increase in intergovernmental cooperation in response to the crisis happened at the expense of a supranational cooperation, as represented by the **European Commission**. The president of the Commission had a weak position vis-à-vis the heads of states or of governments, both institutionally and politically. The Commission's success in realizing new initiatives depended more on the perseverance of individual commissioners than on the entity as a whole. This weakening of the Commission's role also had its impact on the EP, which, after all, was only allowed to provide the Council of Ministers with advisory opinions concerning the proposals of the European Commission.

Although the immediate response to the crisis increased intergovernmental cooperation, it also provoked broader reflections on the future of
integration. At the European Council in Paris in 1974, Leo Tindemans, the
Belgian prime minister, was asked by his colleagues to consider the European
project anew. The **Tindemans Report** of 1975 afforded a guiding role to the
only recently institutionalized European Council, comprising heads of
state and government. At the same time, Tindemans also argued for greater
legislative and supervisory power for a directly elected EP. His proposals
for deepening cooperation were the most disputed. Tindemans put forward
the idea of differentiated integration also known as a multi-speed Europe.
Its supporters argued that this can prevent the vitality of integration from
being reduced to the lowest common denominator of all member states
and that it keeps up the pressure on progress of the EC with initiatives for
intensified cooperation among a few states. Its opponents saw a multi-speed
Europe as an attempt to divide Europe into different ranks of states and
undermine the principle of solidarity.

Another example of larger reflection on the future of European integration
was the **Committee of Three Wise Men**, composed of the former vice-
president of the European Commission, Robert Marjolin of France, the former
British secretary of state for Trade, Edmund Dell, and the former Dutch prime
minister, Barend Biesheuvel. They were appointed by the European Council
in 1978 to draft proposals for improving the consultation and decision-
making structure of the EC, above all with an eye to future enlargements.
The Committee conducted an analysis of the institutional shortcomings of
the EC and concluded that European cooperation at the institutional level ran
the risk of gradually getting bogged down in its own bureaucracy. The EC had
devolved into a hulking ensemble of technical regulations, and distribution
models for incomes and expenditures. The flip side of the Monnet method
of gradual, apolitical integration thus became evident – without larger
goals and the political will to provide a farther-reaching perspective, the EC
apparatus remained trapped in stagnation (CHAPTER 2). Although neither
the Tindemans Report nor the recommendations of the Committee of Three
Wise Men led to any immediate political action, they brought to light the
challenges and dilemmas of European integration.

In addition to deliberations on the EC's institutional architecture and
functioning, member states had to re-evaluate the European economic model
in light of the crisis. This entailed addressing the fundamental question:
'What is Europe for?' Some European politicians would have liked to see
the welfare system that was typical for European economies function at
the European level. In the view of social democratic pro-European parties,

as well as other actors such as trade unions, the common market needed to be complemented with European healthcare, unemployment benefits, and other social provisions and regulations. Taking this direction would also involve increasing the EC budget. From the perspective of supporters of a **'social Europe'**, European integration should focus above all on its citizens. Another possible economic model was a **neo-mercantilist** one. Its supporters cherished the Common Agricultural Policy (CAP) and encouraged the introduction of protectionist measures in other fields of the economy. From their perspective, European integration should provide shelter against rising global competition. The non-EC members often regarded such policies as attempts to build a 'fortress Europe'. Finally, the proponents of a **neoliberal** model considered the postwar European economies to be too rigid to withstand globalization. In their eyes, the welfare system and regulations were obstacles to European competitiveness, a key objective of European integration. For the neoliberals, the EC should enable member states to maintain economic growth, and liberating markets was the best way to achieve that. All three economic models informed EC policymaking to a certain extent. Eventually, the neoliberal model prevailed. However, this was no foregone conclusion during the 1970s crisis, a period of searching for solutions and economic readaptations.

Completion and deepening

The 1969 summit of The Hague took place under the banner of 'completion, deepening, enlargement'. Despite looming economic crisis, the heads of member states successfully navigated deadlocks related to the budget and the CAP. Additionally, they entered new fields of cooperation in monetary affairs and foreign policy and enabled the geographic expansion of the EC.

Budget

Since the initial days of the EC, the Community's budget was a politically sensitive item. The member states regularly negotiated with one another concerning the financing of Community activities and their institutions. Under the heading of **completion**, a decision was finally taken in The Hague concerning the permanent financing of the CAP of which France had long been an ardent advocate, and which had previously led to the Empty Chair Crisis (CHAPTER 3). This decision was part of the wider drive to give the EC a permanent budget, which would be managed by the Commission, and gradually replace member states' contribution from their own resources. It was agreed in a Council decision from 1970 that the EC's own **budget** would consist of agricultural levies and customs duties that would be generated at the external borders of the EC. In addition, there would be a fixed contribution from the member states of at most one percent of the Value Added Tax levied in each country. The Council of Ministers and, to a very limited degree, the EP, too, were designated as assessors of this budget. The further Council's decision from 1975 further increased the EP's powers, giving it the right to reject the draft budget. It also established a new institution- the European Court of Auditors, which has since been responsible for controlling the budget.

The CAP took up the vast majority of the EC's budget, and over the years the costs of this policy only increased. At the same time, however, other internal policies and structural actions started to occupy a more prominent position in the 1970s. The costs of the latter increased in particular once southern enlargement entered the political agenda.

Apart from the budgetary effect, the introduction of this payment plan had important political significance. After all, the member states were transferring their say over their government revenues to Brussels. Even though it had to make do with indirect taxes, the EC had taken the first step to levying taxes supranationally. On top of that, thanks to its own financial means, the European Commission was able to operate more independently. Coordinating economic policies of member states and giving the EC its own budget mattered also in relation to prospects of monetary cooperation.

Monetary policy

Monetary cooperation was an important angle of postwar European integration. The European Payments Union (EPU), created under the auspices of the Organization for European Economic Cooperation (OEEC) in 1951, put in place a multilateral convertibility system which contributed to reinvigorating European trade (CHAPTER 2). Later, the Treaty of Rome made some references to the free movement of payments and capital and common monetary policy. However, as long as the monetary situation was stable, European policymakers felt no need to complement the common market with closer monetary cooperation. In the early days of European integration, the idea of monetary cooperation was popularized above all by European federalists, who saw a common currency as an important economic and symbolic step towards closer unification.

This situation changed with the erosion of the Bretton Woods System, when the devaluation of the dollar posed a threat to European currencies. In particular, the CAP with its fixed pricing required stable exchange rates among the currencies of the six member states. In 1968, when signs of inflation became visible in Europe, Raymond Barre, the vice-president of the European Commission and the commissioner for Economic and Financial Affairs, proposed a joint response. The Barre Plan argued for closer harmonization of economic policies among the member states to avoid economic imbalances undermining trade within the common market. On the basis of this proposal the heads of member states agreed in The Hague in 1969 to pursue the introduction of a monetary union. A separate commission under the leadership of Luxembourg's prime minister, Pierre Werner, was to give an advisory opinion on how this union could best be created. In October 1970, this commission presented the first plan for an **Economic and Monetary Union** (EMU).

The debate on the creation of EMU was between two camps. The first, known as the 'economists', believed that the harmonization of economic policies should precede the establishment of a monetary union. This theory was sometimes called the 'coronation theory', as it viewed the common currency as a crown placed on top of fully harmonized economies. This approach was mainly supported by West Germany and the Netherlands. These countries wanted to avoid the risk of their sound budgetary policy being affected by countries that traditionally compensated for extra expenditure with inflation. In turn, the 'monetarists' believed that monetary integration would lead to harmonization in other areas of the economy. This approach was traditionally supported by France. Monetary cooperation offered the opportunity to tie the West German economy into the rest of Europe and allowed other countries to benefit from the stability of the Deutsche Mark.

The **Werner Plan** was a middle ground between these two camps. Sometimes referred to as a 'parallelist' approach, it proposed the parallel development of economic and monetary cooperation. The harmonization of monetary and economic policy, involving for instance the harmonization of taxes on profits and dividends, was the first step defined by the plan. The second step consisted of fixing the exchange rates of the various European currencies. As a third step, the plan sketched a common central banking system, which was to enter into force from 1980 onward. The plan made no pronouncements on whether this system was supposed to go hand in hand with a common currency. According to Werner, this decision depended so strongly on cultural and political circumstances that it could not be taken until the time was ripe.

The Werner Plan provided a ten-year road map to EMU. However, the collapse of the Bretton Woods System created an acute need for the fixed rates that Werner had planned only for the second step. When the United States cancelled dollar convertibility to gold in August 1971, agreement among the six member states was initially absent. On the initiative of France, the EC countries, together with the United Kingdom, Ireland, and the Scandinavian countries, made arrangements with the United States concerning a maximum bandwidth within which the dollar and the European currencies would be allowed to fluctuate. Currencies were to fluctuate at a maximum of 2.25% above or below the new dollar parity. As a result, the various European currencies were able to gain or lose value at a maximum of 4.5% with respect to one another. Following these arrangements, it was agreed in the spring of 1972 that the EC members' currencies would not be allowed to vary more than 2.25% from one another. This so-called 'snake in the tunnel' –the European currencies would be able to move jointly within the 'tunnel' of the 4.5% – had to be monitored by the central banks of the EC countries, who had the task of stabilizing its exchange rate either by asset purchases or by the devaluation of a currency.

The 'snake' was only allotted a short life, however. Even before arrangements were properly determined, European countries had let go of the common exchange rate. When the economic crisis continued to flare up, they gave priority to national solutions in which domestic policy preferences could more easily play a central role. Whereas West Germany put the stability of its currency first, Italy, France, and the UK, under pressure from strikes, gave priority to social policy, often restoring currency devaluation. As a consequence, although the resolve of the summit conference in The Hague to create EMU in 1980 was still there on paper, in practice, reality dictated economic and monetary cooperation.

After the de facto death of the snake and abandonment of the Werner Plan, the EC members were left without any monetary arrangement. In 1979 West Germany and France embraced the initiative of the British president of the Commission, Roy Jenkins, to launch a **European Monetary System** (EMS) to promote the stability of the exchange rate. In effect, this was about fine-tuning the earlier 'snake in the tunnel'. Participants once again agreed not to allow the exchange rate of their currency to fluctuate upward or downward by more than 2.5%. What was new was the use of the ECU (European Currency Unit) as a unit of account. The ECU was a so-called 'basket currency', put together from the values of the participating national currencies. In this system, each currency had a weighted share, dependent on the quality of the economy of the country concerned. Countries with strong currencies such as West Germany could intervene by purchasing and selling of currencies to ensure that all currency exchange rates remained within range. In exchange, financial reforms were required of weak economies, such as the Italian and the French, in order to consolidate the position of the lira and the franc with respect to the Deutsche Mark.

The EMS was a modest success, both as a result of its direct monetary effect and on account of its significance for the integration process. It did stabilize exchange rates in the EC and helped rein in inflation. The basis for the exchange rate mechanism was intergovernmental – member states voluntarily committed to a few monetary and fiscal arrangements. Greece, Spain, and Portugal did not take part in the EMS until the end of the 1980s. Just like Italy, the United Kingdom was compelled to leave the system temporarily after a brief time (1990–1992), because it could not keep the exchange rate within the prescribed range.

Foreign policy

Foreign policy was the second area in which government leaders aimed to deepen cooperation in The Hague in 1969. The subject of political cooperation had not been debated since talks on the Fouchet Plan were dropped in 1962 (CHAPTER 3). In 1970, ambitions expressed in The Hague resulted in the establishment of the **European Political Cooperation** (EPC). To prevent debates on the transfer of sovereignty, the EPC was limited to voluntary intergovernmental cooperation. The EPC provided for ministers of foreign affairs to attend semi-annual meetings of the member states, at which they were able to exchange standpoints on current international issues as well as coordinate with one another.

The results of the EPC were mixed. Despite the new mechanism, the member states failed to provide a coordinated response to the Yom Kippur War of 1973, or the OPEC oil embargo which followed it. Similarly, the EC states continued to conduct independent foreign policies with regard to their former colonies. At the same time, the EC became an important actor in European détente, and the EPC helped in coordinating policy towards the European socialist regimes.

The Cuban Missile Crisis in 1962, when the Soviet Union and the United States found themselves on the verge of a nuclear war, brought a shift in the Cold War dynamic. The superpowers sought means of cooperation and avoided confrontation. To do so, they opened an era of **détente** marked by Strategic Arms Limitation Talks (SALT) aiming to reduce the threat of a nuclear conflict. The EC member states welcomed this change. Already in the 1960s, some leaders, most famously French President Charles de Gaulle, advocated a cooperative approach towards the socialist regimes. He was sceptical about US influence in Europe, and believed that western European states should not be subject to America's confrontational foreign policy. However, this attitude triumphed only after Willy Brandt's arrival to power in West Germany. Since the end of the Second World War, West German Christian democrat governments had refused to establish diplomatic relations with any country that recognized East Germany, something known as the Hallstein doctrine. The victory of social democrats led by Brandt opened the door to rejection of this doctrine and the introduction of a **Neue Ostpolitik**, a new eastern policy based on the principle of cooperation. Since 1969, West Germany began establishing relations with European socialist regimes, most famously with the Soviet Union in 1970 and East Germany in 1972. In 1970, West Germany did so too with Poland, thus recognizing Poland's western border. After the Second World War, Poland's eastern part was incorporated into the Soviet Union, which was compensated with western territories that had previously belonged to Germany. The acceptance of this border was emblematic of West Germany's new approach, and a broader European trend of coming to terms with the postwar settlement.

The **Conference of Security and Cooperation in Europe** (CSCE) was a high point in this trend and in the European détente. This conference brought together thirty-five countries, including all European states except Albania, and the US and Canada. It started in 1973 and ended in August 1975 with the signing of the Helsinki Final Act. The signatories agreed on the inviolability of the postwar European borders, the development of East-West cooperation in fields such as the economy, technology, and culture, and respect of human rights. For the first time since the end of the Second World War, the leaders of all European states institutionalized a form of pan-European cooperation. The first conference in Helsinki was followed by similar meetings in Belgrade (1977–1978), Madrid (1989–1983), and Vienna (1986–1989). Thanks to the EPC, the EC members were able to successfully coordinate their positions for the CSCE negotiations.

Economic motivations played a big role in the emergence of European détente. On the one hand, European socialist regimes wanted to extend their trade with the West in the hope of acquiring hard-currency revenues and new technology. On the other hand, western European states hit by the crisis looked for new markets and access to resources. The economic entanglement created under the umbrella of European détente led to the indebtedness of the socialist regimes to the West, eventually contributing to their collapse (CHAPTER 5). It also marked the beginning of the EC member states' economic reliance on Soviet oil, which had largely replaced the Middle Eastern sources after the oil crisis.

Widening

In addition to completing and deepening, the summit of The Hague gave the green light to the widening of the EC. Shortly after the first enlargement in 1973, which involved the United Kingdom, Ireland, and Denmark, the prospect of further increase in size appeared on the horizon. The fall of authoritarian regimes in Greece, Spain, and Portugal enabled these countries to seek EC membership, something that materialized in the 1980s. However, the path to these two rounds of enlargement was not an easy one, and this widening changed the EC, bringing not only benefits but also challenges.

First enlargement

The first enlargement from six to nine member states in 1973 followed the 1969 summit conference in The Hague. Shortly after government leaders of the EC agreed to accession of new member states, a Conservative, Edward Heath, became prime minister of the United Kingdom. He knew the problems of accession intimately – during the first British attempt at accession, Heath had led the British negotiation team. In 1970 he noted that the British economy was deteriorating, resulting in high unemployment figures and an unstable currency. Joining the EC seemed the only way out. Together with Ireland, Denmark, and Norway, the UK therefore once again appeared at the gates of the EC. Heath realized very well that he would also have to win the British people over to new developments in the EC, such as the plans for an EMU.

Conversely, the Six were faced with the dilemma of uniting plans for enlargement with the plans for completion and deepening. To secure new arrangements for the EC budget, which was vital to financing the CAP, the Six waited until 1971 to open the official negotiations for accession. To the indignation of the four candidates, the Six began to develop a common fisheries policy, amongst other things. Their intention was that fishers from EC member states would acquire free access to one another's fishing waters. These unexpected plans did not please the candidate countries, as the United Kingdom, Ireland, and Norway had vast fishing regions, and even Denmark had major fishing waters due to its possession of Greenland and the Faroe Islands. Because fisheries were important for the economies of these candidate countries, they demanded adjustments for this intended fisheries policy during the accession negotiations.

However, the most prominent negotiating partner, the United Kingdom, was not in a position to make many demands given its poor economic situation. In areas such as agricultural policy, which had caused problems in earlier rounds of negotiations, (CHAPTER 3) the British were now able to set conditions only for a transitional mechanism. Butter from New Zealand and sugar from the Caribbean in particular came to symbolize trade with countries from the Commonwealth for whom preferential arrangements had applied in the United Kingdom for many years. It was agreed that these preferences would be phased out only in the long term. Additionally, the British contribution to the EC budget, another sensitive question, was made more acceptable by means of transitional arrangements. Because the United Kingdom imported many agricultural products from outside the EC and had a relatively small agricultural sector itself, its net contribution to the EC budget was expected to be relatively high under recent arrangements concerning the budget. After all, a significant part of this was generated by import levies and it was for the most part spent on financing the CAP. The negotiations resulted in an agreement that Britain's contributions would increase gradually over a period of five years, as a transitional mechanism. At the same time, the EC promised to work on structural reforms in agriculture that would cause a reduction in the CAP budget.

After the negotiations were completed, the most challenging task began. British politics was strongly divided concerning the necessity of accession to the EC, so that parliamentary acceptance of the accession treaty was far from certain. Unusually for British politics, the dividing lines cut across the two most important parties. The Labour Party opposed the accession treaty that the Conservative prime minister presented. Heath only succeeded in finding a majority in the House of Commons after months of debates in October 1972, and with the aid of a number of dissident Labour members of parliament.

In Denmark, Ireland, and Norway, referenda gave the people's seal of approval to the negotiations. Apart from hindrances such as the fisheries policy, the negotiations proceeded auspiciously. Accession was not a foregone conclusion, though, on account of the resistance towards the EC that existed among the population in each of these three countries. In **Ireland**, where the first referendum took place, resistance was due above all to concerns about neutrality, its own economic policy, and infractions against the national sovereignty won from the UK in 1921. Given the overwhelming approval of accession in the referendum, however, it has to be noted that these concerns were nothing compared with the prospect of modernization and economic growth that the Irish associated with their accession. In **Norway**, anti-accession sentiment ran deeper. In addition to the feeling that they would again lose the independence acquired 70 years earlier, the notion prevailed that CAP and agreements in the areas of fisheries in particular were less favourable to Norwegians than existing national regulations. Given their solid economic position based on national oil and gas revenues, 53% of the Norwegians voted against accession. In **Denmark**, too, scepticism towards the EC was great. Nonetheless, one week following the Norwegian 'no', 63% of Danes voted for accession to the EC. Membership was economically attractive to the Danes, above all on account of their intense trade with the United Kingdom as well as trading opportunities with West Germany.

Denmark, Ireland, and the United Kingdom became members of the EC as of January 1973. However, this first enlargement coincided with the 1973 oil crisis, which undermined the scale of expected economic benefits emerging from membership in the eyes of the newly integrated states. In the United Kingdom, this fuelled Eurosceptic sentiments. Only two years after joining the EC the United Kingdom, again under Labour leadership, held a referendum on its membership. While the result was 67% in favour of remaining in the EC, the event itself was symptomatic of British attitudes.

These attitudes further increased under the leadership of the Conservative prime minister, **Margaret Thatcher** (1979–1990). The years of her leadership solidified the British position as 'awkward partner' in the EC. On the one hand, the United Kingdom fiercely opposed the increase of supranational-ism and the expansion of the EC into new policy areas. From 1979 to 1984, European Council meetings were dominated by bitter debates concerning the formation and financing of economic cooperation. The biggest differences of opinion on these issues did not occur between France and West Germany, but between the United Kingdom and the member states on the Continent. London, followed by Dublin and Copenhagen, set a strictly intergovernmen-tal course. On the other hand, the UK under Thatcher supported **negative integration**. As a champion of the neoliberal economic approach, Thatcher believed that all barriers to the free movement of goods, people, capital, and services had to be eliminated to advance economic development. In the eyes of the British government, European regulations and protectionist intervention such as the CAP were only market-disrupting mechanisms.

Directly after taking office in 1979, Thatcher, annoyed at rising CAP costs and concerned about the second oil crisis and the economic recession, made revising the budgetary payment plan into the primary objective of her European policy. Rejecting the principle of financial solidarity, the

British government put the accounting principle of 'juste retour' – every member state should be able to profit directly and proportionally from the money it put into the EC. Imbalances would have to be compensated by a **rebate**. In Thatcher's words: 'We are simply asking to have our own money back.' This principle of course ignored the indirect political and economic benefits that could result from a stronger EC as well as the internal market.

Over the following years, this British demand crippled the meetings of government leaders and poisoned their relations with one another. By threatening vetoes on other issues, the British government ultimately forced the other member states to yield to its desired plan for financial compensation. Reform initiatives stood little chance of succeeding again until 1984 at Fontainebleau, when the European Council reached a compromise concerning an annual reduction of the net British contribution.

Second enlargement

Shortly after the first round of enlargement, the issue of the expansion of the EC resurfaced. This prospect arose following the downfall of the Colonels' regime in Greece (1973) and the end of dictatorial rule in the Iberian Peninsula – Salazar's regime in Portugal (1974) and Franco's in Spain (1976). However, it was not a foregone conclusion that an invitation to join the EC would be extended to these newly democratic and structurally different economies. Many member states, including France, were highly apprehensive about enlargement. They cited concerns regarding economic imbalances and plans to deepen integration via EMU or EPC, which would undoubtedly be complicated if the EC was to growth in size. However, during the deliberations on the admission of the southern states to the EC, concerns regarding the future of integration soon took a backseat. Greece, Portugal, and Spain all had strong communist parties that, following suppression during the right-wing dictatorships of the 1970s, were regaining influence. Despite the easing of tensions in Cold War relations, the prospect of these countries declaring neutrality or seeking ties with the Soviet Union was deemed unacceptable by the Western Alliance. The case of Spain, not a member of NATO until 1982, was of particular concern. The United States exerted significant pressure on EC member states to prioritize southern enlargement.

In contrast to the first enlargement, the second one had a political character. In addition to strong anchoring within the Western Alliance, democratic reforms were a hard condition for entry into the EC, a point not even raised during negotiations with Denmark, Ireland, and the UK.

For the countries in southern Europe themselves, this condition was an important motivation as well. A 'return to Europe' would bring them out of their international isolation and give democratic governance a shot in the arm. In the process, they hoped for help from the EC in modernizing their own national economies.

Beginning with the applications of **Portugal and Spain** in 1977, the European Council started to realize what implications this kind of southern enlargement could have. To begin with, for the first time, a considerable difference in prosperity would arise within the Community. This imbalance between northern and southern Europe would directly influence the most important economic sectors. France and Italy foresaw consequences for their competitive position in the area of agriculture. Even the accession of Spain alone would increase agricultural production within the EC by a quarter. The Irish, British, and Danish anticipated a similar development in the fishing industry, and the other northern European countries in the steel industry and shipbuilding. Conversely, there was concern that the Mediterranean countries would not be able to manage competitive pressure from the European internal market. On top of that, the economic crisis of the 1970s sharpened the fear of a massive influx of cheap labour, a politically sensitive point in times of high unemployment in northwest Europe. To accommodate the consequences of this social and economic inequality, the member states set conditions for various transitional regulations and more detailed safeguards. In doing so, a precedent was also created for subsequent enlargement, above all with regard to vulnerable economies and low-wage countries (CHAPTER 5).

The southern enlargement also had consequences for the expenditure pattern of the EC. During the accession negotiations at the beginning of the 1980s, it had become painfully clear that the CAP had brought EC to the brink of the financial abyss. This situation was a direct consequence of the inability of the Community at the end of the 1960s to rein in the two connected problems of overproduction and explosive cost increases. In essence, the EC policy revolved around two market-disrupting mechanisms. On the one hand, it protected the European agricultural market against external imports and, on the other, it guaranteed European farmers permanent sales at a (high) product price. The EC neglected, however, to tie the product increases stimulated by this price fixing to a maximum limit. As a result of this omission, the butter supply, for instance, nearly exceeded annual global consumption. Meanwhile, the EC had to guarantee the costs of both the sales and of a stable price level in member states. With the prospective southern enlargement, images of wine lakes, immeasurable fruit tree acreage, and olive oil overproduction loomed. Reforming the EC budget could not be avoided.

These risk factors considerably delayed accession negotiations with the southern states. The EC tried to get a grip on the economic implications of the enlargement by way of specific and detailed transitional regulations. In doing so, the Communities seemed to gain time to adapt their institutions and decision-making procedures and to solve a number of acute cooperation problems, beginning with the issue of the British rebate. In the end, nearly three years of negotiations preceded the admission of Greece, much longer than the previous enlargement. A new record was achieved with Spain and Portugal. It took more than five years before these two countries were able to accede to the Community, in January 1986.

Greece, as the most recent member state, was to blame for the delay in the last phase of these negotiations. During the initial years of Greek membership, under the leadership of the Socialist Andreas Papandreou – who had only recently entered office and was not very pro-integration – the Greek government assumed an attitude that seemed to be inspired by the British disposition. It made its approval of the admission of the Iberian countries dependent on the granting of financial support to the Greek economy and job creation. Papandreou had set his sights on two funds that were instituted by the EC for the purpose of this sort of structural development. Since the 1960s, the EC has conducted an aid policy for promoting job creation in economically weaker regions and sectors via the **European Social Fund** (ESF). After the first enlargement, it created an even more powerful instrument for reducing economic disparities via monies for structural development and for promoting social cohesion: the **European Fund for Regional Development** (EFRD).

The Greek claim not only made the enlargement of the Community more difficult but also hindered the Council and Commission from being able to deepen cooperation in other areas. At the beginning of 1985, the Commission ultimately managed to eliminate this obstruction in which the Greeks had a substantial share, by setting up an integrated development programme for the Mediterranean Sea region. After intensive talks, the member states agreed on the thorny questions surrounding this enlargement. The European Council subsequently endorsed the accession of the Iberian peninsula to the European alliance in the spring of 1985.

In the same year, and from a similar rationale of self-interest, **Greenland** went down the opposite path and left the EC. This island had entered the Community as a province of Denmark yet mainly experienced the negative consequences of entry. Free access for other fishing fleets to Greenland's waters, which had become part of one major European fishing area, had worsened the competitive position of its own fishers. At the end of the 1970s, after the island had succeeded in obtaining greater autonomy and economic self-governance from its mother country, the population in a referendum opted by a narrow majority, for departure from the EC as of 1985. After complex negotiations, Greenland remained associated with the EC as an overseas territory, with specific provisions concerning the duty-free import of fish.

With the completion of the southern enlargement, the number of member states had doubled in thirteen years. The EC had become the largest market, as well as potentially the most important trading power in the western hemisphere. Yet the Community had also become considerably more heterogeneous in socio-economic respects. The consequences of this development for the project of integration in the long term were ambiguous. More member states and divergent national interests made grand plans for further deepening integration more difficult to realize. At the same time, the vitality of integration was stimulated by those mechanisms created by Brussels to make regional and socio-economic differences smaller. Behind these mechanisms lay the conviction that joint policy and mutual solidarity demanded a large measure of homogeneity. This idea of homogeneity led to a strengthening of competences for Community institutions and of cooperation between the member states.

European identity and democratization

While the crisis of the 1970s did not immediately prompt a major revision of the EC treaties, the direction that integration took during this period revealed gaps in the project. The 1975 Tindemans report had already recognized the problem of a technocratic, faceless Europe, arguing instead that citizens should be able to experience Europe in their daily lives. The progress towards EMU and EPC necessitated a definition of the EC's identity and values, which had not been imperative when the EC was solely a common market. The two rounds of enlargement also raised questions about the nature of the EC and its boundaries. Furthermore, the inclusion of the southern European states positioned the EC as a proponent of democracy, a role it had not previously assumed. In this context, enhancing its own democratic legitimacy emerged as an important task.

In 1973, during the Copenhagen Summit, the heads of the EC member states introduced the **Declaration on European Identity**. This very general document proclaimed a commitment to European unification, declared democracy, rule of law, and human rights to be key elements of European identity, and defined general EC's policy towards the rest of the world. While not having immediate political implications, the declaration had symbolic value. It constituted a first step in the larger task of constructing a European identity and involving European citizens in European integration.

With the same motivation, the EC enhanced its competences in the fields of consumer and environmental policies in the 1970s and early 1980s. For example, the EC introduced the Preliminary Programme for the European Economic Community for a Consumer Protection and Information in 1975. Such steps enabled the involvement of societal actors, such as interest groups and NGOs, in European policymaking. Throughout the 1970s and the 1980s, a growing number of societal actors set up shop in Brussels and became active participants in European debates.

The attempts at strengthening citizens' involvement in the European project multiplied in the 1980s, leading to the introduction of programmes such as the European Capital of Culture in 1985 or the Erasmus student exchange scheme in 1986. The EC also decided to adopt symbols of European identity, with the same goal in mind. The blue flag with twelve stars as the official emblem of the institutions, Beethoven's 'Ode to Joy' as the European anthem and, in addition, the standardized passport, driver's licence, and number plates for cars all contributed to a shared European consciousness.

Creating support for European integration by improving citizens' involvement and identification with this project in the 1980s mattered, as the EC had in the meantime reduced its **democratic deficit**. During the first phase of European integration in the 1950s, those setting up the European Coal and Steel Community (ECSC) and the EC had been rather anxious about democratizing an institution that was still under construction. Initially the dominant notion was that the Communities were about functional, economic projects that had to be organized above all to suit the purpose. Regulations for the common market seemed to be limited and technical in nature, in such a way that democratic control mechanisms would add little and only have a counterproductive effect. Above all, partners, who were disposed to taking an intergovernmental perspective saw this as an excellent argument for limiting the role of the EP to that of a supervisory board that gave advisory opinions and held debates. It was also for this reason that its mandate according to the Treaty of Rome, to 'draw up proposals for elections by direct universal suffrage', did not commit to anything and was not connected to any time frame.

From the very first day of its existence, the EP strove to change this situation. Just like the national parliaments, it also wanted to acquire a voice in determining the budget, designating the Commission, and adopting European regulations. First and foremost, though, the EP pursued the introduction of **European elections** in accordance with its role under the Treaty of Rome. After all, when it came to democratic legitimacy, the EC still had the nature of an international organization, with a parliamentary assembly that was composed of representatives from national parliaments with a double mandate. In 1960, the EP had already presented an initial proposal for elections to the Council of Ministers, which subsequently kept that plan under consideration for three years. For de Gaulle, a democratically legitimized parliament at European level was an unpalatable infringement on French sovereignty.

In spite of persistent attempts by the EP to force a breakthrough, it was only after the departure of de Gaulle that the matter went forward. President Valéry Giscard d'Estaing, a more liberal figure who entered the Élysée in 1974, clearly gave a different shape to French interests. He was less opposed to a directly elected parliament, not least because he had the institutionalization of the European Council in mind. In December 1974, heads of state and government leaders cleared the way for direct general elections for the EP.

Once the European Council gave its green light, the biggest point of contention in the Council of Ministers was the **apportionment of seats**. After it had been decided once and for all to allow the EP to grow from 198 to 410 seats, the question arose as to how to apportion these seats over the nine member states and their very starkly divergent numbers of inhabitants. It was decided to deviate from the democratic ideal that each delegate represented the same number of citizens. A weighted apportionment of seats was chosen on the basis of degressive proportionality. That is to say, the largest countries (France, West Germany, and the United Kingdom) counted the most delegates by far in terms of numbers, but a delegate from Luxembourg represented fewer citizens than his West German colleague. A strictly proportional composition would have yielded an impracticably large parliament or would have completely marginalized the position of the smallest member states (including three of the original Six).

From 7 to 10 June 1979, the citizenry of the nine member states – an electorate amounting in total to more than 192 million people – was allowed to go to the ballot box for the first **European elections**. In reality, however, the elections could barely be called 'European'. They did not take place on one specific day and – contrary to what the Treaty of Rome had suggested – did not proceed according to the same rules. Each member state voted according to national voting procedures, using electoral systems based either on party-list proportional representation or on majoritarian representation, with or without an electoral threshold. National political parties and domestic issues dominated the elections. The turnout was 62%, but there were substantial regional contrasts, ranging from 91% in Belgium, which has compulsory voting, to 32% in the United Kingdom.

The reasoning behind the elections essentially lay in the democratic legitimization of the EP. Although the new group of directly elected European parliamentarians barely had any more authority than their predecessors, they operated with much more self-awareness and self-assurance. This was expressed in growing parliamentary activism. From the end of the 1970s forward, the EP emphatically tried to advance its own economic and reform-oriented agenda through hearings, inquiries, motions, particular commissions, and reports. This activism resulted in an informal power shift in the triangle of Parliament, Commission, and Council of Ministers.

In 1980, recognition of this power shift ensued with a ruling by the European Court of Justice (ECJ). In the **Isoglucose Case,** the Court affirmed the Council's obligation to wait for the advisory opinion of the parliament before taking a decision whenever the Treaty of Rome prescribed that the EP had to be consulted. Besides the fact that this ruling allowed the EP to delay the execution of proposals, the ruling was above all an important moral victory. By issuing this judgement, the Court defended the fundamental principle that citizens should be able to exercise influence over the government by means of an elected representative body, at the European level.

In the following years, the EP would develop more and more initiatives to strengthen its authority to audit and legislate, as well as its position within the Communities. More than 25 years after the establishment of the ECSC, the EP still did not display, many of the characteristics of a fully-fledged, supervisory, and legislative countervailing power. Among other things and in contrast to national parliaments, it lacked the right of initiative, and its right to decide on legislation and the budget was very limited.

Between 1970 and 1986, two fundamental adjustments to institutional procedures would strengthen the supervisory and co-legislative position of the EP. In 1970 and 1975, its authority to audit was expanded somewhat with the introduction of a new budgetary procedure that made the Council of Ministers as well as the EP jointly responsible for determining the annual budget. From that moment forward, the EP had the authority to propose modifications within budgetary frameworks, or to reject the budget in its entirety. Being granted a budgetary right, however, was above all symbolic, because the procedure did not apply to the most important fixed budget items, including those for regional development and the CAP (three-quarters of the total expenditure). This was to change only with the new perspectives in European integration in the 1980s.

Back to Rome: Single European Act

Although the EC developed new fields of cooperation and expanded in size during the 1970s, it did not implement any of the ambitious projects concerning its long-term future. Proposals from the Tindemans Report or Werner Report were put on hold due to difficulties stemming from economic instability. However, the successful implementation of the EMS in 1979 demonstrated the positive effects of economic cooperation, encouraging more ambitious initiatives. In the 1980s, such proposals multiplied, originating from supranational institutions, national governments, and non-state actors. All these actors played a role in the path toward the SEA, the first revision of the EC since the Treaty of Rome.

New perspectives

At the end of the 1970s the Commission had committed to levelling non-tariff (technical and administrative) trade barriers as much as possible. It was encouraged in this objective by an ECJ ruling – the **Cassis de Dijon** case from 1979. The court decided that West Germany's restrictions on the import of the French liquor Cassis de Dijon were unlawful in light of the free movements of goods pronounced in the Treaty of Rome. On the basis of the Community principle of mutual recognition of national regulations, products that were legally produced and traded in one member state also had to be allowed on the market in other member states – a judgement with far-reaching consequences. With this ruling in hand, the Commission managed to effect an initial breakthrough in realizing the common market. This act of jurisprudence made it possible to work toward harmonizing the rules for the free movement of goods without treaty modification. At the beginning of the 1980s, the Commission drafted a large number of proposals for liberalizing trade, harmonizing taxes, making technical standards uniform and enabling European public procurements.

Representatives from the European business world were the first to applaud this new vision for a barrier-free trading community. By the beginning of the 1980s, it had become clear that national investment campaigns and protectionist measures offered little relief in the globalized economy. The

European **business** community attached great importance to tackling global competition jointly and stimulating economic recovery through deregulation at the European level. On this front, the Commission managed to gather support from a circle of leading industrial concerns such as Fiat or Philips, which engaged in active lobbying efforts as the self-appointed European Round Table of Industrialists (ERT) from 1983 onwards. While the involvement of business actors in EC policymaking was not a new phenomenon, for the first time, such a grouping gained wide international visibility. The ERT not only endorsed the initiatives of other actors but also drafted proposals later incorporated into the SEA.

In addition to support from the business world, the Commission gained support from large **networks** of experts and informal groupings. Over the years, an increasingly large number of such actors became involved in drafting proposals or producing campaigns supporting European integration. Examples include the Kangaroo Group, an association of members of European institutions representing different countries and factions but interested in promoting 'jumps' in European integration; or a group of academics and business actors gathered around the economist Robert Triffin debating European monetary cooperation.

During the early 1980s, a feeling of urgency was growing among the politicians in the more integration-minded member states. For them, the EC needed to be made more action-oriented in a political and economic sense, and the intergovernmental model of governance proved ineffective in achieving that. A 1981 initiative from Hans-Dietrich Genscher, the West German minister for Foreign Affairs, and his Italian colleague Emilio Colombo additionally testified to such demands. Building further upon the Tindemans Report, they urged the member states to commit to a 'European Union' by means of strengthened Community entities and more efficient decision-making procedures. Extending cooperation in foreign policy to security policy was pivotal to their proposal. The member states were divided over the desirability of this plan, which would mean sidelining NATO. Again, a non-binding agreement to work towards the coordination of standpoints proved to be the best achievable immediate outcome. Yet the solemn nature of the **Genscher-Colombo Plan** was unable to eliminate the reservations of government leaders. At a summit in Stuttgart in June 1983, the European Council achieved no more than a declaration of intent for closer cooperation.

After the direct elections in 1979, the EP, bolstered by a strengthened sense of self-worth, took initiative, too. Under the leadership of Altiero Spinelli, an Italian federalist from the early days, a group of Members of the European

Parliament (MEPs) conceived the plan of drafting a European constitution. This semi-official plan for a constitution rapidly grew into a broadly backed agenda for the EP. In 1983 a commission for institutional affairs completed a **Draft Treaty Establishing the European Union**, which took as its point of departure a community system with strong federal and democratic elements. The draft also spoke out in favour of the quick completion of the internal market and expansion of the EMS. In February 1984, the EP accepted the treaty proposal by a large majority. Of course, a unanimous EP offered no guarantee of acceptance in the European Council, where national considerations counted more heavily than the visionary rhetoric of the plan for a constitution.

While the new initiatives exerted pressure on European leaders, the changing attitudes towards European integration were also shaped by shifts in the ideological landscape. After attempts to safeguard the European economic model based on regulation and welfare, **neoliberal** ideas began to dominate. This shift was exemplified by President Ronald Reagan in the US (1981–1989) and famously by Thatcher in Europe. While other European states initially resisted deregulation and privatization, they eventually followed the British lead. The most significant transformation occurred in France. Upon assuming the presidency in May 1981, François Mitterrand initially pursued classic neo-mercantilist policies, emphasizing a Keynesian approach that relied on strong government intervention, including higher wages and benefits to stimulate consumption. However, within two years, Mitterrand's *dirigiste* policies pushed the French state to the brink of bankruptcy, endangering the position of the franc within the EMS and straining its relationship of trust with West Germany, where monetary stability was paramount. In order to remain in the EMS, France had to implement drastic budget cuts and align itself with the neoliberal, market-oriented course of the rest of western Europe. Mitterrand made this about-face in 1983, following the direction set by the minister of Finance, Jacques Delors.

Mitterrand made a no less striking about-face in his view on the European project. Convinced that French interests lay in Europe, he exchanged traditional French intergovernmentalism for a more supranational orientation. In the first half of 1984, France seized its six-month presidency to begin clearing the most serious obstacles – the British rebate, the question of CAP expenditures, and southern enlargement. Mitterrand's May 1984 speech before the EP became famous. In this speech, he underscored the necessity of new objectives: 'A quoi sert l'Europe?' (What is Europe for?) Mitterrand spoke out whole-heartedly in favour of the EP's Draft Treaty Establishing the European Union and called for far-reaching institutional reforms and more intensive efforts on the part of the EC in domestic and foreign policy, from environmental protection to defence. Mitterrand found a like-minded partner in the West German Chancellor Helmut Kohl, reviving the powerful impetus for Franco-German leadership.

Single European Act

The final Council summit under the French presidency, at Fontainebleau in June 1984, was crucial for setting in motion the process of integration. To this end, improved Franco-German relations were essential, and a cautious upturn in the economy formed a favourable context. With Mitterrand and Kohl taking the lead, member states proved willing to break through the budgetary impasse, to reduce expenditure for the CAP, and make an arrangement to compensate the United Kingdom.

Furthermore, government leaders decided once again to ask an advisory commission to draft concrete proposals for improving cooperation within the EC, regarding both the economic and monetary area and the political coordination of foreign and security policy. Under the leadership of James Dooge, the former Irish minister of Foreign Affairs, this ad hoc committee of experts was instructed to deal with the institutional barriers that stood in the way of smooth decision-making in the Council of Ministers as well as in the operation of Community institutions. The **Dooge Committee** was an intergovernmental body consisting of experts acting on behalf of member states plus only one representative of the European Commission. It was consciously modelled after the Spaak Committee that had prepared the Treaty of Rome at the end of the 1950s (CHAPTER 2).

The decision to appoint **Jacques Delors,** the French minister for Finance, as the new president of the Commission beginning 1 January 1985, proved to be at least as meaningful. As Mitterrand's right hand, Delors was convinced that the socio-economic problems of the 1980s demanded a joint approach. Delors had developed a vision in regard to the EC that displayed the traits of a model for European society – a social welfare state, based on a mixed economy and modern industrial sector. Such an approach mixed three models of the European economy: social, neo-mercantilist, and neoliberal. In contrast to Jean Monnet's integration strategy, which had focused on practical goals (CHAPTER 2), that of Delors was based on visionary projects – a joint monetary policy, an integrated economic and social policy, and joint foreign and security policy. He was also sketching the contours for a future European Union, in the hope of providing new political verve for the process of integration.

Because his reform agenda was controversial, Delors focused in the first place on the project with the broadest base of support – the completion of the common market. Delors encouraged the vice-president of the Commission, Arthur Cockfield, to draw up a so-called white paper, a technical and substantive document that contained a guide for transforming the common market into a **single market**. This white paper formulated approximately 300 concrete steps and measures for eliminating all non-tariff obstructions. The obstructions he identified included physical barriers such as border controls, technical barriers such as different standards and regulations, and fiscal barriers such as different excise duties. While the common market removed most tariff barriers, such non-tariff barriers still complicated European trade.

Given that the white paper was written by the British commissioner, nominated to this post by Thatcher, it represented negative integration. But this did not automatically secure British support. The bone of contention was whether these kinds of plans for a single market should be laid down in a treaty together with other institutional reforms. Thatcher had clearly spoken out in favour of farther-reaching integration in economic areas at Fontainebleau, though she preferred to see this realized through intergovernmental arrangements rather than treaty modifications. In order to keep the British favourably disposed, Delors presented the internal market as a limited process that had already been implemented much earlier. 'Just as the customs union had to precede economic integration, economic integration has to precede European unity', the white paper argued.

In March 1985, while the European Commission concentrated on harmonization of regulations, the Dooge Committee completed its report with both short- and long-term objectives for the EC. The committee recommended transforming the EC into a European Union with a single market, strengthening the monetary system, and jointly acting on global issues in a more intense manner through coordination in the EPC. In institutional respects, the report argued for extending decision-making by qualified majority to a wider range of issues, limiting the number of commissioners, strengthening the executive competences of the Commission and enhancing the EP's decision-making authority. These same issues would define the agenda again and again at governmental conferences in Maastricht, Amsterdam, and Nice during the 1990s.

Ultimately, the European Council meeting in Milan in June 1985 marked the breakthrough, a year after Fontainebleau and shortly after reaching agreement concerning southern enlargement. The ten member states embraced the white paper's proposals. A single market would have to be in place by the end of 1992 in which the 'four freedoms' –free movement of goods, people, services, and capital were guaranteed. The Dooge Committee's advice to transform the EC into a Union touched upon divergent national interests as well as varying degrees of willingness to commit to majority decision-making at a European level. The British, Danish, and Greeks opposed the proposal to call together a major governmental conference, an **Intergovernmental Conference** (IGC), to draft treaty reforms. In order to avoid another impasse once more, Italy during its six-month presidency decided to break the unwritten rule of unanimous decision-making. The Italian prime minister, with support from Mitterrand and Kohl, forced a simple-majority vote over the implementation of an IGC. This broke the spell of the Luxembourg Compromise of 1966. The United Kingdom, Denmark, and Greece protested heavily, though they did not veto the proposal. They decided to continue working together for the time being on account of the promising vision for a single market.

The IGC that started in September 1985 was a new phenomenon in the EC. Above all, the scope of the agenda was unprecedented. The IGC had a threefold mission to set in motion the completion of an internal market, institutional reforms, and implementation of European foreign and security policy. Earlier governmental conferences had always been limited to a specific, strictly demarcated area. The IGC was an innovation, even regarding its modus operandi. Its tasks were distributed across working groups made up of high-level official representatives who came under the supervision of the ministers of member states yet were given substantive input by the Commission. The EP, in contrast, stood completely on the sideline. The IGC format would become the normal and habitual approach for undertaking treaty amendments.

The interaction of supranational and intergovernmental factors ensured that the first IGC achieved results. After months of preparation by their officials within the IGC, government leaders reached a decision in Luxembourg at the end of 1985 to amend the existing Treaties of Paris and Rome with the SEA. To a significant extent, the creation of this Act was facilitated by the strategic combination of reforms by Delors and his Commission. The prospect of a single market helped overcome resistance from hesitant member states towards the intended institutional adjustments. In order to expedite the establishment of a single market, it was necessary to replace the unanimity rule with majority decisions in this area. The Commission held out promises of financial support for regional development to convince economically weaker (future) member states in southern Europe to back the Act.

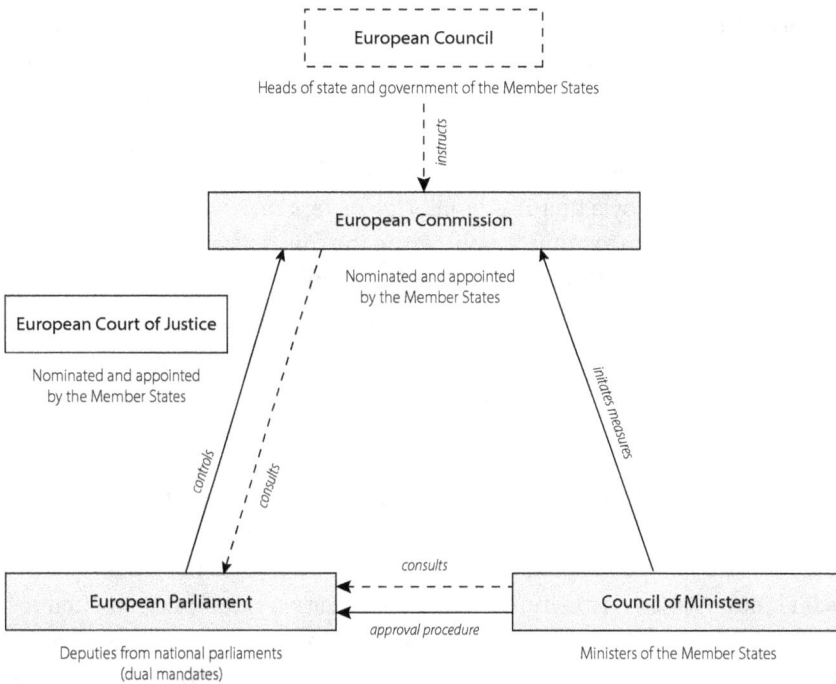

```
                    ┌ ─ ─ ─ ─ ─ ─ ─ ─ ─ ─ ─ ─ ┐
                    │      European Council      │
                    └ ─ ─ ─ ─ ─ ─ ─ ─ ─ ─ ─ ─ ┘
           Heads of state and government of the Member States

                                │  instructs
                                ▼
        ┌──────────────────────────────────────────────┐
        │             European Commission               │
        └──────────────────────────────────────────────┘
                        Nominated and appointed
                          by the Member States

┌──────────────────────────┐
│  European Court of Justice │
└──────────────────────────┘

  Nominated and appointed                          initiates measures
    by the Member States

        controls    consults

                              consults
┌──────────────────────────┐  ◄ ─ ─ ─ ─ ─ ─ ─    ┌──────────────────────────┐
│    European Parliament     │                    │    Council of Ministers    │
└──────────────────────────┘   approval procedure └──────────────────────────┘
  Deputies from national parliaments              Ministers of the Member States
         (dual mandates)
```

European institutions: the Single European Act (1986/1987)

In the end, the final shape of the SEA emerged from negotiations marked by compromises among the twelve government leaders. When it came to solidifying the Act, member states largely reverted to their familiar positions, leading to the failure of ambitious reform aspirations, democratization of decision-making procedures, and deeper monetary cooperation. Unlike the proposals of the Dooge Committee – let alone Genscher and Colombo's advisory opinions, and Spinelli's draft treaty – the outcome of the 1985 IGC was therefore modest. The Act was a brief and somewhat uninspiring document, the maximum number of reforms acceptable to all member state.

However, it has been critical in several respects for the development of the European project. The SEA unified the EC, expanding its objectives beyond just economy and trade. In addition to establishing a single market for over 300 million consumers, it granted European institutions authority over aspects of social policy, socioeconomic cohesion, and matters concerning technology, the sciences, and the environment. The EPC was introduced into a European treaty for the first time. Furthermore, the SEA brought significant changes to the institutional arrangements of the EC, incorporating the European Council and EP into the Community's legal framework. The EP gained new avenues for influencing legislation, although these were limited to certain policy areas and subject to specific procedures. Henceforth, the EP could amend proposals and contribute to the final decision-making process. It introduced a major breakthrough in the Council of Ministers' decision-making procedure, with member states relinquishing their veto power concerning measures related to the internal market, allowing the Council to decide by a qualified majority, except on sovereignty-sensitive issues like indirect taxation. Lastly, while the Commission did not acquire additional formal authority, it expanded its sphere of influence with the broadening of the EC's scope of operations.

Conclusion

Before the SEA, the years 1969–1986 did not witness any major revisions to the EC legal framework. However, this period saw a substantial increase in the EC's role and size. Many of these developments took place in response to the economic crisis. On an institutional level, the creation of the European Council aimed to effectively coordinate these efforts. The collapse of the Bretton Woods System laid the foundation for cooperation in the monetary field. Similarly, in addition to political considerations, economic problems drove the expansion of contacts with socialist regimes, partly coordinated within the EPC. Eventually, neoliberalism, which dominated the search for a new economic approach, was one of the factors that enabled the adoption of the SEA. Other international developments also influenced European integration. The end of authoritarian regimes in southern Europe resulted in major territorial expansion for the EC, initiated with the accession of the UK, Ireland, and Denmark in 1973. This increase in the EC's competences and size underscored efforts to bind citizens closer to the European institutions and necessitated the democratization of the latter. Between 1969 and 1986, a period marked by crisis and globalization, the EC emerged as the primary forum for European integration. By 1986, it was much more than a technocratically governed common market.

Further reading

- Ballor, Grace, *Enterprise and Integration: Big Business and the Making of the Single European Market* (Cambridge: Cambridge University Press, forthcoming).
- Bussière, Éric, Vincent Dujardin, Michel Dumoulin, N. Piers Ludlow, Jan Willem Brouwer, and Pierre Tilly, eds. *The European Commission,*

1958–72: History and Memories of an Institution. Luxembourg: Office for Official Publications of the European Communities, 2007.

– Eichengreen, Barry. *The European Economy since 1945: Coordinated Capitalism and Beyond* (Cambridge: Cambridge University Press, 2007.

– Geddes, Andrew Peter. *Britain and the European Union.* The European Union Series. Basingstoke: Palgrave Macmillan, 2013.

– Hiepel, Claudia, ed. *Europe in a Globalising World: Global Challenges and European Responses in the 'Long' 1970s.* Veröffentlichungen der Historiker-Verbindungsgruppe bei der Kommission der EG, vol. 15. Baden-Baden: Nomos, 2014.

– Ludlow, N. Piers. 'From Deadlock to Dynamism: The European Community in the 1980s.' In *The Origins and Evolution of the EU,* edited by Desmond Dinan, 218–32. Oxford: Oxford University Press.

– Krotz, Ulrich, Kiran Klaus Patel, and Federico Romero. *Europe's Cold War Relations: The EC towards a Global Role.* London: Bloomsbury, 2020.

– Laursen, Johnny, ed. *The Institutions and Dynamics of the European Community, 1973–83.* Baden-Baden: Nomos, 2014.

– Mourlon-Druol, Emmanuel. *A Europe Made of Money: The Emergence of the European Monetary System.* Cornell Studies in Money. Ithaca: Cornell University Press, 2012.

– Mourlon-Druol, Emmanuel. 'Steering Europe: Explaining the Rise of the European Council, 1975–1986.' *Contemporary European History* 25, no. 3 (2016): 409–37.

– Romano, Angela. 'Untying Cold War Knots: The EEC and Eastern Europe in the Long 1970s.' *Cold War History* 14, no. 2 (2014): 153–73.

– Warlouzet, Laurent. *Governing Europe in a Globalizing World: Neoliberalism and Its Alternatives Following the 1973 Oil Crisis.* London: Routledge, 2017.

Map of Europe with accession years marked in circles: 1995, 1995, 1995, 2004 (multiple), 2007, 2007, 2004, 2004.

Timeline:

1989	Aid programme for Eastern Europe (PHARE)
1990	First phase of the Economic and Monetary Union (EMU)
1992	Treaty of Maastricht signed / European Economic Area (EEA) agreement signed
1993	Copenhagen criteria established
1995	Accession of Austria, Finland and Sweden
1997	Agenda 2000 on eastern enlargement / Treaty of Amsterdam signed
1999	Resignation of the Santer Commission
2000	Proclamation of the Charter of Fundamental Rights
2001	Treaty of Nice signed
2004	Accession of Cyprus, Estonia, Hungary, Latvia, Lithuania, Malta, Poland, Slovenia, Slovakia and Czech Republic / Treaty establishing a Constitution for Europe signed
2007	Lisbon Treaty signed / Accession of Bulgaria and Romania

5. The era of transformation and treaties, 1987–2007

Nearly three decades separated the birth of the Treaty of Rome from its first major revision, the Single European Act (SEA), signed in February 1986. By contrast, the passage of the SEA instigated a frenetic period in European treaty making. Within just a few years, the Maastricht Treaty, signed in February 1992, remodelled the European Community (EC) into a wide-ranging European Union (EU). Over the next fifteen years, Maastricht would itself be amended by the treaties of Amsterdam (signed in 1997), Nice (2001), and Lisbon (2007) – the latter emerging only after the failure of the Constitutional Treaty agreed in 2004. These alterations arose amid a dramatic transformation in European and international politics caused by German reunification, the end of the Cold War, and the disintegration of the Soviet Union and Yugoslavia. The next two or so decades were in effect spent responding to the implications of these events.

One of the most prominent was **enlargement.** The end of Cold War ushered in a debate about where the EU's borders lay and how the EU should interact with countries around it. Was it possible, for instance, to incorporate the poorer, only recently democratic countries of central and eastern Europe (CEE) while at the same time maintaining the efficiency of European institutions? Another challenge arose because the Maastricht Treaty dramatically expanded the EU's competences. It included provisions for a common currency, closer coordination of social policies, and deeper cooperation in areas such as justice, security, immigration, and foreign policy. Precisely what this cooperation entailed and how it worked in practice was however all up for debate.

As more issues began to be decided upon in Brussels, the EU's structure became increasingly complex. One potential implication was a stronger Commission and Parliament. Yet member states remained wary of ceding greater powers to the supranational level. Subsequent treaties thus became little more than convoluted compromises designed to guarantee the functioning of the EU while simultaneously safeguarding their national sovereignty. Throughout, these arguments at the political level also took place against a backdrop of discontent with European integration among ordinary citizens. As the EU after 1989 became geographically larger, institutionally stronger, and its policy remit more wide-ranging, it was also increasingly contested by these Eurosceptic forces.

The end of the Cold War and the beginning of a new Europe

It might seem self-evident that the end of the Cold War marked a turning point in the decision to draw up the Treaty of Maastricht. But there were indications well before the **fall of the Berlin Wall** on 9 November 1989 that a new treaty might be necessary. Three stand out.

First, the Single European Act was generally considered a success. Not only was it negotiated relatively quickly, but it described in one clear text what the EC should do and how it should function. For instance, it laid the foundations for shared decision-making by the Council of Ministers and Parliament (the 'co-decision procedure') and greater use of qualified majority voting (QMV). Most notably, the SEA committed member states to the '**1992 Project**' for completing the EC's internal market by 1992. All this highlighted the significance of treaties, as opposed to piecemeal agreements, as a device to spur on further developments in European cooperation. This set in train what would become the Maastricht Treaty well before the fall of the Iron Curtain. It also inaugurated the era of treaty making that would last through to the Lisbon Treaty.

Second, key European leaders had long been aware of the necessity of further cooperation. Since the signing of the Treaty of Rome, the EC had struggled to become little more than a trade and commercial bloc. Over the years, plans for monetary cooperation and foreign policy coordination (among other things) had repeatedly failed. Even internal EC trade was sometimes not easy. The **Cassis de Dijon case** (1979) about a French-made fruit liqueur banned by West Germany because of its low alcohol content, proved that many physical barriers and technical limitations continued to exist. Crucially, French President François Mitterrand and German Chancellor Helmut Kohl expressed a desire to resolve these issues and deepen ties. To this end, the SEA was considered simply one step towards still closer unity. Their relationship would become an important engine for further integration.

Third, there was the unbridled ambition of Jacques Delors, the Commission president (1985–1995). Delors had already played a major role in the '1992 Project'; he would prove similarly crucial in planning the route towards the Maastricht Treaty (CHAPTER 4). He did so in the Delors Report, submitted to governments on 12 April 1989, which included another timetable – this time for full monetary union, ending up with the introduction of a single currency. Delors' status – he was trusted by both the French and German leaders – and his economic knowledge as a former French finance minister, helped ensure the report was accepted by member states at the

June 1989 Madrid European Council. He was also a highly skilled politician. For instance, although the report carried his name, Delors worked with a committee comprising the presidents of the European national banks, which lent gravitas to his arguments. Moreover, the report itself did not ask whether a single currency was theoretically necessary but rather how a single currency could be practically achieved, thereby taking political drama out of the decision. All this elevated the influence of the European Commission and made a supranational body out of it with the aid of non-political, technocratic reforms. In doing so, Delors set in motion a process that could not easily be stopped.

Combined, these factors explain why the Treaty of Maastricht has been called both the last treaty of the Cold War and the first treaty of a new European era. The ending of the Cold War would of course come to have a major impact on the pace and shape of European integration throughout the 1990s and 2000s. And it brought new opportunities and challenges that would need to be dealt with by successive Intergovernmental Conferences and treaty changes. But behind the Maastricht Treaty evidently lay longer-term drivers.

The end of the Cold War nevertheless gave extra urgency to a new treaty. With good reason, too: by the end of 1989, the socialist regimes in Poland, Hungary, the German Democratic Republic (GDR, or East Germany), Romania, Czechoslovakia, and Bulgaria had all fallen. In the event, EC leaders responded quickly. As early as June 1989, at the Madrid European Council, ministers welcomed signs of democratic renewal. A month later, an aid programme called the Poland and Hungary Assistance for Reconstruction of Economy (PHARE) was established to reconstruct these countries' economies. And later in December, the Strasbourg European Council accepted that the EC would actively contribute to economic reconstruction and political stability in the CEE countries as well as deepen ties with them. This intervention showed that the then twelve members of the EC – which had increasingly been speaking with one voice on international matters since the 1970s – were ever more comfortable with being a single geopolitical actor (CHAPTER 4).

At the same time, there was great uncertainty. The collapse of the Berlin Wall led to immediate questions over the possible **reunification of Germany**. Not every European leader supported reunification: Margaret Thatcher (Britain), Ruud Lubbers (the Netherlands), and Giulio Andreotti (Italy) all feared the consequences of a bigger, more powerful German nation. Even Mitterrand privately expressed concerns. The question only became more urgent as developments continued apace. In March 1990, the first democratic election took place in the GDR. Two months later there was an agreement on a monetary union between East and West Germany. And complete reunification followed on 3 October 1990. In the end, and despite British, Dutch, and Italian apprehensions, a united Germany assumed what was previously West Germany's seat in the EC. Here, the support for reunification of the United States and even of the Soviet leader Mikhail Gorbachev proved key. It was also a further reminder of the historic role played by the US in providing momentum to European cooperation.

Also crucial to this decision was a letter sent earlier, on 18 April 1990, by Kohl and Mitterrand to their fellow leaders inviting them to discuss fundamental changes to the EC. Mitterrand was already known to support a single currency to help French competitiveness. For his part, Kohl shared his predecessors' traditional scepticism about monetary integration (CHAPTER 4). Yet he was otherwise a passionate advocate of integration, in part because he felt a strong Europe was crucial to uniting Germany. As he declared in 1989, 'Germany's house can be built only under a European roof'. Both leaders, moreover, were firm believers in Franco-German rapprochement, given the experiences of the Second World War and half a century of European division. Their letter thus explicitly called for the 'establishment of the internal market and the realization of the economic and monetary union (EMU)'. This was to be flanked by a political union. This idea had been around since the early 1960s and had gone through numerous iterations in the intervening years, notably in the form of European Political Cooperation (EPC) (CHAPTER 4). Kohl and Mitterrand were themselves vague about its meaning or intent, but used their letter to say that such a union would give 'democratic legitimization' to the Community, make its common institutions more efficient, and help in 'defining and implementing a common foreign and defence policy'. According to both leaders, the 'profound changes in Europe' now made a political union and EMU essential. The future progress of the EC and German reunification thus became closely entwined.

Delors agreed. Support was less of a foregone conclusion among member states, however. Thatcher maintained that German reunification did not necessitate political unification. What made progress possible was when Kohl expressed his wish that the European Council – that is, member states – should remain powerful in any new political union. Because of this, the European Council, meeting in Dublin on 25–26 June 1990, agreed to accept Kohl and Mitterrand's invitation, initiating two Intergovernmental Conferences (IGCs). One, concerning monetary union, started work on 13 December. The other, on political union, began the following day.

Negotiating the Maastricht Treaty

Judged against the ambitions outlined by Kohl and Mitterrand in their April 1990 letter, the Maastricht Treaty can be characterized as a failure. Most of the historiography would certainly agree with this point. Looking back, however, the IGCs were nonetheless a watershed moment. Innovations in new policy areas, notably a single currency overseen by state-like structures, marked the turning point from an economic Europe to a more political Europe. Yet member states manoeuvred cautiously, and a common impression emerged that leaders acquiesced because it was a stripped-down Treaty that had its sharper edges removed.

In terms of successes, plans for monetary union came out of the negotiations relatively unscathed, for at least three reasons. First, monetary union was seen as the best instrument for dealing with a reunified Germany. It helped to anchor the country in Europe, but also stopped the Deutsche Mark acquiring hegemony. Second, plans for monetary union were well established thanks to the Delors Report but also to the long history of monetary discussions stretching back to the Werner Plan (CHAPTER 4). Finally, the plan could be phased in, which provide room for alterations as well as moments when states could decide not to progress further.

The idea of a phased implementation was outlined in the **Delors Report**. In the first of three phases, the initially envisaged the alignment of the economic and monetary policies of member states. Thus, they would adopt common policies to combat inflation and manage their budgets. Phase two included the establishment of the European Monetary Institute – the precursor to the European Central Bank (ECB). The subsequent introduction of the single currency constituted the final phase. This would only start if the so-called 'convergence criteria' (or Maastricht criteria) – including a deficit of maximum 3% and public debt of no more than 60% of gross domestic product (GDP) – had been met. This was designed to ensure the stability of the new currency and the economies that were going to use it. Despite agreement in these areas, there were some difficulties. The United Kingdom won assurances that it was not obligated to move to the final stage, ensuring an opt-out from the single currency. The final product, too, was a compromise between France as the most ardent proponent of the monetary union, and Germany, which was only won over with the concession that the union be set up according to the German model – that is, with an independent, supranational central bank.

Movement towards political union was less straightforward. One problem was that it was rarely clear what political union would entail.

For some, it had unmistakable associations with federalism, something countries such as Britain had fundamental objections to. It was all the more remarkable, therefore, that federal solutions were openly discussed during the negotiations. In one speech, for instance, Delors portrayed the Commission as the true 'government' and the European Parliament and the Council of Ministers as a bicameral model of a federal union. Because of this, Delors increasingly became the target of parody, especially in the British press. In turn, this meant that reference in the first draft of the treaty to a 'federal objective' was categorically rejected by British political opinion. For much the same reason, the British would also object later to the inclusion of the Social Chapter covering matters such as health and safety in the workplace, rules on redundancy, and social security rights. Instead, the Social Chapter had to be annexed to the treaty rather than be incorporated into the main text.

Because of the position of countries such as Britain, but driven also by concerns elsewhere about Delors' comments on greater Commission control, Luxembourg, during its presidency of the Council of Ministers in the first half of 1991, proposed a compromise plan on a new institutional structure. Three domains or '**pillars**' were proposed, which would each have its own competences and decision-making processes. The first 'Community' pillar would consist of existing policies such as agriculture as well as economic and monetary union; a second concerned a Common Foreign and Security Policy (CFSP); and the third dealt with cooperation in Justice and Home Affairs (JHA). Crucially, while in the first pillar it was expected that national sovereignty would slowly be transferred to the supranational level, the second and third pillars would be governed by intergovernmental cooperation. Luxembourg's original proposal even sought to limit the influence of the Commission in the first pillar in favour of the Council and Parliament. While this last suggestion was later revised following protests by Delors at what he saw as the neutering of the Commission, the pillar system remained. Even then, the whole plan was unacceptable to those who, like the Dutch, the Belgians, and the Commission, felt this was moving too far away from federalist aspirations. But despite attempts to push their case and create one single 'Community' unit, few other governments expressed support. The result was that the Luxembourg option of three pillars, standing separately but all under one roof in the shape of a temple, endured.

Although criticized by some, this temple structure meant that several new areas finally acquired a basis in a European treaty. JHA comprised, for example, migration policy and cooperation in combating organized

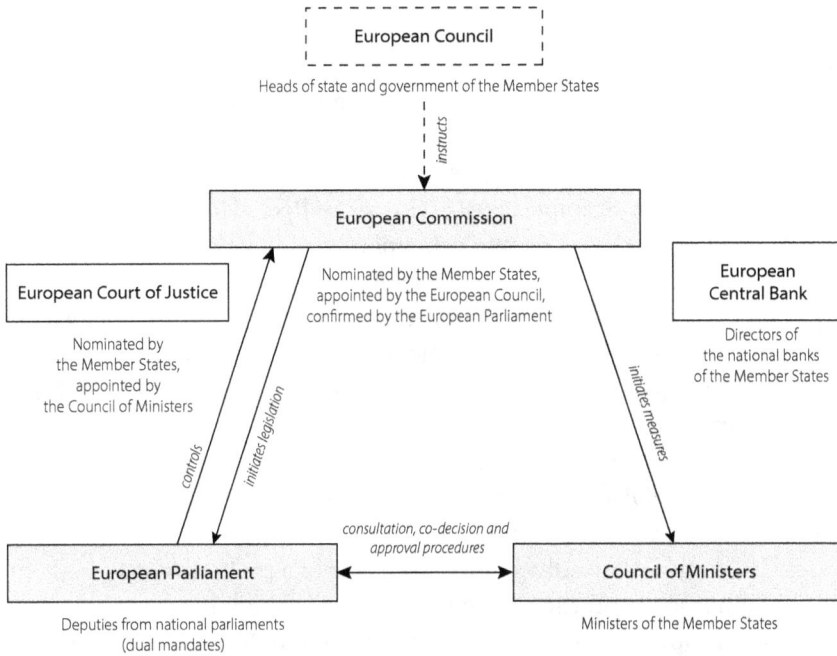

European institutions: Treaties of Maastricht (1992/1993), Amsterdam (1997/1999) and Nice (2001/2003)

crime (eventually leading to the creation of Europol) and terrorism. In the CFSP pillar, the most important point of debate was the question of how far European states should be able to develop their own defence initiatives. The United States was opposed to this idea because it would create a rival to its own power. For that reason, member states with strong transatlantic bonds withdrew their support. There would therefore be no majority decisions on defence policy, although the treaty still allowed other states to take 'joint action' should they wish to. In the process, this latter element helped strengthen the image of the EU as more than just a trade bloc with a single currency.

The catch came in the decision-making process applied to these areas. Building upon the SEA, the Maastricht Treaty ensured that legislation had to be approved not just by the Council of Ministers but also by the Parliament – termed the **co-decision procedure**. Yet this was restricted to the first pillar, while some key areas such as agriculture within the first pillar would remain the sole domain of governments. Contrary to Kohl and Mitterrand's letter, which hoped to democratize the Community, plans to empower Parliament through the right to initiate legislation were also watered down. In this way, the pillars led to an extraordinarily complex legal situation. It also meant the Treaty of Maastricht consisted of two treaties: the first pillar revised the Treaty of Rome into the 'Treaty establishing the European Community', while the second and third pillar were governed by the 'Treaty on European Union' (TEU).

Viewed in this way, the TEU was an explicit recognition of intergovernmentalism. The lasting importance of this was reflected in the incorporation of **subsidiarity** as a fundamental principle. Subsidiarity ensures decisions are taken at the lowest possible level of administration. For instance, policy areas such as education, healthcare, and culture were defined exclusively as competences of member states, and a new Committee of the Regions – comprising, for instance, mayors and regional governments – was established to safeguard subsidiarity.

Because of this, Maastricht overall suggested a middle ground between the grand design of a federal union with its own currency and the sort of sector-based functionalist integration that had dominated prior to the 1990s. This was, admittedly, sufficient to lead to a preliminary agreement in December 1991 and the signing of the treaty the following February. Ratification, however, was slow and contentious. In Britain, the governing Conservative Party was heavily split. Some countries held a referendum, either because it was a constitutional requirement convention or because of domestic pressure. The first referendum in Denmark in June 1992 signified immediate stagnation when the treaty was voted down by 50.7% of the population, caused in part by the argument that European leaders were ignoring the concerns of citizens. A positive outcome in France averted catastrophe, but the *petit oui* vote, with just 51.05% in favour, nonetheless suggested growing societal concerns over the direction of European integration. Because of these tough ratification battles, it was not until November 1993 that Maastricht entered into force. Before then, the Danish referendum had required politicians to go back to the drawing board. Only when the **Edinburgh Agreement** (December 1992) gave Denmark opt-outs from participating in a single currency, home affairs, common citizenship, and any possible future defence policy, did the public vote in favour.

Two challenges

The decade following the Treaty of Maastricht was marked by at least two challenges, which in turn formed the backdrop to the treaties of Amsterdam, Nice, and Lisbon.

Changed nature of international relations

The first was the dramatically changed nature of international relations. The consequences from the ending of the Cold War initially remained unclear. Outside Europe, the balance of power between the United States and the Soviet Union was disrupted. While the former soon affirmed its hegemony with the Gulf War (1990–91), the latter dissolved. This radically changed international relations from a 'bipolar' to a 'unipolar' world order – all while European leaders were preoccupied with negotiating and ratifying the Maastricht Treaty.

Within Europe, the fall of the Soviet Union occasioned the **independence of the Baltic states**, which almost immediately oriented themselves towards the EU. Political fragmentation was witnessed elsewhere on the borders of the EU with, for example, Czechoslovakia's velvet divorce (1993) resulting in the formation of two new independent states. Whereas, as the word 'velvet' implies, this was a peaceful transition, the Balkan peninsula soon saw more violent tensions. Slovenia, Croatia, and Macedonia declared their independence from the Yugoslav Federation in 1991, followed by the then Republic of Bosnia and Herzegovina in 1992. The ethnic mix in Croatia and Bosnia and Herzegovina, lack of strong common national identity, and disputes over borders, meant that their secession resulted in bloody wars. These lasted until the Dayton Accords, enforced by the United States, finally produced a ceasefire at the end of 1995. The **Bosnian War** resulted in scenes recalling the Second World War; ethnic cleansing around Prijedor and Srebrenica even evoked memories of the Holocaust.

Conflict in southeast Europe was of crucial importance to European integration. Not only had it opened everyone's eyes to the fact that political fragmentation and bloody fighting were still possible on the European continent, but it also called for active intervention to help democratize the region. This suggested that the EU's foreign policy should acquire an ethical and humanitarian dimension to help end ethnic cleansing. Yet, the Treaty of Maastricht's stipulations on foreign policy meant that the EU's capability was too limited to allow it to play any central role during the wars in Yugoslavia. There were also diverging European interests on the matter and a general lack of willingness by some governments to intervene, exacerbated by the lack of a political culture among European leaders to undertake joint action without the United States. And several EU member states with large ethnic minorities of their own were reluctant to recognize the self-determination movements in Yugoslavia because of the consequences for their own countries. Together, this meant it was the US-led

North Atlantic Treaty Organization (NATO) which instead took a leading role in combating the violence in Bosnia and Herzegovina.

On paper at least, NATO's rapprochement with the CEE countries at times also seemed to go further than the EU's. The Partnership for Peace programme (1994) attracted headlines for promoting trust, understanding, and security cooperation via defence agreements with, and military aid for, post-Soviet countries. NATO also expanded at a faster rate, initially including Poland, the newly named Czech Republic, and Hungary (in 1999). This was a significant moment; after the fall of the Berlin Wall, former socialist countries had initially been reluctant to engage with NATO as a product of the Cold War. Instead, they had sought more 'European' solutions such as the Organization for Security and Cooperation in Europe (OSCE) – which had emerged from the Conference for Security and Cooperation in Europe opened in the 1970s (CHAPTER 4) – with its remit to maintain human rights and monitor elections and the media. Quickly, however, these European organizations – like the EU itself – proved incapable of taking on the job of their defence. This is not to say the EU was completely unsuccessful in this field, as its mediation of the Ohrid Agreement (2001) relating to the Albanian minority in Macedonia showed. But the CEE countries realized that genuine guarantees of security with respect to any possible new threat from Russia (which would deploy military force in Transnistria, Moldova, (1990–1992) and in Chechnya (1994–1996)) could only be given by the United States. There was little doubt therefore that NATO remained the cornerstone of European security.

Enlargement

The second challenge was enlargement. CEE countries had made appeals for closer relations immediately upon achieving independence. But the first post-Cold War enlargement, in 1995, saw Austria, Finland, and Sweden join. During the Cold War, their neutral status had prevented membership; instead, they had created the European Free Trade Association (EFTA), a looser intergovernmental free trade organization set up in 1959–1960. Excluded from the Community's internal market, the EFTA states – which also included Norway, Switzerland, and Iceland – by the late 1980s initiated discussions for a new association, the **European Economic Area (EEA)**, eventually established in 1992. The EEA allowed non-EU member states to benefit from the free movement of persons, goods, services, and capital, on the condition that they would adopt a portion of EU regulations.

From the start, the EEA was seen as inferior to full EU membership. It meant having to adopt EU rules without having a say in writing them. Once the Soviet Union – which had always demanded their neutrality – collapsed, Austria, Finland, and Sweden therefore sought rapprochement with the EU. The limitations of the EEA also meant that Norway again applied to join the EU as a full member, having rejected membership in a referendum in 1972. Although Switzerland decided that its neutrality prohibited it from joining the EU, it wished to become an EEA member.

This process did not go entirely smoothly. Switzerland dropped out because of the negative outcome of a referendum on the EEA. Norway completed negotiations for EU membership yet ran into major difficulties in talks about its fishing sector. While most of the Norwegian political elite remained in favour of accession, the electorate once more vetoed EU membership in a referendum in 1994 (CHAPTER 4). Sweden, for its part, did enter the EU. But political neutrality was deeply rooted in this country and had been part of the national culture since the nineteenth century. For that reason, sharing of sovereignty, a single currency, and foreign policy coordination all aroused suspicion. Although it did not negotiate an opt-out, Sweden chose not to meet the conditions for participation in the euro. After joining, Sweden's neutrality also caused it to emphasize the voluntary nature of its involvement in foreign policy cooperation and 'softer' elements such as championing cooperation with the United Nations and humanitarian peacekeeping missions. Since the EU has eventually become more active in these areas, Sweden is a good example of how enlargement not only influences new members but also of how new members influence internal EU processes and policies.

The 1995 enlargement was otherwise unproblematic from the standpoint of the EU. Austria, Finland, and Sweden were politically stable with strong service economies and a per capita income that was 103.6% of the EU average. This meant they would have limited demands on EU spending. By contrast, the integration of CEE countries proved more complex. Upon accession, they stood to add just 5% of GDP to the EU but over 20% to its population. Expectations were nevertheless high. The PHARE aid programme had quickly expanded beyond Poland and Hungary to nearly all the countries of the former Warsaw Pact. The hope was that this was a first step in preparing them for accepting the obligations of full EU membership.

The prospect of enlargement was given an early boost when from 1991 onwards the countries concerned gradually concluded more ambitious association agreements with the EU, known as the Europe Agreements. The countries concerned were Hungary, Poland, the Czech Republic, and

Slovakia (referred to as the 'Visegrád countries' based on their own separate cooperative trade association), as well as Bulgaria and Romania. Since the Europe Agreements contained provisions on political, economic, and technical reforms, it was expected that these countries would become ever more compatible with the EU. Poland and Hungary submitted their membership applications on the back of this as early as 1994, followed a year later by Bulgaria, Estonia, Latvia, Lithuania, Romania, and Slovakia, and in 1996 by Slovenia and the Czech Republic.

It further helped that countries such as Germany became a major engine behind enlargement. Even before the Treaty of Maastricht, Hans-Dietrich Genscher, the German foreign minister, had expressed his desire that CEE countries should become members 'before the end of the decade'. This made sense. Germany not only had to defend a long boundary with the CEE states but, as a neighbouring country, also had major economic interests in the region. For instance, German companies established themselves in these countries to benefit from low wages. In turn, this interaction would steadily strengthen Germany's position in European affairs.

This process initially did not acquire any real momentum, for three reasons. First, the CEE countries were transitioning from one-party systems with planned economies to democracies and mixed market economies, a transition that caused great upheaval and short-term hardship. Czecho-slovakia fell apart, and Slovakia grappled with right-wing authoritarian regimes. Economically, the shock therapy used in Poland in particular saw standards of living fall below pre-1989 levels. While the Baltic states became relatively prosperous – helped by their budding technological sector – they too had to manoeuvre cautiously in their rapprochement with the EU so as not to invoke a harsh reaction from Moscow. And in Romania and Bulgaria, many socialist-era elites initially remained in power, which caused reforms to stagnate. This made the task of absorbing these countries into the EU far more complex than it had been for the former EFTA countries.

Second, the Treaty of Maastricht said very little about enlargement. The treaty's 'Article O' merely stated that any European state could join providing there was unanimous support. Neither the precise steps to be followed nor the minimum political and economic conditions expected of a country before it could join, were spelt out. This risked the accession of countries that could destabilize the EU's cohesion and threaten its very existence. Knowing this, in July 1993 – even before the Treaty of Maastricht came into effect on 1 November 1993 – the European Council agreed the **Copenhagen criteria** laying down preconditions for membership. To join, a country needed to have: (1) 'stability of institutions guaranteeing democracy, rule of law, human rights, and respect for and protection of minorities'; (2) 'a functioning market economy and the capacity to cope with competitive pressure and market forces'; and (3) the capacity to 'take on the obligations of membership, including adherence to the aims of political, economic and monetary union'. After these conditions, the final declaration stated: 'the European Council today agreed that the associated countries in central and eastern Europe that so desire shall become members of the European Union'. Critically, there was relatively little mention of what would later be called absorption capacity – that is, the ability to integrate new member states while maintaining the effectiveness of the EU's functions and decision-making processes. With Maastricht otherwise silent on the subject, the issue of how to reform the EU's institutions would become the central point of debate during negotiations for the treaties of Amsterdam, Nice, and Lisbon.

Third, in the years following the realization of the Treaty of Maastricht, the EU, as we shall see below, was busy reforming its own ways of working. Often, therefore, it was too distracted to deal with enlargement. This provoked criticisms from within CEE countries. Václav Havel – the celebrated Czech president who had led the struggle against Czechoslovakia's former socialist regime – argued that Maastricht was too technical and lacked stipulations on the meaning of European culture or the nature of a common future.

Eventually, though, enlargement did become a reality. In part this was due to the way in which the Copenhagen criteria were managed. The European Commission came to occupy a central role in deciding whether an applicant satisfied the accession criteria and in supervising countries as they sought to meet those standards. The Commission was also key in implementing, for instance, the Europe Agreements. As a result of these developments, the European Commission became a major player when the official negotiations began in 1998. This led to the enlargement process becoming more technical and less an exclusively political issue susceptible to vetoes and infighting. This was clear when negotiations began first with Poland, the Czech Republic, Hungary, Estonia, and Slovenia, along with Cyprus, followed by Malta and the remaining five former socialist states: Bulgaria, Latvia, Lithuania, Romania, and Slovakia. It was the European Commission that conducted the negotiations and drew up progress reports. Even the final decision of the European Parliament and the Council of Ministers was based on an advisory opinion from the European Commission. In the accession countries, this helped form the impression that Günther Verheugen, the European commissioner responsible for enlargement (1999–2004), had the deciding vote on accession. This contrasted with a perceived decline in influence in other areas after 1995 when Jacques Delors was succeeded by the rather less dynamic Jacques Santer of Luxembourg.

In part, too, enlargement was given greater urgency by growing instability in southeast Europe. In 1999, when NATO bombed Serbian targets as a reaction to **ethnic cleansing in Kosovo** by Slobodan Milošević's regime, the situation in former Yugoslavia had again reached a low point. There were fears in the West that conflict would escalate if there was no economic as well as military integration in Europe. This provided an impetus for accelerating talks with applicants, notably Bulgaria, Latvia, Lithuania, Romania, and Slovakia.

Since Greece had joined, enlargement was also seen as a way of helping enforce domestic reforms and promote democratization. This was a further factor in hastening talks with the Baltic countries because, it was felt, the opening of enlargement negotiations would itself offer some protection against any future threat of democratic backsliding. Similarly, it could further help protect these countries from a potentially revanchist Russia, since the prospect of accession would increase domestic efforts to restructure their economies, societies, and politics towards a Western model. Inevitably, this caused friction between a formal reading of whether the accession criteria had been met and the overwhelming political advantages that could be accrued from allowing enlargement to proceed.

Resolving Maastricht's open questions: the Treaty of Amsterdam

The failure of Maastricht to fully prepare the EU to respond to the changing nature of global politics and properly confront the prospect of enlargement made new treaty reform essential. Just eighteen months after Maastricht came into force, the European Council, meeting in Corfu in June 1994, therefore established a Reflection Group to identify the matters which needed to be resolved. This started work in 1995, and in addition to representatives from member states, such as ministers and diplomats, as well as from the European institutions, it also included former politicians and specialists. The broad nature of the **Reflection Group** set the tone for its final report, which sought to push the EU in a more supranational direction. The ensuing IGC commenced work in March 1996 in Turin and was concluded in Amsterdam in June 1997.

It soon became obvious that the Reflection Group and European leaders did not always agree on what was needed. Many institutional modifications necessary to prepare for enlargement remained disputed. The problem was simple: in many ways the EU was still governed by the decision-making structure that had been developed by the six original member states, but these 'older' members were loath to give up rights such as the number of commissioners per state – even though there was a risk of the Commission becoming impractically large if enlargement took place. While member states agreed that something needed to change, it was decided that the exact composition of the Commission would have to be dealt with in a future treaty. Decisions concerning a new formula for distribution and weighting of votes in the Council and the allocation of seats in Parliament were similarly postponed. Admittedly, it was agreed that a few new areas such as research would be governed by QMV, although this was a lot less than had originally been hoped for. Several policy areas were also transferred to Maastricht's first pillar and, with that, to the co-decision procedure, of which the most important was migration policy. As far as institutional reforms were concerned, however, the Treaty of Amsterdam achieved only incremental steps.

One area where greater progress was made was how to manage future disagreement. Looking back in particular at the negotiations concerning monetary union, it was obvious that not every country necessarily wanted or was able to progress towards integration at the same pace. Because of this, the Reflection Group had floated the possibility of forming a 'lead group' within the EU, allowing countries, should they so wish, to deepen ties faster and further than others. There was a great deal of concern over whether this might lead to fragmentation, but the final treaty nevertheless introduced the concept of 'closer cooperation' (later 'enhanced cooperation') to reflect a situation in which most member states wanted to move at different speeds.

There was also approval for integrating the **Schengen Agreement** into the EU Treaty. Schengen had emerged in June 1985 as an intergovernmental agreement outside the EC, designed to eliminate passport controls and border checks between Belgium, France, West Germany, Luxembourg, and the Netherlands. In effect these countries were together moving ahead of their peers. But they were also moving rather slowly: not until June 1990 did these five countries, joined by Portugal and Spain, set down rules for how the plan would work. And Schengen only entered into force in March 1995. Given that enlargement was likely to make border controls and migration an important consideration, the transfer of the Schengen Agreement to the EU was crucial groundwork for its future. Even though the Schengen Area would not comprise all EU member states (it also included some countries not belonging to the EU, such as Iceland, Norway, Liechtenstein, and Switzerland), it further suggested that the message of the Amsterdam Treaty was one of wanting to reduce the different treaties and organizations that governed European cooperation.

Preparing for enlargement also underlay the decision of the Madrid European Council in 1995 to have the European Commission draw up a plan, parallel to its work on the Amsterdam Treaty, to identify other areas where the EU might need to be reformed as part of its expansion. The result was **Agenda 2000** 'for a stronger and wider Union', which was presented by the European Commission approximately a month after the signing of the Treaty of Amsterdam on 2 October 1997. Agenda 2000 included an extensive revision of the funding and functioning of agriculture and cohesion policy – two areas that would come under the most pressure during the accession of the poorer, agrarian economies of eastern and southeast Europe. The plan for the reforms was officially accepted in 1999. Apart from the content of the plan, the process again manifested the distribution of roles in the institutions, since it showed that if the European Council chose to mandate it, the Commission could propose alterations to the EU's functioning without undergoing treaty amendments. Despite the limitations of the Amsterdam Treaty with regard to revision of the EU's decision-making processes and institutions, the late 1990s were thus not a period completely without institutional innovation.

Amsterdam is remembered above all for its innovations in foreign policy. The most striking change was the introduction of a **High Representative** for foreign affairs to support the Foreign Affairs Council in international crises, a position that was previously in the hands of the country holding the rotating presidency of the Council of Ministers. The High Representative would be joined by the president of the Council and a commissioner for external policy (mostly dealing with trade and enlargement) as the troika representing the EU abroad. Since it remained intergovernmental, however, the Commission still had no formal mandate to act on foreign non-trade matters.

The nomination of the first High Representative was very telling. The post went to the Spaniard Javier Solana, who had just served a term as secretary-general of NATO. This underscored that foreign and security policy would develop in addition to and in cooperation with NATO. This arrangement owed much to pressure from Britain and, to a lesser degree, Germany. For the British, it provided a way to anchor its transatlantic preferences more strongly in the EU and not allow the EU to take a competing route of its own. Meanwhile, Germany was reticent to develop military competences for historical and political reasons. An indication of how politically sensitive defence still was for Germany came when European leaders decided to support the United States in its plans to bomb Serbia in 1999, a move designed to prevent further catastrophe in Kosovo. This precipitated fierce debates because it was the first time since the Second World War that a German government deployed the country's military forces in what was an act of war. Several political parties demanded that Germany instead adopt a policy of pacifism.

This dual ambition for the EU to develop defence cooperation while continuing to lean on NATO, led to the resurgence of the **Western European Union** (WEU) as an important forum. The WEU – itself an update of the Treaty of Brussels agreed in 1948 – had emerged back in 1954 between Belgium, Britain, Germany, France, Italy, Luxembourg, and the Netherlands to help guarantee western European security. While it had always stood in NATO's shadow, by the 1990s the idea emerged of the WEU developing into the operational arm of NATO member states in Europe. To understand why, it is worth remembering that at the end of the Cold War (and notwithstanding its later involvement in areas such as Kosovo) NATO was experiencing an identity crisis. After all, why have a defensive military alliance when your main antagonist, the Soviet Union, had disintegrated? The possibility therefore arose of using the WEU as a different kind of European security structure. With this in mind, the WEU member states in 1992 formulated the **Petersberg tasks**, which sought to identify areas where European states could cooperate in other areas than NATO. Three 'tasks' centred on what were now perceived to be the main 'threats' to European security: 'peacekeeping' missions, 'peacemaking' missions, and humanitarian missions. All this matters because in the Treaty of Amsterdam, these tasks were effectively absorbed into the EU, becoming the foundation of a distinctively EU foreign policy. So much so, indeed, that in 2011 the decision was taken to formally terminate the WEU and incorporate its remaining functions into the EU system. As with Schengen, the aim here was also to declutter Europe's institutional landscape.

What the Petersberg tasks symbolized was that while Europe's collective defence would continue to be served by NATO, the EU would play an increasing role in the less conventional military aspects of national security. In short, its task would be keeping armed opponents apart and helping to calm situations of tension. However, the conflict in Kosovo had shown its capacity to do this to be remarkably limited by. This spurred on the EU's two largest military powers, Britain and France, to sign a new accord. Meeting in the French spa town of **Saint-Malo** in December 1998, their respective leaders – Tony Blair and Jacques Chirac – signed a new declaration. They agreed that the EU should be able to undertake 'autonomous' actions as well as have the 'military capacity' for doing so. These plans were elaborated on during the European Council meetings in Cologne (June 1999) and Helsinki (December 1999). At the latter meeting, a concrete structure was developed: the EU should be able to mobilize 60,000 armed personnel within 60 days for a duration of at least a year. This was expected to be functional from 2003.

The Treaty of Nice

Despite innovation in foreign policy and in enhanced cooperation, and despite the work preparing for enlargement, the EU faced many difficulties following the signing of the Treaty of Amsterdam. Its status internationally had already taken a knock because of its hesitant attitude towards events in Kosovo. This was exacerbated by a major scandal involving allegations of nepotism and corruption by Édith Cresson, a European commissioner and a former prime minister of France. These accusations led to the European Parliament refusing to approve the budget until the matter was investigated. Because individual commissioners could not be dismissed, the saga was only brought to an end on 15 March 1999, when the **entire Commission resigned**, something that had never happened before. Santer was eventually replaced by Italy's Romano Prodi. It was a major victory for the European Parliament and a recognition of its power and importance, yet it was disastrous in terms of public faith in European institutions. Increasingly, the image came to prevail that the Commission lacked oversight and was interested only in self-aggrandizement.

Ongoing debates about institutional power made the situation worse. Like Maastricht, Amsterdam had failed to enact the bureaucratic reforms necessary to ensure that an enlarged EU would run efficiently. This was symptomatic of the different ways in which European leaders continued to think about integration. While they seemed to agree that it was an ever-evolving process, not every member state wanted to pursue *more* or *deeper* integration. In practice, this translated into disputes over whether reforms should benefit the supranational or intergovernmental level.

Nice brought these divisions out into the open. From the off, Chirac was keen for more power to be concentrated in the hands of member states. By contrast, Prodi was an advocate of strengthening supranational Commission influence. Motivated by the need to find a solution before the accession of ten new member states, Joschka Fischer, Germany's foreign minister, championed a different integration strategy entirely. His speech at Berlin's Humboldt University in May 2000 in effect advocated for a parliamentary

European federation which, he felt, was the only fitting model for a future EU with 30 or more members. This would have a chamber of deputies (i.e., the European Parliament, with members who would also have seats in their respective national parliaments), a senate (the Council) and a 'European government' (i.e. the Council *or* the Commission). Reaction to Fischer's proposals was rather reserved, but it nevertheless served to highlight fragmentation in the views of EU members. It was little surprise that it took over 300 hours for member states to agree on the agenda of the European Council due to meet in Nice on 7–9 December 2000. At the summit itself, after another marathon round of talks, only a few concrete steps towards reforming the EU were taken.

Again, there was not complete stalemate. One of the most important items for negotiation was the expansion of policy areas decided by qualified majority in the Council as well as the weighting of votes in that procedure, so that the latter would better reflect the populations of individual countries. Some cautious success was achieved when Britain, Germany, France, Italy, and Spain made a major concession by relinquishing the right to have two European commissioners. In view of the fallout of the Cresson case, the Commission president also gained new powers to dismiss individual commissioners. And agreement was finally reached on increasing the overall size of the European Parliament to 732 members. In addition, closer, or enhanced, cooperation was reformed to allow a minimum of eight states to push ahead with cooperation in a particular field rather than needing a majority as stipulated by Amsterdam. Each of these were important steps prior to the EU's eastern enlargement.

Yet behind these changes there were signs of tension and, ultimately, lack of substantial progress. In terms of QMV, Britain was quick to object to majority decisions applying to matters of security and taxation, while Germany raised questions in the case of supranational migrant policy. Meanwhile, France (which wanted parity) and Germany (with its larger population) battled hard over the weighting of QMV. A double majority of votes and population provided a compromise but, in the process, set the threshold (in effect, two-thirds) for majority decisions unreasonably high. Far from introducing a more streamlined procedure, gridlock threatened to become the norm. Like at Amsterdam, member states in Nice again postponed other reforms of the Commission. It was all very well for the larger member states to forgo their second commissioner, but retaining the rule of one commissioner per country still meant a scenario was likely in which the Commission would become unwieldy if the EU were to grow to perhaps as many as 27 members if not more. The solution was to put a ceiling – 27 commissioners – on the size of the Commission, but the Nice Treaty left it unclear how the EU would achieve fewer commissioners or indeed what system could be used to ensure all countries were fairly represented. The same problem emerged from the decision to stop the EP from growing beyond its 732 members.

In the end, the Nice Treaty – signed in February 2001 – was regarded as something of a disappointment. Despite the time pressure due to the upcoming enlargement, governments failed to come up with convincing answers to topics left over from Amsterdam. If anything, some institutional changes seemed to make the functioning of the Council and Commission more, not less complicated. Important suggestions by the Commission such as the creation of a European Public Prosecutor's Office (EPPO) to overcome national fragmentation of law enforcement were also ignored. And the status of the Charter of Fundamental Rights of the European Union (see below) was similarly left unresolved. Yet another round of discussions therefore seemed likely.

The birth and failure of the European Constitution

In retrospect, it was fortunate that the Nice Treaty emerged at all. As in 1992 when the Danish public voted against the Maastricht Treaty, in June 2001 voters in Ireland **rejected the Nice Treaty**. The reasons were numerous, but some argued that the EU was becoming ever more remote from the citizens it was meant to serve. Although the result was reversed in a second referendum held eighteen months later, and the treaty eventually entered into force in February 2003, this event was the latest example of a more general disenchantment with European politics. Two years earlier, parties critical of the EU, including the United Kingdom Independence Party (UKIP) and the French Mouvement pour la France (Movement for France, MPF), had gained ground in the European Parliament elections. At the same election, turnout had fallen to below 50% for the first time, highlighting if not scepticism then certainly apathy among European voters. These trends would only accelerate in the coming years.

Such challenges did not go unnoticed by political elites. During the 1990s, the EU's perceived lack of democratic legitimacy in fact became subject to ever more frequent criticism. This was symbolized by a new phase in which European leaders began serious attempts to reduce the gap between 'Europe' and its citizens. The result was that democracy and participation moved up the political agenda, in marked contrast to earlier years when political discussions often revolved around institutional power and policy fields. Thus, as early as 1999, on the advice of the European Parliament, EU member states had met to discuss writing a document that would outline all the rights of European citizens and residents. Out of this emerged a 62-person group of politicians, experts, and civil society actors – who called themselves 'the Convention' – tasked with drafting this document. By the time of the Nice Council meeting in December 2000 they had succeeded in producing a draft covering everything from rules on unfair dismissal and guarantees for the freedom of religion and assembly, to stating an individual's right to free expression, social assistance, a family life, and parental leave. Thus, the **Charter of Fundamental Rights of the European Union** was born.

From the start, the idea of a document was controversial. It evoked the illusion of a nation state governed by central constitutional principles. It also risked replicating the European Court of Human Rights at the Council of Europe in Strasbourg. Resistance to the provisions meant that at the December 2000 Nice European Council meeting, member states could not agree to give the document legal status or even make formal reference to it in the Nice Treaty. Yet this did not stop states such as Germany and the Benelux countries, which were determined to push ahead. Just a year later, with Belgium holding the rotating presidency, the European Council in Laeken consequently heard calls for a new 'Convention' of experts under the leadership of former French leader Valéry Giscard d'Estaing. Soon enough, he was given the ambitious task not simply of writing an amending treaty along the lines of Amsterdam and Nice but establishing a full-scale European Constitution. This, it was hoped, would tackle the limitations of previous treaties, identify where the EU could benefit from new shared competences, solve once-and-for-all the role and workings of EU institutions to best guarantee their efficiency in the face of enlargement, and more clearly bring citizens into policymaking – including by giving the Charter of Fundamental Rights legal standing within the EU. It was out of this process that the European Constitution, officially the **Treaty Establishing a Constitution for Europe** (TCE), would eventually emerge.

Giscard's 'Convention' expert group was similar in composition to the first, but it was also innovative: it held public meetings, internet forums, and media campaigns in effort to get the European public involved. But for all its good intentions, the difficulty of explaining complex content soon became apparent. Once the Convention reached the stage of drafting a text, Giscard felt the need to tighten the reins. Consequently, the draft of the TCE reflected Giscard's vision for a much stronger, more cohesive EU rather than the concerns of ordinary Europeans. When some – notably the

French, British, and Spanish governments – saw this as an opportunity to strengthen the Council and reduce the influence of the Commission instead, the same old arguments over supranationalism resurfaced.

The scepticism of European citizens grew amid the ensuing, closed negotiations. Not even the symbolic significance of the place where the Constitution was signed on 29 October 2004 – in the very same location where the Treaty of Rome had been signed in 1957 – could allay these anxieties. It was no surprise that **two referendums** – in France on 29 May 2005 and in the Netherlands three days later – brought ratification to a crashing halt. Given the earlier Danish and Irish referendums, the sense of *déjà vu* was palpable. But this time there would be no second vote: the TCE was dead in the water.

Enlargement and the Treaty of Lisbon

By the time French and Dutch voters rejected the TCE, the first stage of the **'big bang' enlargement** of 1 May 2004 had already seen the EU expand from fifteen member states to 25. Accession negotiations with six countries – Poland, Hungary, the Czech Republic, Estonia, Slovenia, and Cyprus – had opened back in 1998. As this process got underway, few doubted that these countries were in a good position to fulfil the Copenhagen criteria and absorb the vast body of EU rules – the *acquis communautaire* – into national law. But this was not necessarily the case for others. Analysis by the Commission, published in the first of its annual progress reports, pointed out concerns over Slovakia's stagnant democratization process. Beyond the benefits of enlargement discussed above, two more immediate pragmatic considerations prompted the decision to invite not only Slovakia but also five other countries – Malta, Latvia, Lithuania, Romania, and Bulgaria – to open negotiations. First, additional delay would have created a long, temporary outer border of the EU, which would have been costly in terms of infrastructure for customs and border control. Second, accession in two or more waves would run counter to the idea of regional cooperation and suggest instead a two-tier ranking of countries, something that Brussels sought to avoid. Come December 2002, the EU had thus concluded negotiations with all but two of these twelve countries.

The two countries excluded were Romania and Bulgaria. Initially, this decision came as a shock to them both. Yet the EU's thinking was understandable: the Commission's October 2002 progress reports had argued that while both needed investment in agriculture, transport infrastructure, and environmental protections of the sort that EU membership could provide, their stagnant political and administrative reform processes remained a cause for concern. Even the prospect of enlargement, rather than enlargement itself, it was suspected, would compel them to continue making progress in these areas. At the same time, existing member states were unwilling to risk the EU's internal cohesion or spend money while inefficiency and corruption remained rife. To push them further towards reform, Brussels therefore opted to continue monitoring the level of their compliance with EU norms – observations that would continue even after Romania and Bulgaria finally joined the EU in 2007.

Even so, EU membership was widely perceived as crowning ten long years of post-socialist political and economic reforms. True, enlargement has not been without its challenges. Membership of Estonia and Latvia, each with large Russian minority populations, as well as the historic Cyprus question, immediately involved the EU in tricky strategic questions and massively complicated its external relations with Russia and Turkey respectively. Longer-term issues relating to freedom of movement, the broader costs of absorbing so many relatively poor countries (by Western standards), and the ability of the EU framework to preserve the democratic standards of its newer members, have all cast a shadow over enlargement as a foreign policy device. Without diminishing these issues, the 2004 and 2007 enlargements were doubtless a historic moment. They united once hostile societies and nations. And they brought various political, economic, social, and cultural opportunities to both acceding and existing member states.

After the French and Dutch referendums, such positive readings of the EU's achievements was not in ready supply. Following these referendums, EU leaders prescribed a 'period of reflection' to take stock of events. Come September 2006, this led to yet another group of seasoned politicians being asked to find a way out of yet another crisis, headed this time by the former Italian Prime Minister Giuliano Amato, who had previously been involved in the Convention overseen by Giscard. Amato's approach could not have been more different from Giscard's, however: citizen participation was taboo for him. With enlargement now a reality, there was an added urgency to work as swiftly as possible. Within just nine months, **the Amato group** had drafted its report. The group's recommendations would ultimately form the basis of the present Treaty of Lisbon, signed on 13 December 2007.

In place of a single codified constitution covering every aspect of the EU's workings, Lisbon was a revision of two existing treaties. There would be a modified Treaty on European Union – the intergovernmental elements of Maastricht – containing text from the first section of the failed

Constitutional Treaty. Alongside this, a modified Treaty Establishing the European Community – the first 'pillar' of Maastricht comprising the original Treaty of Rome – was renamed the **Treaty on the Functioning of the European Union** (TFEU). Signed in Lisbon, this included many elements in the latter half of the abortive Constitution.

On the face of it, this revision suggested a high degree of overlap between Lisbon and the unsuccessful Constitutional Treaty. But it was not a precise carbon copy. Lisbon reflected the reality that Europeans were increasingly averse to 'more Europe' and it minimized the TCE's constitutional ambitions accordingly. No reference was made for instance to a European flag or anthem. Nor was there any invocation of God. Moreover, the person in charge of foreign policy was not referred to as a minister. Compared to the Constitution, Lisbon also enhanced intergovernmental guarantees on several strategic issues. For example, the 'yellow card' and 'orange card' procedures in Lisbon were a much-revised reversion of the TCE's early warning system designed to reinforce the national level: if a certain number of national parliaments protest, the Commission must review any proposals it has made. In this same vein, the Charter of Fundamental Rights was not integrated into the Lisbon Treaty itself, although it was recognized as legally binding. For similar symbolic reasons, the primacy of European law over national law was relegated to an annex, while the main text underlined national sovereignty. And for the first time, the Treaty laid down that countries could not just accede to the EU but member states could also undertake an 'orderly exit' from the EU – a stipulation which, when written, seemed hypothetical.

In other ways, the Constitutional Treaty's innovations were upheld. This was true of areas such as enhanced cooperation, where both the TCE and Lisbon specified objectives and expanded it to areas including defence. It was equally true for institutional changes. One example is differentiation between the Council of Ministers and the European Council – long recognized but never fully incorporated into a treaty – which was first proposed in the TCE only to reappear in Lisbon. Lisbon similarly included plans to create a permanent president of the European Council appointed for a term of two and a half years – a position which threatened to overshadow the Commission as the main external face of the EU – at the same time reducing the significance of the rotating presidency. Like the TCE, too, Lisbon merged the High Representative for CFSP and the commissioner for external relations (although it gave the new official a different name). As also envisaged by the European Constitution, this single foreign affairs post was to be supported by a new diplomatic service, the European External Action Service (EEAS), which was expected to work at bridging the gap between the communitarian structures of the Commission and the intergovernmental ideas of the Council. Both texts further mentioned that the choice of president of the Commission would be made with reference to the performance of parties in European parliamentary elections, replacing the previous practice of merely asking for the Parliament's consent for whomever was nominated. Alongside an extension of the co-decision procedure, this provision seemed to add additional weight to the Parliament at the expense of EU governments.

Both texts also sought to answer questions left unresolved by earlier treaties. They tackled QMV in similar ways, after several years of criticisms that the two-third majority set out in the Nice Treaty was impracticable. So too did the spirit of 'one citizen, one vote' appear in both texts, with at least 55% of member states and 65% of the population required to win approval. And in finally agreeing a formula to settle the size of the European Parliament and the Commission, both the failed Constitutional Treaty and the Treaty of Lisbon sought to succeed where Maastricht, Amsterdam, and Nice had failed.

Given this overlap, it is perhaps not surprising that ratification was again not straightforward. National parliamentary ratification did admittedly proceed much more smoothly. Yet the governments of Poland and the Czech Republic extracted additional concessions from Brussels in exchange for their consent. And once again the Irish were compelled to hold a second referendum in October 2009 after voters rejected the treaty in June 2008. It was in part because of this experience that when the ratification process was finally completed at the end of 2009, government leaders and the Commission agreed that the **days of major treaty reform were over**. These sorts of referendum results, and the growth of Eurosceptic forces throughout the 1990s and 2000s, suggested that another such endeavour could jeopardize the EU's past achievements.

At the same time, the existing treaties appeared to offer ample room to deepen integration without needing to resort to full-scale treaty change. Few better examples exist than **differentiated integration**, of which two main types have emerged. The first – deepening differentiation – allows EU member states to pursue integration without others. Enhanced cooperation most obviously provides a ready-made avenue for closer ties while recognizing the reluctance of some to move forward. Outside the treaties, a practical if inelegant solution has also emerged allowing for ad-hoc coalitions to tackle specific, urgent problems.

The second form is enlargement differentiation. At first sight, a country is either a member or not. Yet by the mid-2000s it was obvious that the EU was an ever-more complicated matrix. Norway is not a member proper but is part of Schengen; non-EU member Turkey now participates in the Customs Union; the non-EU states Vatican City, Monaco, and San Marino participate in the euro but Denmark and Sweden do not; and the western Balkans and Ukraine have degrees of association beyond free trade cooperation, but short of membership proper.

Differentiated integration is not without its critics. It might well facilitate deepening but is interpreted by some as being liable to make EU decision-making still more convoluted and inefficient and potentially less transparent. In this argument, differentiation is an example of EU actors taking continued strides to streamline the EU's institutional architecture without ensuring that these efforts are in lockstep with the strengthening or guaranteeing of the Union's democratic legitimacy.

Conclusion

How, then, should this period of treaties and transformation be interpreted? The era of Maastricht, Amsterdam, Nice and Lisbon was doubtless marked by successes regarding *how* the EU functioned and *who* made policies. The long-awaited EMU was realized, as was a European foreign policy. Both European and national parliaments strengthened their positions. All of this came during, and in many ways because of, the various waves of enlargement during the 1990s and 2000s. That expansion not only saw the EU's competences grow but also involved a restructuring of the decision-making process that governed them. New competences such as security and democratization meanwhile highlighted the EU's undoubted emergence as a, if not *the*, major player in European politics.

But the EU was in some ways an imperfect union. Enlargement was realized but not everyone agreed about *what* 'Europe' is or should be. Relations between EU member states were characterized by a powerful appeal to national interests. As new policy areas increased the Commission's influence because of the need for technical support, the Council remained an intergovernmental counterweight; intergovernmentalism and supranationalism thus went hand in hand. And the citizen became both more central to the EU's functioning and a major risk to its stability and cohesion – it was not obvious that the answer to *why* the EU existed would always be affirmative. Yet, however transformative and testing this period was, in retrospect the greatest challenges and controversies the EU faced were still to come.

Further reading

– Bicchi, Federica, and Daniel Schade. 'Whither European Diplomacy? Long-Term Trends and the Impact of the Lisbon Treaty.' *Cooperation and Conflict* 57, no. 1 (2022): 3–24.
– Bickerton, Christopher J., Dermot Hodson, and Uwe Puetter, eds. *The New Intergovernmentalism: States and Supranational Actors in the Post-Maastricht Era*. Oxford: Oxford University Press, 2015.
– Gray, Mark, and Alexander Stubb. 'The Treaty of Nice: Negotiating a Poisoned Chalice?' *Journal of Common Market Studies* 392, vol. 1 (2001): 5–23.
– Ludlow, N. Piers. 'European Integration in the 1980s: On the Way to Maastricht?' *Journal of European Integration History* 19, no. 1 (2013): 11–22.
– Moravcsik, Andrew, and Kalypso Nicolaïdis. 'Explaining the Treaty of Amsterdam: Interests, Influence, Institutions.' *Journal of Common Market Studies* 37, no. 1 (1999): 59–85.
– Smith, Karen. *The Making of EU Foreign Policy: The Case of Eastern Europe*. Basingstoke: Palgrave Macmillan, 1999.
– Usherwood, Simon. 'Realists, Sceptics and Opponents: Opposition to the EU's Constitutional Treaty.' *Journal of Contemporary European Research* 1, no. 2 (2005): 4–12.

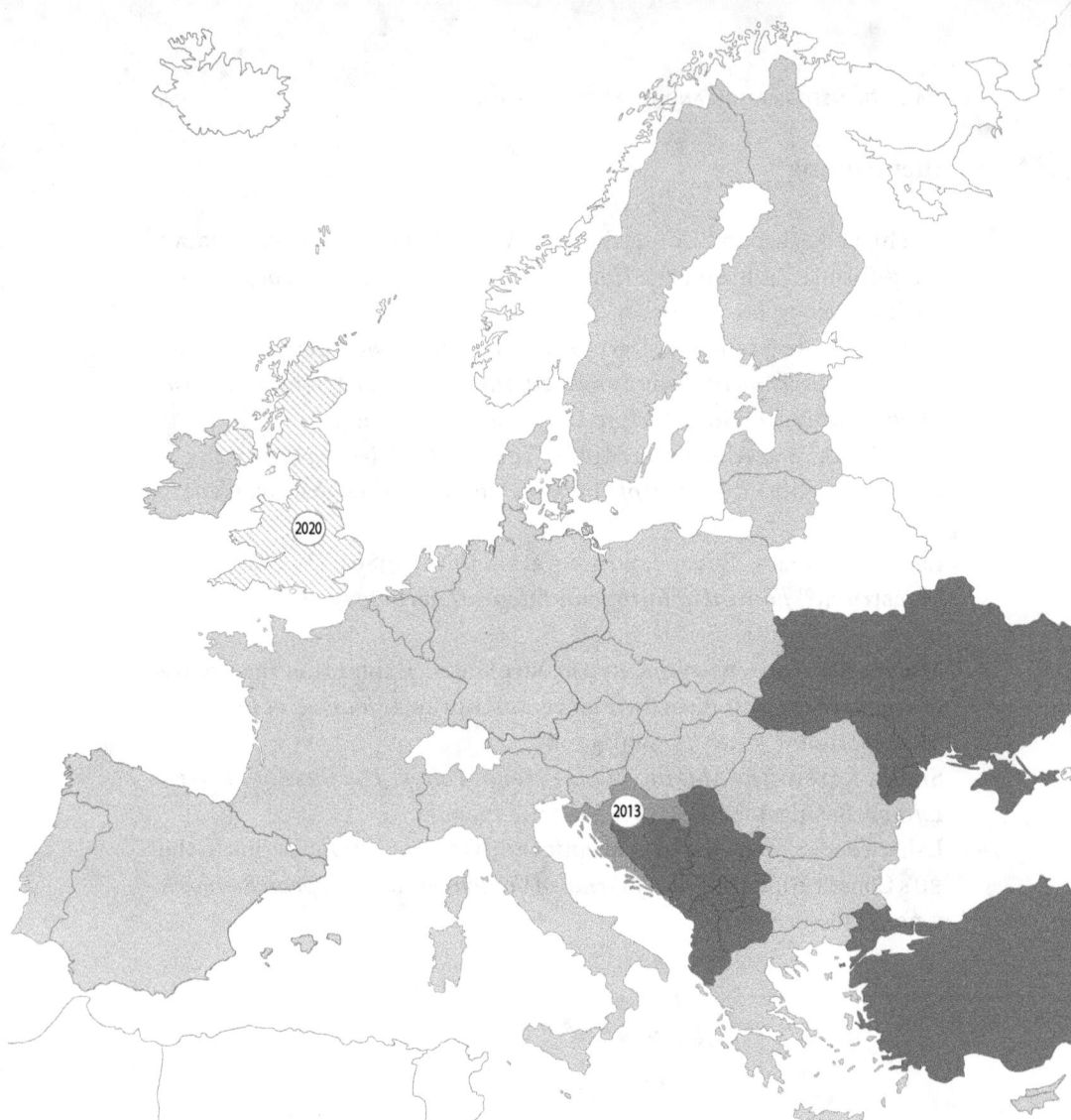

2009 Start eurozone sovereign debt crisis
      Eastern Partnership programme launched

2010 First bailout package Greece; bailout Ireland
      Viktor Orbán's Fidesz party in power

2012 'Whatever it takes' speech by ECB president Mario Draghi
      Introduction European Stability Mechanism

2013 Accession of Croatia

2014 Russian invasion of Ukraine and annexation of Crimea
      EU Association Agreements with Georgia, Moldova, Ukraine
      Opening of accession negotiations with Serbia

2015 Quantitative easing by ECB; end eurozone crisis
      Start migrant 'crisis'
      Juncker Commission launches Digital Single Market Strategy

2016 United Kingdom votes to leave EU in membership
      referendum
      Migration deal between EU and Turkey
      Commission announces EU Global Strategy

2019 Von der Leyen Commission launches European Green Deal

2020 Start COVID-19 pandemic
      Commission initiates Next Generation EU recovery plan
      United Kingdom departs from EU

2022 Renewed Russian invasion of Ukraine
      Opening of accession negotiations with Albania and
      North Macedonia

2023 Opening of accession negotiations with Georgia,
      Moldova, Ukraine

2024 Opening of accession negotiations with Bosnia and
      Herzegovina

6. From crises to new directions? Contemporary European integration, 2007–2024

Since the conclusion of the Lisbon Treaty, the European Union (EU) has been confronted by significant new challenges, ranging from the eurozone sovereign debt crisis and Brexit to the COVID-19 pandemic and the Russian invasions of Ukraine. Many EU analysts suggest that such crises often drive deeper European integration, suggesting a pattern of 'failing forward' (CHAPTER 7). This chapter argues that both internal and external crises have played a pivotal role in influencing European integration dynamics during the 2010s and 2020s, echoing the 1970s (CHAPTER 4). Also, the chapter examines how key actors have shaped as well as contested the EU's responses to these challenges, highlighting that the EU does not automatically gravitate towards further crisis-induced integration. The focus lies on the period between 2008 and 2024, which was marked by a number of interconnected developments, namely major crises, a fundamental deepening and broadening of European integration, key changes in EU foreign policy and geopolitics, and a new scope and level of politicization of the EU.

The chapter is organized chronologically around four thematic sections. First, it covers the EU's answer to the financial and eurozone crises and its aftermath. Second, it addresses three other major challenges of the 2010s: the so-called migrant 'crisis' of 2015–2016, the United Kingdom's (UK) departure in 2016, and democratic backsliding. Combined with the euro crisis, they have contributed to a rise in Euroscepticism and EU politicization as well as to debates over European *dis*integration. Third, the chapter discusses foreign policy and enlargement. While a sense of enlargement fatigue set in after 2007, rising geopolitical tensions and events such as the Russian invasion of Ukraine in 2014 gave a newfound urgency to initiatives for greater 'strategic autonomy' of the EU in foreign and security policy. Lastly, the chapter argues that there are a number of new directions and important shifts in the dynamics of European integration in the early 2020s, reflecting on the observation in the introduction that the EU is at a crossroads. After years of fiscal restraint, the EU's reaction to the COVID-19 pandemic and the European Green Deal (EGD) indicate a move away from neoliberal austerity to more neomercantilist policies, which are also aimed at strengthening competitiveness with the United States and China. Moreover, the renewed

Russian invasion of Ukraine in 2022 has marked a turning point in post-Cold War European integration and underscored the need to reconsider European foreign and security policy. In light of these developments, the questions of how the EU should function and what its purpose should be in a changing world have become pertinent once again. The answers to these questions are deeply political and constantly evolving, as can be seen in the EU's response to the euro crisis.

The eurozone crisis and economic divergence

The **financial crisis** of 2007–2008 was the most severe global economic downturn since the Great Depression of the 1930s. It was triggered by the collapse of the United States housing bubble. The crisis swiftly spread to the EU since many member states' financial sectors were deeply intertwined with the American economy and housing market. Moreover, these financial sectors had expanded significantly in the years before the crisis. Banks in western European member states such as the UK, Ireland, France, Spain, the Netherlands, and Germany had liabilities and balance sheets that far outstripped their respective countries' entire gross domestic product (GDP). The financial crisis disrupted global trade and the transnational flow of capital, which critically threatened the liquidity of the European financial sectors. To prevent collapse, member states either nationalized banks or provided substantial amounts of money for bank recapitalization and debt guarantees. The European Central Bank (ECB) responded swiftly by providing funds to support EU banks as interbank lending became increasingly hesitant. However, Germany's opposition to a unified approach by European institutions, such as common bank bailout programmes, set the tone for how it would operate as the eurozone's largest economy.

The crisis exposed several fundamental imbalances within the European Monetary Union (EMU). First, it revealed the imperfections of the union. Unlike national central banks, the ECB had few fiscal tools and primarily focused on maintaining price stability. Additionally, there was limited monetary integration, leading to a lack of coordination on economic policies, taxation, and fiscal transfers. Second, the EMU saw export-oriented economies such as Germany sharing the same currency with less competitive economies in southern Europe. Since these economies had given up their sovereignty in monetary affairs, they could no longer devalue their currencies in response. Third, the Maastricht criteria of the Stability and Growth Pact (SGP) (CHAPTER 5) were not rigorously enforced. When France and

Germany failed to adhere to these criteria, there was a lack of political will in the European Council to enforce them. Fourth, all eurozone members could borrow money at low interest rates, backed by the productivity of northwestern European members and their reputation as dependable debtors. Combined with the lax regulation of the Maastricht criteria, this led to southern European members accumulating large debts, often issued by French and German private banks.

From financial crisis to eurozone crisis

The financial crisis evolved into a **eurozone sovereign debt crisis** in 2009 when Greece faced a serious risk of defaulting on its debt. The newly elected Greek government disclosed that Greece's budget deficit was four times higher than previously reported. Consequently, interest rates on Greek bonds surged and credit rating agencies downgraded Greece, which already had the highest debt-to-GDP ratio in the eurozone. A Greek bankruptcy would threaten the entire eurozone. However, the ECB lacked a ready-made toolbox to address the crisis. When the euro was introduced, it was not anticipated that a country would be unable to pay its debts. Furthermore, the Treaty of the Functioning of the European Union prohibited bailouts. Eurozone member states initially disagreed on how to respond to the Greek debt crisis. German Chancellor Angela Merkel led opposition to both a bailout and a debt write-off. This stance was influenced by a critical German electorate and concerns about potential losses from German and northern European banks, totalling tens of billions of euros.

Financial assistance to Greece came at the price of **austerity** and loss of sovereignty to a newly established institutional arrangement known as the Troika, comprised of the ECB, the International Monetary Fund (IMF), and the European Commission. Merkel insisted on including the IMF due to concerns that the Commission might be too lenient. Additionally, she valued the expertise and additional funding provided by the IMF, hoping it would appease German public opinion. The Troika's initial rescue package for Greece amounted to 110 billion euros and was conditional upon extensive reforms, austerity measures, privatization, and budget cuts to align with the Maastricht criteria. Despite widespread protests and nationwide strikes in Greece, the **bailout** was ultimately accepted. Under pressure from financial markets and after intense negotiations, the European Council established the European Financial Stability Facility (EFSF). The EFSF was a temporary support mechanism for eurozone members which issued bonds or other debt instruments guaranteed by the ECB to raise funds to provide loans to

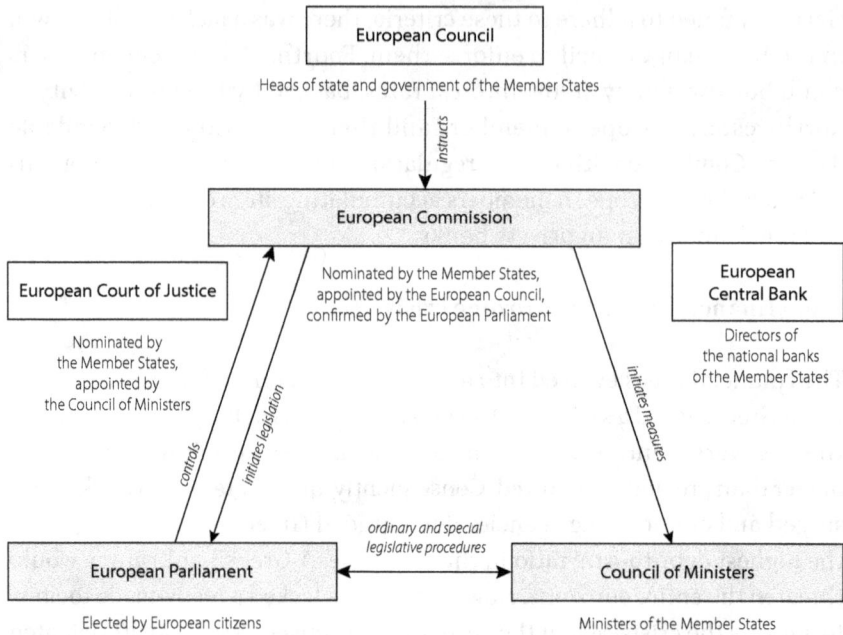

European institutions: Treaty of Lisbon 2007/2009

eurozone countries, a significant new competence for the institution. In 2012, the Troika oversaw a second bailout of 130 billion euros provided by the EFSF, coupled with private debt write-offs. These measures prevented a Greek bankruptcy and reduced Greece's budget deficit. However, they came at a significant social cost, including a deepening recession, a 40% decrease in purchasing power, and a 24% unemployment rate by 2012. In response the Greek prime minister initially proposed a referendum on the second bailout program but eventually backed down under pressure from other European Council members.

Greece was not the sole eurozone member facing financial difficulties. Ireland and Portugal also applied for bailout packages from the EFSF. Concerns of the financial markets extended to Italy too. Although the Italian economy was not yet in severe crisis, high levels of debt raised alarm and led to a sharp increase in interest rates on Italian bonds. A more pressing issue than Italy's debt was the bursting of Spain's real estate bubble. This caused a near-collapse of Spain's financial sector and an economic downturn including a staggering youth unemployment rate of 55%. To avert a crash of the eurozone's fourth-largest economy, the Troika approved a 100 billion euros assistance package under the EFSF. Although Italy did not have to seek aid, the ECB demanded that Italy, like Spain and others facing economic difficulties, implement austerity measures and reforms as crisis response efforts.

Mounting concerns over the future of the euro prompted the implementation of new EU measures. However, in northern European countries with high credit ratings, such as Germany, the Netherlands, or Finland, public debate was often characterized by stereotypical references to corruption and tax evasion in the so-called 'PIIGS' countries: Portugal, Ireland, Italy, Greece, and Spain. During the 2012 Dutch election campaign, the incumbent Prime Minister Mark Rutte opposed a third Greek bailout and even speculated on a Greek eurozone exit. However, despite such critiques and strong domestic opposition, Chancellor Merkel managed to maintain eurozone cohesion on the response to the crisis, although this often leaned towards fiscal conservativism and austerity measures. After lengthy negotiations, the European Council finally agreed on the establishment of the **European Stability Mechanism** (ESM). With a maximum lending capacity of 500 billion euros, the ESM replaced the EFSF as a permanent intergovernmental organization for instant financial assistance. It was accompanied by a new, stricter version of the SGP. The Commission now monitored states' debts and budgets and had the authority to impose measures if these exceeded established norms. The ESM constituted a stepping stone towards a closer, but still incomplete fiscal union, focusing primarily on budget restraint rather than converging economic policies or transfer payments.

The ECB began to take significantly more initiative to save the euro. In 2012, newly appointed ECB President Mario Draghi declared that 'Within our mandate, the ECB is ready to do whatever it takes to preserve the euro. And believe me, it will be enough.' Under Draghi's leadership, the ECB transformed from a distant central bank into an institution dedicated to safeguarding the overall financial and macroeconomic stability of the eurozone. First, it demanded that eurozone members adhere to budget norms and implement austerity to prevent excessive debt accumulation. Second, it committed to purchasing bonds issued by members without a predetermined limit, overcoming initial German opposition. Thus, the ECB injected up to 500 billion euros into 800 eurozone banks. Third, it implemented a fully-fledged **quantitative easing** policy aimed at increasing the money supply in the economy and stimulating lending and economic growth by injecting well over one trillion euros into the economy by regular purchases of state and corporate bonds. Quantitative easing followed earlier policies by the ECB aimed at lowering interest rates to nearly zero to increase money supply. Finally, strides were made towards a European Banking Union (EBU). Although the EBU remains incomplete, the ECB assumed oversight of systemically significant eurozone banks from national central banks and implemented mechanisms to manage bank failure.

Economic divergence

The economic crisis in central and eastern Europe usually receives less attention in narratives of the euro crisis. Before 2007, member states from this region were making significant progress towards reaching economic parity with western Europe. This was in no small part due to EU financial assistance which, proportionally speaking, exceeded that of the Marshall Plan. Between 2007 and 2013, Poland alone received 40 billion euros, nearly matching foreign investments in the country. However, the booming economies of these new member states were hit harshly by the crisis. Among those most affected were Lithuania and Estonia, where GDP shrunk by respectively 14.8% and 14.6% in 2009, while Hungary and Romania experienced decreases of 6.6% and 5.5%. Foreign investment, crucial for sustaining growth, came to a virtual standstill and in several countries, real estate bubbles burst. Furthermore, many citizens had taken out loans in foreign currencies arranged by Austrian and Swedish banks, which accounted for up to half of all private credit in Hungary and Romania. These loans became almost impossible to repay when the exchange rates of their domestic currencies depreciated.

Since the newly acceded member states were not yet eurozone members they received less EU aid in practice. Austrian and Hungarian proposals for a collective EU response to the economic crisis in central and eastern Europe were rejected by Germany. Still, the IMF and the European Commission intervened with aid packages to prevent bankruptcies, contingent upon the implementation of neoliberal reforms and austerity measures. Poland, the largest new member state, fared better during the crisis and adopted a more stimulus-focused approach while maintaining GDP growth. Conversely, states subjected to stringent financial austerity performed significantly worse. In Latvia, for instance, unemployment surged to 20%. Another consequence of this severe recession was large-scale emigration from particularly the Baltic states and Romania. In the long term, the crisis, coupled with limited EU support, halted the economic convergence of many central and eastern European member states with western Europe. Additionally, the subdued EU response dispelled the belief that merely joining the EU would inevitably bring prosperity and that the West held all the solutions.

The choice for severe austerity had a similar negative long-term impact on southern Europe. Both Italy's and Spain's GDP and GDP per capita have remained stagnant since 2007. The situation is even worse in Greece. In 2008, Greece had a GDP of 356 billion US dollars and a GDP per capita of 32,128 US dollars, which plummeted to 219 billion US dollars and 20,732 US dollars by 2022. In western Europe, the adoption of neoliberal measures and budget cuts also had detrimental consequences, such as a double-dip recession in the Netherlands, while the British Conservative government implemented deeper public sector cuts than even Prime Minister Margaret Thatcher did in the 1980s. Moreover, the narrative of European solidarity suffered serious damage. Discriminatory remarks made by northern European politicians exacerbated tensions. For example, in 2017, the Dutch Minister of Finance and Eurogroup chair Jeroen Dijsselbloem chided southern Europeans by stating, 'You cannot spend all the money on alcohol and women and then ask for help' – a remark for which he refused to apologize.

The EU's crisis response and perceived shortcomings in national democratic control triggered a **political backlash** that often took on a Eurosceptic tone. In southern Europe, far-left parties such as Podemos in Spain or Syriza in Greece capitalized on discontent at EU-imposed austerity. In 2015, Syriza succeeded in forming a coalition government but failed to renegotiate bailout packages with Brussels. Additionally, support grew for other Eurosceptic populist parties such as Five Star Movement (M5S) in Italy, which advocated a referendum on leaving the eurozone. In western Europe, populist radical right-wing parties such as the Freedom Party (PVV) in the Netherlands, the United Kingdom Independence Party (UKIP) in Britain, the National Front in France, and the Alternative for Germany (AfD), sought to exploit dissatisfaction with the handling of the euro crisis. These parties also made large gains during the 2014 European Parliament elections. In central and eastern Europe, there was a smaller increase in Euroscepticism with a less clear correlation with the crisis. However, in economically hard-hit Hungary, Viktor Orbán's populist radical right-wing Fidesz party returned to power with an overtly Eurosceptic agenda, also partly fuelled by dissatisfaction with the previous government. Another crisis that soon followed the euro crisis would reinforce this EU-critical trend in politics.

The migrant 'crisis' of 2015–2016

From 2012 onwards, there was a significant increase in the number of **refugees and migrants** arriving in the EU. This surge was primarily driven by the aftermath of the popular uprisings in the Middle East and North

Africa, known as the 'Arab Spring', which led to destabilization in several countries in the region, notably Syria, Libya, and Yemen. Many refugees, particularly those fleeing the prolonged Syrian civil war, initially sought refuge in neighbouring countries. However, these countries could only accommodate a limited number of refugees, prompting many to look towards Europe for a brighter future. Additionally, the collapse of Libya's government resulted in the breakdown of controls on trans-Mediterranean boat migration. In 2015 and 2016, a record 1.3 million and 1.2 million people respectively applied for asylum in the EU, marking the highest numbers since the Yugoslav Wars of the early 1990s. According to the EU's Dublin Regulation, asylum seekers must be processed in the member state of their arrival unless specific criteria, such as family reunification, are met. The majority of arrivals were concentrated in a few entry points in Greece and Italy, which were quickly overwhelmed. Unable to manage all asylum applications and grappling with economic difficulties, Greece and Italy appealed to the EU for support, particularly in terms of relocating migrants. Other member states situated along the main migratory routes towards northwestern Europe, such as Hungary, also faced challenges in accommodating tens of thousands of migrants.

The surge in migrant numbers created a **political crisis** primarily because several member states opposed EU-wide schemes aimed at resettling asylum seekers or preventing their arrival altogether. As tensions escalated over the migrant issue and the deplorable conditions in which many migrants were accommodated worsened, Chancellor Merkel announced that Germany would start accepting all asylum seekers and would temporarily suspend implementing the Dublin Regulation. Consequently, a significant number of migrants turned to Germany, which received circa 1.5 million asylum requests in 2015–2016, along with Sweden, which was similarly welcoming. Later the Commission's proposal to proportionally relocate asylum seekers from Italy and Greece to other member states was approved by the Council of Ministers. Hungary openly contested this proposal, but other member states such as Poland also obstructed its implementation, and it was never fully carried out as a result. For a while, even the Schengen Agreement and the EU's principle of free movement seemed in jeopardy. The movement of migrants to Sweden and Germany prompted several countries, including Austria, Denmark, France, Germany, Norway, Poland, and Sweden to temporarily reintroduce border controls. Meanwhile, the construction of border fences was initiated by other member states such as Hungary, Bulgaria, and also by the UK and France at the Channel Tunnel and port of Calais. The reluctance of many member states to accept migrants and the insufficient aid provided to countries overwhelmed by migrant arrivals not only undermined the EU's reputation as a defender of human rights but also eroded European solidarity.

The politicization of migration in 2015 and 2016 correlated with a further rise in Euroscepticism, particularly on the populist and radical right. Populist radical right-wing parties across Europe contended that the EU had lost control of its borders to waves of migrants. From 2015 onwards, populist and radical right-wing Eurosceptic parties made significant electoral gains. In Germany, the AfD secured 12.6% of the vote during the 2017 general election, compared to 4.7% in 2013, by capitalizing on discontent at Merkel's migration policies. In neighbouring Denmark, the Danish People's Party became the second-largest party in 2015. Italy's 2018 general election saw the Eurosceptic and anti-immigrant M5S emerge victorious, alongside substantial electoral gains for the populist radical right-wing parties Lega Nord and Brothers of Italy (FdI). Consequently, concerns among EU leaders regarding potential electoral losses prompted a shift towards more restrictive immigration policies. In central and eastern Europe, where popular reluctance at immigration was more prevalent, various governments adopted hard anti-immigration measures coupled with sharp criticism of 'Brussels', viewing its demands for migrant relocation as undermining national sovereignty. Hungary, under Orbán's leadership, championed this approach, and was joined increasingly by Poland, where the right-wing populist and Eurosceptic Law and Justice Party (PiS) assumed power in 2015. The political dynamics surrounding the migrant 'crisis' also shaped political discourse in Britain.

European disintegration: Brexit

The decision to organize a **British referendum** on EU membership in 2016 was largely driven by contingent factors and short-term political calculations rather than deep-seated, long-term reasons. For forty years the UK had been a member of the European Community (EC)/EU. However, during the 1990s and 2000s, the UK opted out of various key new common policies, most notably concerning fiscal and monetary integration. Additionally, the handling of the euro crisis and later the migrant 'crisis' strengthened Eurosceptic sentiments in the country. When Conservative Party leader David Cameron became prime minister in 2010, he faced pressure from within his party to negotiate better terms for the UK 'in Europe'. This pressure intensified with the rise of the Eurosceptic and radical right-wing UKIP, which became the largest British party in the European Parliament after the 2014 elections. Consequently, Cameron renegotiated several concessions, including formal recognition that British taxpayers would not contribute to eurozone bailouts, a potential temporary brake on full access to in-work benefits for newly arriving EU migrant workers, and symbolic exemption from references to an 'ever closer union' in future EU treaty amendments. Claiming to have secured a 'special status' for the UK, Cameron entered debates on the membership referendum on the 'Remain' side.

In 2016, 51.89% of the British electorate voted for **Brexit** – much to the surprise of both the British and European political elite. This outcome was markedly different from the 1975 referendum, when 67% had voted in favour of remaining in the EC (CHAPTER 4). Like during the 1975 referendum, the Remain campaign emphasized economic arguments for membership. By contrast, the 'Leave' side centred its campaign on opposition to migration from eastern Europe and Turkey. Other key themes were the notion of being a net contributor to the EU, including the dubious claim that the UK spent £350 million per week on EU membership, and fears of losing sovereignty. Moreover, the Leave campaign successfully tapped into anti-immigration sentiments that had been intensified since the migrant 'crisis' of 2015–2016 by projecting these concerns onto 'Brussels.' However, it is important not to view the Brexit referendum as the inevitable culmination of four decades of an 'awkward partnership' with the EU. Instead, it should be understood largely as the result of political manoeuvring and specific debates tied to the mid-2010s.

The process of leaving the European Union proved to be lengthy and complex, although on paper, Article 50 of the Lisbon Treaty provided a framework for leaving and a two-year withdrawal period. Brexit presented the EU with a dilemma: it needed to maintain a close relationship with the UK as a key partner while also setting a precedent to discourage other member states from following suit. From the onset, the EU adopted a moderate stance, with the Polish European Council President Donald Tusk stressing that the EU-27 would not take a 'punitive approach.' Key EU demands included minimizing disruption, preserving an open Irish border, and ensuring British commitment on remaining financial obligations. Conversely, the British government lacked clarity on its Brexit strategy. In 2019, the British Parliament rejected a proposed withdrawal agreement, resulting in the collapse of the government. Eventually, a new agreement was reached, postponing the UK's departure until 2020 after multiple extensions granted by the EU. Despite concerns, a hard border between Ireland and the UK was avoided, but the UK did leave both the single market and the customs union. The chaotic way the UK departed paradoxically underscored the benefits of EU membership. Unexpectedly, the EU-27 maintained cohesion and solidarity, with Eurobarometer polls showing increased overall support for EU membership after 2016. Nevertheless, Brexit marked the first time a sovereign EU member state chose to leave, even though the UK remained deeply involved in European and transatlantic integration through other forums. Contrary to fears at the time, Brexit did not inspire plans to leave the EU elsewhere and, in fact, many Eurosceptic parties abandoned such plans over time. However, some of these parties would undermine the EU in a different way.

Democratic backsliding

During the 2010s, political parties came to power in various European Union member states that undermined the rule of law and democratic governance at large. This trend is usually defined as **democratic backsliding**, which denotes the erosion or reversal of democratic institutions, norms, and practices. The most severe cases of democratic backsliding occurred in Hungary, governed by Orbán's Fidesz Party since 2010, and Poland under coalition governments led by PiS between 2015–2023. Orbán's regime in Hungary undermined liberal democratic checks and balances, curtailed media freedom, skewed the electoral process, weakened judicial independence, extended partisan control over the state, and fostered corruption. Embracing populist nationalist rhetoric, Orbán designated Hungary an 'illiberal democracy' while denouncing minorities, opposition voices, and the EU. In many ways PiS adopted Orbán's playbook, especially regarding the frontal attack on judicial independence. Elements of democratic backsliding have also been observed in Bulgaria, the Czech Republic Romania, and Slovenia among other countries, while in Slovakia and Malta, journalists investigating government corruption were even murdered. However, in the early 2020s voters in the Czech Republic Slovenia, and Poland elected parties to power which strongly opposed further erosion of democratic norms. This demonstrates that democratic backsliding is not necessarily permanent or irreversible and underlines the non-linear nature of the development as well as the contestation of democracies.

It should not be forgotten that western European member states also faced claims of democratic backsliding, particularly in terms of the rule of law and the treatment of non-nationals. Moreover, some older EU members rank lower on democratic indexes than newer members in the Baltics and central Europe. For instance, the Netherlands, which has frequently criticized Hungary and Poland on democratic standards, saw Mark Rutte's cabinet resign in 2021 due to discriminatory practices by tax authorities which systematically targeted citizens with a migration background. While the Commission's focus on Hungary and Poland is justified given their severe democratic backsliding, there is a noticeable normative and geographic bias on which countries are scrutinized for their democratic merits.

The EU has long struggled to do more than merely condemn democratic backsliding. As early as 2013, the foreign ministers of Germany, Denmark, Finland, and the Netherlands urged the Commission to establish procedures for safeguarding democratic norms in response to controversial constitutional reforms in Hungary. Consequently, in 2014 the Commission introduced the Rule of Law Framework to engage with member states that face systemic threats to the rule of law, although it lacked binding enforcement mechanisms. However, more substantial responses were long absent due to different reasons. First, the EU's **intergovernmental structure** hindered harder measures which are dependent on qualified majority voting (QMV) or unanimity – minus the accused country – within the European Council. Additionally, Hungary and Poland influenced European institutions through their appointments. Second, given the succession of crises, concerns about further EU destabilization tempered responses. Third, there were limited legal options to deal with democratic backsliding, and those that did exist had scarcely been tested in practice. Theoretically, Article 7 of the Treaty on European Union provides a sanctioning mechanism when the EU's democratic norms are breached, with the suspension of voting rights in the European Council as the ultimate sanction. Following consultations in line with the Rule of Law Framework, the Commission applied Article 7 proceedings against Poland in 2017. These included regular hearings but failed to yield tangible results, also because the European Council was unwilling to push for further action.

Under its German President Ursula von der Leyen, the European Commission has increasingly adopted a confrontational stance against democratic backsliding. The Hungarian and Polish governments' blatant disregard for EU warnings and democratic norms also forced a response. For example, in 2021, the Hungarian parliament passed legislation that banned all content from education or television that the Hungarian government considered to 'promote' homosexuality after the example of a similar Russian law. In response, von der Leyen denounced the law while Dutch Prime Minister Rutte even stated that Hungary 'has no business being in the European Union anymore.' From 2021 onwards, the EU moved beyond rhetoric by commencing infringement procedures against Polish violations of EU law and challenges of the primacy of EU law at the European Court of Justice (ECJ). The ECJ has subsequently delivered multiple judgments affirming that member states are legally obligated to uphold the EU's rule of law principles as outlined in the treaties. Crucially, the Commission took the unprecedented step of withholding tens of billions of euros to Hungary and Poland from the COVID-19 recovery programme and structural and cohesion funds, making this conditional on reform. When PiS was ousted from power at the 2023 Polish general election, a first part of these subsidies was redirected to the new government led by Tusk, contingent on promised reforms.

However, this more confrontational approach has not yet halted the threat of democratic backsliding. Nor does the Polish opposition's 2023 election victory, and similar election results in other central and eastern European countries, guarantee an end to democratic backsliding elsewhere. Furthermore, Hungary has leveraged the power it has in the European Council to veto aid to Ukraine following Russia's renewed invasion in order to gain access to withheld EU funding; this will be discussed below. The normalization and rise to power of populist radical right parties in ever more EU member states could potentially reduce the European Council's willingness to confront leaders like Orbán, with whom many of these parties have cultivated close ties. In 2024, Giorgia Meloni from the FdI leads a coalition government in Italy, while the Finns Party participates in a coalition in Finland and the Sweden Democrats support the government in Sweden. It remains a possibility that parties such as Wilders' PVV or Le Pen's National Rally (known as National Front before 2018) will gain power in other key EU member states. Additionally, since Brexit, many of these EU-critical parties no longer seek to leave the EU but to reform it, although many of these parties' plans are fundamentally at odds with professed EU core values and its legal fabric. However, it is important to underline that democratic backsliding should not be equated with populist radical right-wing parties: such parties are far from being the only ones to have enabled democratic backsliding, and some, moreover, have not in fact done so at all. In the end, even though new steps by the Commission and other EU institutions have created precedents for action, further democratic backsliding and the accompanied risk of European disintegration remain a concern.

From enlargement fatigue to enlargement resistance

The 2007 accession of Romania and Bulgaria marked the end of an era for the European Union, concluding the 'big bang' enlargement. By leveraging membership, the EU successfully motivated central and eastern European countries to implement and maintain political and economic reforms during their transition from socialist regimes. However, prospective members in the **western Balkans** faced more daunting challenges in their post-socialist transitions, exacerbated by the wars and conflicts of the 1990s and early 2000s. After the EU's relative failure to insert itself as an actor into the wars in former Yugoslavia, it did subsequently increase efforts in crisis management and diplomacy (CHAPTER 5). The EU initiated civil police missions and deployed troops to Macedonia and Bosnia and Herzegovina, where Operation Althea, started in 2004 to secure stability, is still ongoing as of 2024. Notwithstanding these important EU-led contributions to peace, many EU citizens and leaders remained unconvinced of the merits of further EU expansion in the area. Contemporaries often spoke of '**enlargement fatigue**', the idea that after 2007 the EU was not (yet) ready to absorb new members with much less developed economies and still fragile democratic systems. Fear of increased immigration and an unwillingness to support structural reforms and development efforts added to this fatigue.

At the 2003 European Council summit in Thessaloniki, all western Balkan states received a commitment regarding their future in the EU. However, two decades later, only Croatia has joined the EU. Croatia's accession process was heavily politicized, contrasting with the usually more technocratic approach supervised by the Commission as seen in central and eastern Europe. Political dynamics were evident early on, as Austria demanded that Croatia could start negotiations early in 2004 under threat of vetoing membership talks with Turkey. Additionally, Croatia's neighbour Slovenia leveraged accession negotiations to settle disputed maritime borders, and several western European governments used the negotiations to pressure Croatia to cooperate fully with the International Criminal Tribunal for the former Yugoslavia. Despite these and other political complexities, Croatia became the 28th EU member state in 2013.

The accession process for southeastern European countries has been protracted and heavily politicized. Several factors contributed to this. Member states frequently bypassed the Commission, of which the most obvious example is Greece's veto of Macedonian membership due to a dispute over the latter country's name and historical claims. After the Socialist Republic of Macedonia gained independence in 1991, it used 'Republic of Macedonia' as the country's new official name until 2019. This was contested by Greece, resulting in many international organizations using a compromise name. Despite some important successes, such as the EU's role in rapprochement between Kosovo and Serbia, accession talks have been hindered by their formalistic and technical nature, failing to induce necessary reforms. This is particularly evident in countries where political parties have captured institutions, diminishing the perceived benefits of EU membership which brings scrutiny to corruption and undermining of the rule of law. Moreover, the EU's inconsistent approach to enlargement strategy and democratic backsliding may have inadvertently legitimized autocratic tendencies in some prospective member states. For example, under the increasingly authoritarian Serbian Prime Minister Aleksander Vučić, negotiations have all but stalled. In Macedonia, the then Austrian Foreign Minister Sebastian Kurz supported the incumbent Prime Minister Nikola Gruevski at an election rally, despite Gruevski's involvement in a wiretapping and corruption scandal, in order to secure a deal on blocking migrants which he desired for the upcoming Austrian elections. Gruevski later fled to Hungary which, under Orbán's leadership, has also strengthened its ties with Serbia.

In southeastern Europe, enlargement faces further complexity due to the growing involvement of **external actors**, chiefly Turkey, Russia, and China during the 2010s. Russia in particular has opposed EU and North Atlantic Treaty Organization (NATO) enlargement, cultivating closer ties with Serbia and attempting to interfere directly, as evidenced by a failed Russian-backed coup attempt in Montenegro in 2016. Meanwhile, China has gained significant economic influence in the region. However, the EU has struggled to devise a unified response to this geopolitical competition. For example, when Greece resolved its disputes with Macedonia, which was subsequently renamed North Macedonia, Bulgaria used accession talks to demand concessions from the renamed country. Furthermore, in 2019 the French President Emmanuel Macron outright vetoed making Albania and North Macedonia official candidate member states. This trepidation in the ranks of the EU is one of the reasons many potential member states have been either unwilling or unable to make the necessary changes required for accession.

The potential **accession of Turkey** has faced many delays and political hurdles to the point that it seems unlikely in the near future. Turkey, which had been an associate EC member since 1963, began actively pursuing full membership in the 1980s. After Greece lifted its veto in 1999, the European Council recognized Turkey as a candidate. Subsequently the Turkish government implemented key reforms, including abolishing the death penalty and allowing the Kurdish language in broadcasting and private education. After Recep Tayyip Erdoğan came to power in 2003, further reforms were undertaken. These efforts led to the start of membership negotiations in 2004, albeit amid opposition from politicians and voters in many EU member states. For example, Wilders founded his PVV as a reaction to Turkey's prospective membership. Over time, the German and French governments also became much more critical of Turkish entry. A key reason for the public and political contestation of Turkey's membership was its majority Muslim population. In addition, its population size – circa 70 million in the mid-2000s – would fundamentally alter the EU's power balance, while the poorer Anatolian provinces would require substantial funding. By the early 2010s, resistance to enlargement intensified, and several EU member states blocked opening new chapters in accession negotiations. Meanwhile, Turkey's enthusiasm for EU membership waned as it explored other geopolitical options amid continued economic growth during the eurozone crisis.

While enlargement efforts have all but grounded to a halt, the EU has expanded its influence in neighbouring states through other means. In 2004, the **European Neighbourhood Policy** (ENP) was established in anticipation of eastern enlargement. The ENP involved sixteen countries in eastern Europe and North Africa that could or would not become EU members soon, unlike the countries in the western Balkans. In fact, the EU remained extremely hesitant to offer concrete prospects of membership, even following the 2004 Orange Revolution in Ukraine. Launched in 2009, the Eastern Partnership aimed at fostering reforms related to the rule of law, democracy, and economy in the former Soviet republics Armenia, Azerbaijan, Belarus, Georgia, Moldova, and Ukraine in exchange for benefits such as a free trade zone with the EU, visa-free travel, and ultimately the possibility of full membership. This included a substantial budget of 1.9 billion euros for the 2010–2013 period. However, the Commission often selectively applied sanctions for non-compliance and has tended to favour regional stability over democratization, particularly in the absence of a strong democratic opposition. For example, the EU has intensified economic relations with oil-rich, authoritarian Azerbaijan. Moreover, Russia's hostile position on EU enlargement in the former Soviet Union has remained the elephant in the room of the Eastern Partnership. The ENP also extended to states in North Africa and the Middle East, due to France's historical ties to this region and its concerns over the EU's political centre moving east, to the benefit of Germany. Unlike the Eastern Partnership, the ENP's focus on the Mediterranean did not foreground democratization but focused on providing stability and security on the EU's southern external border, which would come under new pressure in the early 2010s.

The Arab Spring and its impact on EU foreign policy

Since 2011, the **Arab Spring** uprisings across North Africa and the Middle East forced the EU to reassess its regional foreign policy. Particularly in Syria and Libya, these uprisings resulted in severe destabilization. While the Commission in response announced a review of the ENP, it was not initially designed to oversee crises and few substantial changes happened. The Lisbon Treaty had created new foreign policy instruments, chiefly the European External Action Service and the High Representative of the Union for foreign affairs and security policy/vice-president of the European Commission (CHAPTER 5). However, these mechanisms were not yet well-established, and the inexperienced British High Representative Catherine Ashton struggled to maintain unity between member states. For instance, during the Libyan civil war, Britain and France supported a US-led military intervention but Germany did not. Similarly, as the Syrian civil war escalated into a lengthy conflict and humanitarian crisis, some EU states participated in US-led NATO operations, particularly against Islamic State. Complementing NATO, the EU continued to focus its diplomatic efforts on soft power and humanitarian aid. However, the complex implementation of EU funds limited their effectiveness in this context. Additionally, the complex situation in Syria and Russian and Turkish interventions strained the EU's relationship with Moscow and Ankara.

The EU's main focus since 2011 has been on restraining the uncontrolled arrival of refugees and migrants from the Middle East and North Africa. One key element of this was securing the EU's external borders. This task was performed by the European Border and Coast Guard which is more commonly known as **Frontex** (derived from the French Frontières extérieures). Starting with Operation Hermes in 2011, Frontex began surveillance of the Mediterranean Sea between Italy and North Africa. Since then, Frontex's role has grown exponentially, which is reflected by an extension of its mandate in 2015 for border control and management and a sevenfold budget increase between 2011 and 2022, with future growth anticipated. Frontex is facing criticism for its involvement in human rights violations. This particularly pertains to Frontex's role in lethal so-called pushbacks of migrants at sea but also to the EU's Data Protection Supervisor's criticism of how Frontex processes personal data of migrants, in breach with the EU data protection framework. However, given the political salience of curtailing migration the chances of significant policy changes seem unlikely.

To address migration, the EU has increasingly pursued **bilateral agreements** with third states. At the height of the European migrant 'crisis' in

2015, and in light of the deaths of hundreds of migrants attempting to cross the Mediterranean, European and African leaders held a migration summit in Malta. African countries were to receive aid, development assistance, and easier legal migration in exchange for halting migration and readmitting illegal migrants. Subsequently, the EU began striking bilateral deals with for example Libya, which drew criticism for inhumane detention centres and lethal pushbacks on sea. Nevertheless, with migration remaining a key political issue, the EU has sought similar agreements to curtail migration with Tunisia (in 2023) and Egypt (in 2024) in exchange for substantial sums of money, even though their implementation and human rights implications remain uncertain. The deal struck between the European Council and Turkey in 2016 has proven to be more successful. In exchange for six billion euros between 2016 and 2020 and other benefits such as visa liberalization and re-energizing accession negotiations, Turkey agreed to halt migrants from crossing the Aegean Sea, effectively ending this migration route, notwithstanding international humanitarian concerns. Despite at times tense relations between the EU and Turkey, the agreement has endured. However, dealing with other neighbouring powers has proven more challenging for the EU.

The Russian invasion of Ukraine in 2014

By the mid-2000s, under President Vladimir Putin, **a revanchist Russia** aimed to reassert its influence in the post-Soviet space. Bolstered by income from oil exports, Putin brought more prosperity to the country, but this went hand in hand with an increasingly authoritarian and oligarchic rule. Addressing the nation in 2005, Putin stated 'that the collapse of the Soviet Union was the major geopolitical disaster of the century. As for the Russian nation, it became a genuine drama. Tens of millions of our co-citizens and compatriots found themselves outside Russian territory.' Russia began opposing further EU and NATO enlargement, instead favouring the expansion of the Russian-dominated Eurasian Economic Union (before 2015, the Eurasian Economic Community) which is partly modelled on the EU and comprises several former Soviet states. This was precisely at the time that NATO considered granting membership to Georgia, which had been liberal and pro-Western since a 2003 non-violent regime change. While the US supported Georgian membership, Germany and France feared provoking Russia. However, Russia perceived the open debate about this issue as a direct encroachment upon its sphere of interest. In 2008, Russian armed forces invaded

Georgia under the pretext of protecting minority rights in two breakaway Georgian regions. This was the first time Russia invaded a former Soviet state, although it had previously intervened to secure Transnistria's secession from Moldova (CHAPTER 5). Bypassing EU channels, the French President Nicholas Sarkozy flew to Moscow to negotiate a ceasefire, although he did consult with European partners. However, the Kremlin almost immediately undermined this ceasefire by unilaterally recognizing the independence of the breakaway provinces. Georgia remained in the Eastern Partnership, but the EU did not increase its Caucasian presence or impose sanctions on Russia, despite warnings from central and eastern European members in particular that Russian aggression required deterrence.

The 2014 Russian invasion of Ukraine marked the end of the post-Cold War European security order that the EU had pursued since the Yugoslav Wars. In 2013, the Ukrainian President Viktor Yanukovych was on the brink of signing an association agreement with the EU but succumbed to pressure from the Kremlin. This move towards the EU was generally popular in Ukraine, which had been severely affected by the 2007–2008 economic crisis, although opinions were more divided in the eastern parts of Ukraine where there were closer economic ties with Russia. Yanukovych's refusal to sign triggered protests on Kyiv's Maidan Square, which soon came to be known as the Euromaidan, since protesters waved EU flags and demanded that Yanukovych sign the agreement. Yanukovych was ousted from power after his government lost popular support by condoning the use of targeted fire, resulting in the deaths of over 100 protesters. In the ensuing turmoil, Russia invaded Ukraine and seized Crimea, contending that the Maidan protests were a Western-backed coup and that it had to protect the rights of Russian speakers. In an orchestrated action, Russian armed forces and Russian-backed local mercenaries achieved the secession of Crimea and the so-called Donetsk and Lugansk People's Republics in eastern Ukraine, although the Kremlin denied direct involvement.

Unlike in 2008, there was a shared sense of urgency that the EU had to respond, but debates raged as to how. The EU's heavy reliance on Russian energy, which started in the 1970s, accounted up to 40% of gas and 25% of overall EU oil imports and caused internal divisions between countries that were more or less dependent on Russia (CHAPTER 4). While the Scandinavian member states, many central and eastern European countries, and the UK advocated for a robust response, others, such as Germany and Italy, feared potential economic consequences. These divisions extended to public debates, which were often dominated by a Moscow-centric perspective, portraying Ukraine as a failed state plagued by far-right politicians with an eastern half that was supposedly predominantly Russian given the prevalence of Russian speakers. Fears over Russian retaliation, including armed or nuclear action, further undermined calls for hard measures.

The downing of Malaysian Airways flight MH17 at the command of the Russian army on 17 July 2014, and the ensuing death of all on board, including 211 EU citizens, galvanized the EU into a more forceful response. The presidents of the European Council and Commission announced additional **sanctions** targeting Putin's inner circle, while the EU member states also agreed on stricter economic measures, including an arms embargo, curtailing Russian access to some advanced technologies, and limiting EU deals with major Russian banks as well as energy and defence groups. However, it soon became apparent that many companies were able to evade sanctions, and the reluctance of states to enforce them further hampered the effectiveness of the EU's response.

Tensions within the EU on a shared foreign policy towards Russia are exemplified by Germany's ambiguous role as the de facto leading state of the EU following the eurozone crisis. On the one hand, Chancellor Merkel seized the initiative on behalf of the EU alongside the French President François Hollande to negotiate a peace settlement for Ukraine. Merkel estimated that due to the lack of Western resolve to support Ukraine and its limited military capacity, a ceasefire, even if advantageous to Russia, was necessary. Together with Hollande, she brokered the Minsk Peace Agreements in 2014 and 2015, essentially turning the war into a **frozen conflict**. Although Ukrainian and especially Russian forces would frequently violate the ceasefire, open conflict did not break out. On the other hand, however, Germany simultaneously deepened economic ties with Russia, most prominently by agreeing to the start of construction on **Nord Stream 2** in 2015, a pipeline between Russia and Germany through the Baltic Sea. It would be operated by a consortium of German, Austrian, Dutch, and French energy companies with a Russian state-owned company as the main shareholder. Crucially, this pipeline bypassed existing Ukrainian ones, diminishing the European need to maintain Ukrainian security while increasing western European dependence on Russian energy. Notwithstanding Merkel's diplomatic efforts, Nord Stream 2, and other actions by a German political elite supportive of Russia ultimately undermined the EU's attempt at creating a united front. Moreover, it signalled to Russia that it could use force without any all too detrimental consequences.

If the resurgence of war in Europe had not already forced the EU to reassess its geopolitical position, the dual shock of Brexit and Donald Trump's election as president of the US certainly did. Despite earlier indications of a

US pivot away from Europe, the continent still heavily relied on the US and NATO for security after the Cold War. Nevertheless, the election of Trump, a radical right-wing populist and isolationist, a self-avowed Putin admirer and critic of NATO, represented a disruptive change. The 2016 EU Global Strategy (EUGS) made the timely assertion, 'We need a stronger Europe.' Prepared by the Italian High Representative Federica Mogherini, the EUGS urged for **strategic autonomy**, meaning the capacity to independently address security issues, a unified foreign policy, and enhanced economic and technological independence. Additionally, the EUGS foregrounded 'principled pragmatism': the EU remained committed to multilateralism, human rights, and climate action, but also to securing stability in neighbouring states via the ENP. The Trump administration's unilateral actions, such as ending a planned free trade zone with the EU and the Iran nuclear deal, intensified calls for strategic autonomy, with French President Macron even expressing concerns over the 'brain death' of NATO. Notwithstanding progress in establishing new steps in common foreign and security policies, divisions persisted among EU members. While some hesitated to increase defence spending, particularly central and eastern European states such as Poland continued to prioritize transatlantic security cooperation via NATO. Although the EU increased support for Ukraine after 2014, its foreign policy remained focused on non-military issues such as trade. Nonetheless, the EU did reassert its leading role in global climate policies, which will also be discussed below. When member states' interests converged the EU could act as a global actor, as seen by the growing role of the High Representative and the Commission. However, diverging national interests hindered many efforts towards strategic autonomy, which also became evident in navigating relations with another global power.

Debates within the EU on relations with **China** highlight this lack of coherence in EU foreign policy. In short, EU foreign policy has had to strike a balance between self-professed democratic values and the economic benefits of close EU-China relations. By the turn of the millennium, China had become the world's second-largest economy and it was increasingly asserting its political power. A good example is the Chinese Belt and Road Initiative launched in 2013, which aimed to improve infrastructure, stimulate Chinese trade, and gain political influence. China initiated proportionally large investments in southeastern Europe and it became the majority stakeholder in Greece's largest port in 2016. Western European states have, however, also welcomed Chinese investments. Like its approach to Russia, Germany during this period preferred dialogue to confrontation and profoundly deepened economic ties with China to benefit the country's export-oriented economy.

However, Chancellor Merkel's decision to pursue this independently, including her solo visit to China without EU representatives and partners in 2019, drew criticism for undermining a coordinated EU response. Nevertheless, there was growing momentum within the EU to present a more coherent front in its dealings with an increasingly assertive China, as illustrated by a joint communication by High Representative Mogherini and the Commission on the strategic relationship between the EU and China which designated China as a 'systemic rival' in 2019. However, significant shifts in the EU's approach to relations with competing powers would mainly come in response to new external shocks during the early 2020s.

From austerity to pandemic stimulus and the European Green Deal

Originating in China, the COVID-19 pandemic brought international travel and the global economy to a standstill in 2020. Initially, EU member states resorted to national measures, as necessitated by the lack of European solidarity in delivering medical supplies to countries such as Italy that were first hit by the disease. Several member states – principally France, Germany, Italy, and the Netherlands – pursued individual deals with vaccine procedures. Since this undermined not only EU solidarity but also the internal market, the Commission was able to step up by establishing a joint vaccine procurement programme. Calls for a European financial stimulus to address the pandemic-induced economic slump were initially met with scepticism from the 'frugal four', Austria, Denmark, the Netherlands, and Sweden, which alleged that in the aftermath of the euro crisis, southern European member states should have improved their budget to withstand shocks. However, due the unprecedented nature of the pandemic crisis and the EU's experience in managing past crises, such concerns were quickly sidelined, and the European institutions were able to take swift and far-reaching measures.

The response of the EU to the pandemic marked a major change in the design of the EU and the eurozone. In stark contrast to the eurozone crisis, the Maastricht criteria were put on hold and austerity policies abandoned in favour of large-scale stimulus programmes. Already in March 2020, the ECB intervened with a generous financial support programme amounting to 750 billion euros. The Commission also announced the **Next Generation EU** (NGEU) as an aid package for EU economies to recover from the pandemic of up to 750 billion euros. Crucially, the NGEU was primarily funded by issuing common debt at the EU level. During the euro crisis, aid packages were largely paid for by contributions directly from the member states – common debts were anathema, especially for northern European members. The NGEU marked a major change in European integration and increase in supranational competences, which to a certain extent went unnoticed during the pandemic, and by signalling the shift from neoliberal austerity to economic stimulus and increased market intervention. Lastly, in addition to the Commission's vaccine procurement programme, the pandemic also deepened integration in public health policies by strengthening the authority and funding of the European Medicine Agency and the European Centre for Disease Prevention and Control, also to be prepared for future pandemics.

Even before the pandemic, the EU broke new ground by assuming competences over the **digital dimensions** of European integration. Under President Jean-Claude Juncker, the Commission established the Digital Single Market strategy, which aimed to remove virtual borders and improve access to cross-border online goods and services, fostering innovation and competitiveness in the digital sector. Perhaps the most tangible impact for citizens has been the end of roaming charges for mobile data. A landmark achievement was the implementation of the General Data Protection Regulation (GDPR) in 2018, which provided a comprehensive data protection regulatory framework for the EU. Moreover, the GDPR harmonized data privacy laws and established new measures for data protection and transparency. The GDPR has had a veritable 'Brussels effect' (CHAPTER 7) as a consequential regulatory step for (digital) information policy elsewhere, although shortcomings and inconsistencies in its application remain. Building on this, the von der Leyen Commission introduced the Digital Markets Act in 2022 to encourage fairness, transparency, and competitiveness, by targeting non-EU tech giants such as Meta in the US or ByteDance in China, which owns TikTok. Additionally, the Commission is developing the Cyber Resilience Act to bolster cybersecurity, also in response to, for example, Russian cyberattacks and Chinese corporate cyberespionage. The subsequent **Artificial Intelligence** (AI) Act is also linked to concerns over Europe's competitiveness in the digital domain, gaining a new urgency with the introduction of generative AI. It provides a common regulatory and legal framework for AI and identifies risks in its usage. Together, these new forays into digital common policies highlight the EU's turn to strategic autonomy, market intervention and more neomercantilist policies. Also, to secure Europe's position amid these rapid advances in digital technologies and strategic digital chip industry, the von der Leyen Commission implemented Horizon Europe as a flagship research and innovation programme, replacing Horizon 2020. Horizon

Europe aims to stimulate European science and innovation with a budget of close to 100 billion euros for the 2021–2027 period, not least of all in the realm of sustainability.

Climate policy is another area in which the EU has significantly increased its role in recent years. European environmental policies originated in the 1970s and were long relatively limited (CHAPTER 4), but this changed when **climate change** became a major issue in the 1990s. During this decade, the EU asserted itself as a global actor in climate policy by representing the interests of member states at the third United Nations (UN) Climate Change Conference in Kyoto, at which the EU committed itself to a 9% reduction in greenhouse gas emissions by 2012 compared to 1990 levels. In 2005, the EU introduced the Emissions Trading System (ETS). The ETS was a market-oriented mechanism that aimed to promote cost-effective measures by establishing an emissions cap for specific polluters, who must trade allowances if they exceed their limits. Building on this, the EU set more ambitious targets in 2007, including a 20% reduction in greenhouse gas emissions by 2020. Initially, some central and eastern European member states that were more reliant on coal opposed these measures, but they eventually agreed after receiving assurances of subsidies and exemptions to mitigate economic impacts. The economic downturn after 2007 dampened the political appetite for climate policies, which were largely perceived as economic disadvantages by member states. However, the economic crisis also decreased overall carbon emissions. This led to a surplus of allowances that reduced the effectiveness of the ETS, many exemptions to which had been secured by national and corporate lobbying efforts.

In 2019, the von der Leyen Commission with much fanfare announced the **European Green Deal.** The EGD pledged to make the EU climate-neutral by 2050, surpassing the targets set by the Paris Agreement of 2015. Unlike previous policies, the EGD approaches climate action holistically, incorporating environmental sustainability, energy policies, and agricultural policies. The EGD's Farm to Fork Strategy aims to make food systems more sustainable, with fewer pesticides, better animal welfare and cyclical and less polluting agriculture. Moreover, the EGD embraces a green-growth strategy focused on innovation and a just social transition to create new 'green' jobs. In 2021, the Commission presented a policy package to decrease carbon emissions by 55% in 2030, which included a fundamental reform of the ETS and funds to compensate poorer households. The implementation of COVID-19 stimulus packages was also used to further EU climate ambitions. For example, 30% of NGEU funding is raised by issuing green bonds, which are investments or loans directed at projects with a positive environmental impact. However, the allocation of one trillion euros of planned EGD investments and the criteria for determining a positive environmental impact remain unclear and face questions about due diligence and implementation.

The EGD aims to position the EU as a global leader in climate policy, as well as in green technologies and the transition towards a climate-neutral economy. This is closely aligned with debates on strategic autonomy and indicates a shift from more neoliberal and market-oriented policies to neomercantilist policies and market intervention. The Carbon Border Adjustment Mechanism (CBAM) illustrates this approach by imposing a special tax on carbon-intensive imports. On the one hand, CBAM leverages the EU's market power or 'Brussels effect' to raise global standards. On the other hand, it serves a protectionist purpose by shielding transitioning European industries from competition. In this sense, the EGD's industrial policies and subsidies are also a response to large-scale US climate transition stimulus policies, again marking a turn to strategic economic planning. Importantly, the EGD also has other, more negative external impacts by encouraging the offshoring of carbon emissions and pollution, potentially hindering climate-neutral transitions elsewhere, and causing additional environmental degradation from the extraction of resources which fuel the EU's transition efforts.

Lastly, the implementation of the Commission's EGD is shaped by the increasing politicization of European policymaking. For example, initial plans to exclude nuclear energy from the renewable energy taxonomy were halted by a French-led lobby. Similarly, pressure from the powerful German automobile industry weakened a Commission proposal to phase out fossil fuel cars. Since 2023, farmer protests across Europe have contested efforts to sustainably reform the Common Agricultural Policy, leading to concessions ahead of the 2024 European Parliamentary elections. In short, these developments underscore the profound challenges of navigating competing interests and ideological pressures in the pursuit of a carbon-neutral Europe. Crucially, the agency of the EU to face these challenges is heavily shaped by external factors, such as energy imports from Russia.

Zeitenwende? The renewed Russian invasion of Ukraine in 2022

The renewed **Russian invasion of Ukraine** on 24 February 2022 is a turning point in European history. Russia's military invasion came as a shock when Europe was recovering from the after-effects of the pandemic. It was also a more ambitious invasion on a much grander scale than in 2014, with goals including regime change and the occupation and integration of large portions of Ukraine into Russia. Three days after the invasion, the German Chancellor Olaf Scholz gave a speech in which he called the invasion a *Zeitenwende* or historical turning point, a characterization indicative of how most European leaders and citizens perceived the war. In response to Russia's aggression, Scholz announced that Germany would depart from its post-Cold War diplomacy by pledging 100 billion euros on strengthening its military. Additionally, he advocated a fundamental revaluation of European security policy. The brutality inflicted on Ukrainian civilians, such as the massacre in Bucha, further galvanized European solidarity in support of Ukraine. Unlike in 2014, the impact of the war was felt much more directly by the calculated Russian reduction of energy exports, which, in addition to sanctions, contributed to an energy price crisis in the EU. The German decision to cancel the permits for Nord Stream 2 also exemplifies the changed European approach to Russia. However, although Germany has provided more support than any other EU member state in absolute terms, Chancellor Scholz and a significant section of German society have found it difficult to supply more offensive arms, resulting in heavy criticism from NATO allies.

EU member states have displayed remarkable unity in condemning Russia's invasion of Ukraine. As of early 2024, the EU has committed substantial economic, humanitarian, and military aid to Ukraine, totalling over 88 billion euros – an unprecedented level of support for any third state. Moreover, EU member states have taken in over six million Ukrainian refugees, which further underlines solidarity with Ukraine, while it also stands in contrast with the migrant 'crisis' of 2015–2016. Another indicator of this unity is that the European Council has agreed on thirteen sanction packages of a far larger scope than those adopted in the aftermath of 2014. These sanctions target hundreds of individuals and companies associated with the Russian military complex, implement export bans on advanced technology, and import bans on coal and luxury goods. The EU furthermore collaborated with the G7 to freeze offshore Russian central bank assets and exclude Russia and Belarus from the SWIFT international payments system.

Despite strong intergovernmental support for EU actions in support of Ukraine, there have been few clear indications of deeper integration through strengthening EU regulatory powers or supranational institutions. However, new policies and instruments are being implemented, such as the Commission's Ukraine Facility to provide constant financial aid to Ukraine between 2024 and 2027. Although some argued that treaty reforms are necessary before further enlargement can be contemplated, so far more far-reaching reform proposals, such as Scholz' suggestion to implement QMV for foreign policy in the European Council have faced opposition, particularly from Hungary. Circumvention of sanctions and internal EU opposition have undermined the effectiveness of the sanction packages. Hungary has not been alone in seeking to evade or limit sanctions, but it has been the most vocal in opposing sanctions against Russia, as the country is fully dependent on Russian energy imports and given Orbán's ideological affinity with Putin's authoritarian government. Moreover, there have been growing signs of fatigue concerning the economic burden of refugee care and economic sanctions in European public debates. Voices advocating a settlement with Russia, previously marginalized, have been gaining traction, particularly but not only among Eurosceptic and populist radical right-wing parties.

The Russian war on Ukraine has caused a paradigm shift in debates on European foreign policy, by comparison with discussions on **strategic autonomy** since the mid-2010s. For one, the war provided a newfound geopolitical impetus for overcoming resistance to European enlargement and for accelerating this process. Since 2022, the European Council has given the green light for membership negotiations with Albania, Bosnia and Herzegovina, Georgia, Moldova, North Macedonia, *and* Ukraine. In addition, the ongoing war highlighted the pressing need for further military European autonomy and integration. In this sense, the political centre of the EU has moved eastwards since 2022. Notably, Finland and Sweden have abandoned their foreign policy of neutrality to become members of NATO, while the French President Macron has apologized to central and eastern Europeans for not taking their concerns on Russia seriously. EU member states have also pledged major increases in defence spending and investment in armaments industries. While the US has by far given the most military aid to Ukraine, the politicization of this aid and serious concerns over Trump's potential re-election in 2024 mean that debates over strategic autonomy are not likely to fade any time soon. Crucially, beyond Ukraine, political and ethnic tensions have also risen in other neighbouring states, ranging from the ethnic cleansing of Armenians from Nagorno-Karabakh by Azerbaijan in 2023 to Serbian separatism in Kosovo and Bosnia and Herzegovina, and the war between Israel and Hamas and the Israeli invasion and ethnic cleansing of Gaza. Given the growingly hostile geopolitical climate and rising tensions with Russia, China, and the United States across the diplomatic, economic, and technological spheres, the EU faces mounting external pressures to take decisive action on achieving strategic autonomy.

Conclusion

In short, this chapter has shown how European integration has both deepened and broadened in response to the challenges faced by the EU since 2007. This includes the fundamental deepening and widening of monetary and fiscal policy as well as the issuance of common EU debt, the establishment of novel digital regulatory frameworks and policies, climate policies, and initiatives on foreign policy. Although the intergovernmental dynamics behind the EU's response to the crises of this period have remained strong, the Commission, as well as other European institutions such as the ECB and Frontex, have acquired major new competences and instruments. Undeniably, Germany has played a dominant role in deciding the direction of the EU in the past two decades. Germany has enforced austerity and fiscal restraint and undermined a common approach to China and Russia by deepening bilateral economic ties, while also playing a pivotal role in the migrant 'crisis' and in establishing pandemic stimulus programmes. It should not be forgotten that the impact of these crises and how they have been handled contributed to new levels of politicization of the EU and Euroscepticism. Additionally, there has been a significant shift in the attitude of many Eurosceptic parties to the EU, no longer principally rejecting the EU after Brexit, but seeking to act through it. Paradoxically, this is a testimony to the political staying power of the EU, despite many of these parties' tendencies to undermine the democratic norms and framework of the EU.

The EU is at a critical juncture point at the beginning of the third decade of the twenty-first century. The early 2020s saw indications of **new directions** and shifts, marked by renewed but often selective efforts to counter democratic backsliding in member states, a turn from neoliberal austerity to neomercantilism and market interventions, ambitious climate and digital policies, and new ventures in the realm of foreign policy. Amid rising geopolitical tensions and heightened economic and technological competition, the EU finds itself at a crossroads. Will debates over strategic autonomy break with decades of path dependency and a reliance on NATO to forge a more independent union in terms of military and security policy? Is the EU still a community grounded in shared democratic values? Or does it remain a collection of different interests, which may temporarily converge to counter external pressures? So far, debates over climate change and the Russian invasions of Ukraine have foregrounded both support for new initiatives to deepen European integration and vastly diverging national interests. This chapter also addressed the increased public scrutiny and politicization of EU-level policymaking and decision-making. Politicization and public debate on the EU can be interpreted in their own right as signs of a closing 'democratic deficit', although a genuine European public sphere has yet to emerge. This especially applies to the fundamental questions on the EU's purpose and functioning that are on the table. After all, the past two decades of the EU's history have shown that crises do not automatically induce a widening and deepening of integration. The Russian invasion of Ukraine serves as a stark reminder that the European Union remains an inherently political and perpetually evolving project, which by its very nature remains an unfinished one with an open-ended future.

Further reading

- Börzel, Tanja A. 'European Integration and the War in Ukraine: Just Another Crisis?' *Journal of Common Market Studies* 61, no. 1 (2023): 14–30
- Cianetti, Licia, James Dawson, and Seán Hanley. 'Rethinking "Democratic Backsliding" in Central and Eastern Europe – Looking Beyond Hungary and Poland.' *East European Politics* 34, no. 3 (2018): 243–56.
- Dinan, Desmond, Neill Nugent, and William E. Paterson, eds. *The European Union in Crisis*. London: Palgrave, 2017.
- Hodson, Dermot. *Circle of Stars: A History of the EU and the People Who Made It*. New Haven: Yale University Press, 2023.
- Kelemen, R. Daniel. 'Will the European Union Escape its Autocracy Trap?' *Journal of European Public Policy*. Advance online publication (2024).
- Laczó, Ferenc. 'Moderately Failing Forward: The EU in the Years 2004–2019.' In *European Integration Outside-In*, edited by Mathieu Segers and Steven Van Hecke. Vol. 1 of *The Cambridge History of the European Union*. Cambridge: Cambridge University Press, 2023. 163–186.
- Middelaar, Luuk van. *Alarums and Excursions: Improvising Politics on the European Stage*. Newcastle upon Tyne: Agenda Publishing, 2019.
- Popova, Maria, and Oxana Shevel. *Russia and Ukraine: Entangled Histories, Diverging States*. Cambridge: Polity Press, 2024.
- Ther, Philipp. *Europe since 1989: A History*. Translated by Charlotte Hughes-Kreutzmüller. Princeton: Princeton University Press, 2016.
- Tooze, Adam. *Crashed: How a Decade of Financial Crises Changed the World*. New York: Viking, 2018.

7.   Theoretical perspectives on European integration

Seven decades into the existence of the EU, thinking about European integration spans a history that dates even further back. This chapter charts that history, and offers a chronological survey of the key social science research and theory that has shaped thinking about European integration. Like the work of historians of European integration, this scholarship emerged in the context of the integration process as it unfolded. Their work does not just reflect the academic priorities of the age, but political, institutional, and policy priorities as well. Some political scientists actually make this explicit by prescribing and theorizing about what they think the EU should do or look like – so-called normative scholarship. Others merely describe what they observe in European integration, so-called empirical scholarship. In addition, there is also political science scholarship that makes predictions about European integration – it extrapolates from quantitative data or observed developments to argue where it is headed. Political science theories often have a normative or predictive element to them, and in order to understand them, it is key to comprehend the context in which they emerged. In other words: what was the background of the scholar in question, and in what context did they develop their theories?

For the first decades, the theories discussed in this chapter were primarily concerned with the *what* and *why* of European integration: what kind of organization was this European Community (EC) exactly, and why did member states invest in this project? These theories sought to explain European integration as it happened, but also to predict where it was headed. In the wake of the Maastricht Treaty and the end of the Cold War, as European integration and the world within which it operated became increasingly complex, it became harder to capture European integration in a single theory. From the 1990s onward, theories of European integration therefore became increasingly interested in the *how* and *who* of European integration: how did the EU impact the functioning of lower levels of government or global governance? And, related to this, who had a say or should have a say in shaping European integration – in other words: how democratic was it? This chapter therefore consists of two parts: that of the classical 'grand theories' pre-Maastricht and the more diverse scholarship that followed it, as the study of European integration professionalized, expanded, and diversified.

Pre-war ideas on European unity: federalism and functionalism

Throughout history, a host of different thinkers have played around with the idea of European unity. It gained real traction, however, when these ideas materialized with the creation of international organizations such as the League of Nations. As the first global forum set up for the pursuit of peace, it inspired scholars to think how this new internationalism could also provide an impetus for European unification in the wake of the First World War. The most popular idea in this regard was not so much a political science theory, but a longstanding political ideal, namely that of **federalism**. Just as there were federal national states, this model could be applied on a larger scale, encompassing continents or even the entire world. The League of Nations, while not approximating the kind of centralized government that a federation required, fuelled this ideal. In the interwar years, the most prominent thinker on European federalism was Richard Nicolaus Coudenhove-Kalergi, who also strived to bring it about through his Pan-European Movement (CHAPTER 1).

The aim of Coudenhove-Kalergi and his movement was to establish a federation of European states with a centralized democratic government. The basis for this federal Europe would be a constitution, which would prevent signatory states from ever waging war on each other again and form a single bloc in geopolitics and the world economy. In essence, Coudenhove-Kalergi thus sought to replicate the nineteenth-century process of state building – but then at the European level and in accelerated fashion. This idealist thinking elicited many critical responses, the most groundbreaking of which was that by the Anglo-Romanian political theorist David Mitrany. With his critique of Coudenhove-Kalergi's ideas, Mitrany laid the foundation for the theory of **functionalism**. Over the years, he developed this into a fully-fledged theory, which he outlined in his book *A Working Peace System*, published in 1943 as a pamphlet for organizing durable peace after the end of the Second World War.

The theory of functionalism held that states could choose to work together on a technical basis, within clearly delimited areas of policy, such as transport, infrastructure, or industry. This, Mitrany argued, would form a steady basis for international cooperation that could inspire nation states to transfer parts of their sovereignty to an international organization – something that Mitrany believed Coudenhove-Kalergi's federalist plans could never achieve. Mitrany thus criticized Coudenhove-Kalergi on the question *what* European unity should look like, but also on *why* states would want to join the international organization they proposed. Mitrany did not develop his theory out of thin air – he drew inspiration from longstanding international organizations such as the Central Commission for the Navigation of the Rhine (1815), the International Telegraph Union (1865), and work done by the Secretariat of the League of Nations. These organizations showed that Mitrany's proposals were not just some idealist scheme, but responded to real-world interests and challenges of states.

At the core, the difference between federalism and functionalism was that Coudenhove-Kalergi advocated form over function. Much of his theorizing therefore went into designing the ideal European constitution and federal structure. Mitrany, by contrast, put function over form – hence functionalism. He did not exclude the possibility that functionalist initiatives could culminate into a federal union over time. In principle, after all, functional forms of cooperation were compatible with each other, and could coalesce into a single central organization. Rather than creating an instant political union, however, this would result in a gradual path towards federation.

In the years following the Second World War, Coudenhove-Kalergi's idealist plans resonated with advocates for European unity. Mitrany's more technical approach found greater appeal among policymakers, however. His work was an inspiration for those who already worked towards the economic organization of postwar Europe during the Second World War (CHAPTER 1). Indeed, the Schuman Declaration, as devised by Jean Monnet, corresponds entirely with functionalist logic. The 1951 Treaty of Paris had achieved what had seemed unlikely up to then: that signatory states would transfer part of their sovereignty to a newly created international body. It ushered in a new era of political thought. The subject of European unity was no longer a subject for pamphleteers, but for academics.

Interestingly, the basis for this new scholarship lay in the United States, not in Europe itself. For one thing, this was because political science was more established as a science in the US than it was in Europe, and often had a focus on the study of international relations. The study of politics and government in Europe, by contrast, was often geared toward domestic affairs. In the context of the Cold War, scholarship in the US was more outward-looking, since expertise on different world regions was in high demand in foreign policy circles. The 1950s therefore saw the emergence of so-called area studies, where US-based scholars would study European affairs on a regional scale, beyond the nation state. Finally, the US was the destination for many students and scholars who fled wartime Europe and would go on to make a career out of looking at Europe from the outside in, rather than the other way around. Many social scientists from Germany and Austria moved to the US in the run-up to and during the Second World War.

Among them was also Coudenhove-Kalergi, who became a professor at New York University. Another was Ernst B. Haas. Hailing from a German Jewish family, he fled to the US in 1938, where he ultimately became a professor at the University of California, Berkeley. As a German expatriate, he was personally invested in the European pursuit of integration and peace. He would go on to become the founder of the first of the grand political science theories of European integration, neofunctionalism.

The grand theories: neofunctionalism and intergovernmentalism

There was already a basis for scholarly thought about European integration before the postwar period saw some of these older ideas come to fruition. The creation of the European Coal and Steel Community (ECSC) ushered in a new phase of theorizing about European integration. No longer was it a mere theoretical ideal: now, it was a real-world achievement that required explaining. Federalism and functionalism provided models for *what* European unity could look like, but not for what European integration through the ECSC would look like. The creation of the ECSC raised questions, moreover, of where this new organization was headed. The Schuman Declaration suggested that European integration would continue to expand and deepen, but if this were to be the case, *why*? These questions inspired the two theories of the 1950s and 1960s that, in hindsight, have been branded as the grand theories of European integration: **neofunctionalism** and **intergovernmentalism**.

Neofunctionalism

At the heart of the Schuman Declaration was the idea that a functional approach to European integration, through coal and steel, could over time result in a federalist Europe (CHAPTER 1 and 2). Mitrany's theory of functionalism certainly came closest to capturing the logic behind the ECSC, but it was too general to explain what European integration through the ECSC would look like and how this federalist end goal could be achieved. The experience of the ECSC inspired a number of US-based political scientists to adapt the theory of functionalism to tailor it to the specific experience of the ECSC, resulting in the theory of neofunctionalism.

Ernst B. Haas pioneered the theory of neofunctionalism. His book *The Uniting of Europe* (1958) was a detailed survey of the first years of the ECSC and a projection of what it would go on to be. It is to neofunctionalists such as Haas that we largely owe the idea of European integration as a progressive process. The theory predicts that the ECSC's humble beginnings in coal and steel would, step by step, spill over into other areas of the economies of its member states. After all, sectoral integration in the area of coal and steel was inextricably tied up with sectors such as transport, energy, and trade. As Mitrany had already argued, it would make sense to incorporate these adjacent fields into the existing organization, thus expanding its scope. The concept of spillover theorized this process and explained that political and economic elites would be compelled to pursue further integration in other areas. For economic elites in neighbouring sectors, for example, there would be 'functional pressures' to seek closer cooperation with the ECSC, because of the benefits of scale and efficiency this would yield.

In Haas' account, European integration was predominantly an affair of changing elite attitudes. Economic elites would not be the only ones to gradually gravitate towards the ECSC. Political parties, civil servants, and civil society actors such as trade unionists in the member states would also increasingly become oriented toward the ECSC institutions. Since these elites were opinion leaders in their respective member states, citizens would follow in due course and start to identify with the European project, bringing a federal Europe closer. In this sense, Haas observed spillovers not just in the economy, but in politics as well. As a theory, neofunctionalism is very much top-down, in that it hardly engages with the role of the public. This is of course indicative of the postwar period in which neofunctionalism emerged, when politics was considered to be an essentially elitist affair and opinion polls did not play the role in either politics or political science that they do nowadays. The ECSC was also very much a reflection of this conception of democracy. In the 1970s, the fellow neofunctionalists Leon Lindberg and Stuart Scheingold characterized the relation between political elites and citizens in European integration as a **permissive consensus**: elites drove European integration forward based on implied, tacit support from their electorates. This concept would become highly debated in later decades, as European integration became increasingly politicized.

Neofunctionalism has had many critics over the years – not least from intergovernmentalist scholars, who will be discussed below. The main criticism centres around the unidirectional and indeed inevitable character of the integration process that Haas described. According to neofunctionalists, member states were unable to stop European integration and its progressive deepening and widening once it had been set in motion. Not only does this reveal Haas' strong idealist leaning towards the end goal of a federal Europe, his characterization of actors operating within this process also deprives them of their agency to steer European integration through political decisions. Haas' theory of neofunctionalism does not account for actors making their own choices, especially not decisions that deviate from the progressive character of European integration. Neofunctionalists who built on Haas' work, such as Lindberg and Scheingold, have therefore done more to highlight the agency that actors have to work with the mechanisms of European integration rather than being subjected to them.

Clearly, the advancement of European integration relied not just on functional pressures and incentives, as Haas argued, but also on political commitments and decisions. At the same time, there was indeed evidence that integration, especially with regard to the common market, spilled over into other areas. After the failure of the European Defence Community, the ECSC organization was expanded with the European Economic Community (EEC) and Euratom. This in itself attested to the progressive character of European integration. Economic integration on the common market, moreover, spilled over into other areas such as consumer and environmental policy in the 1970s. The making of the common market, after all, required a regulatory level playing field for economic actors to operate on without causing harm to consumers, public health, and the environment. These policies also played to a growing demand in European society at the time for policies that went beyond economic integration (CHAPTER 4).

Another criticism of neofunctionalism is its regional, indeed rather isolated character. As conceived by Haas, the world outside the Six played no discernible role in shaping European integration: there were only internal functional incentives and pressures pushing it forward. According to neofunctionalism, however, the EC did exert influence on the countries surrounding it. Successful economic cooperation compelled third countries to associate themselves with the EC, either by joining it or by developing initiatives for economic cooperation of their own, such as the British initiative for what became known as the European Free Trade Association (EFTA). Haas' theory was therefore very EC-centric.

Considered in a wider global context, theories of European integration such as neofunctionalism often share one characteristic: they underline the unique character of the project. This idea was prevalent at the time in political science as well as in legal studies. Legal scholars stressed that the EC was what they called **sui generis**, or one of a kind. Like political scientists, legal scholars engaged in discussions about the question *what* the EC actually was. This idea caught on in legal studies as well as in other disciplines and even the European institutions themselves. The first Commission president, Walter Hallstein, himself a legal scholar, liked to present the EC as 'a new kind of political animal'. It was no traditional intergovernmental international organization because its member states transferred sovereignty to joint institutions. Neither was it a fully-fledged federal system, however, given its limited functions and the fact that its member states remained sovereign in crucial state domains such as taxation, foreign policy, and defence. As neofunctionalists projected, however, its path would inevitably take it to becoming a federal system. This conceptualization of the EC as a *sui generis* entity reflected the great expectations that surrounded European integration up to the 1970s.

As European integration progressed, there was mounting evidence that, contrary to what neofunctionalists claimed, the process had no momentum of its own. The 1965 Empty Chair Crisis was the most obvious evidence for this. Haas himself was the first to admit that neofunctionalism only accounted for progressive integration and that it could not explain this interruption of a hitherto smooth process. Indeed, the fact that this episode is still referred to as a crisis, much like the 1970s have often been characterized as a period of 'Eurosclerosis', shows that scholars thought of European integration as a progressive process, as did actors in the institutions themselves (CHAPTER 8). Even though this progressive and autonomous logic discredited neofunctionalism as a theory that could predict the future course of the EC, it did continue to inspire new thinkers to study the functioning of EC institutions and policies, and especially the ways in which integration in some areas spilled over into others.

Intergovernmentalist approaches: the central role of states

As a response to neofunctionalism and challenges such as the Empty Chair Crisis, the 1960s saw the rise of a competing theory: intergovernmentalism. Building on the so-called realist tradition in international relations theory, intergovernmentalists challenged the notion that European integration was a self-propelling process. By their account, the EC was far from self-evident, but was a marvel of international relations. It was an entirely different response to the question of *why* states integrate. Intergovernmentalists posited that European integration was a way for member states to actively pursue their national interests. There was no predetermined end goal, only the pursuit of international relations by entirely new means.

Intergovernmentalists put governments and ministries of foreign affairs back at the heart of analysing the *why* of European integration. They determined the development of European integration. Where their interests converged, integration could move forward. Where they diverged, however, integration could stagnate or even fall apart. To intergovernmentalists, then, there was nothing definite about the EC. Whereas neofunctionalists saw European integration as a process of slow but inevitable convergence and alignment of national preferences, intergovernmentalists argued that the EC simply was a collection of disparate national interests that were continuously being debated and (re)negotiated. The theory suited the 1960s and 1970s, the period of its dominance, when there was a pervasive sense of stagnation in European integration, later described as Eurosclerosis.

The political scientist Stanley Hoffmann was the most prominent theorist of intergovernmentalism. He was born in Europe like Haas, having grown up in Paris in an Austro-American household. Hoffmann drew attention to what was lacking in the theory proposed by Haas and others, namely the political culture of the EC's member states and the role they sought to play in geopolitics. Unlike neofunctionalists, intergovernmentalists thus situated European integration in a global context, which at the time was dominated by the Cold War. In analysing the EC, Hoffmann drew a clear distinction between 'high politics' – issues of peace and security – and 'low politics' – matters of economic regulation. What characterized European integration, according to Hoffmann, was that states ceded power in the area of low politics, but wanted to remain in control with regard to high politics. It was in the area of low politics, therefore, that European integration could progress, as long as it did not interfere with matters of high politics for member states.

Hoffmann's distinction explained why Charles de Gaulle abandoned his chair on the Council of Ministers and twice vetoed British membership of the EC: these were not mere matters of low politics, but touched upon the French government's conception of peace, security, and sovereignty (CHAPTER 3). More than other government leaders at the time, de Gaulle regarded the EC as a forum for France to project its power – vis-à-vis the European Commission and the United Kingdom. Intergovernmentalism also explained why EC member states chose to cooperate in areas of low politics, such as rules for trade: it simply served national interests. It was therefore very possible that states would continue to integrate in these areas, but this process would inevitably run into difficulties once it touched upon high politics.

With the rise of neofunctionalism and intergovernmentalism, there were thus two dominant theories by the 1970s for explaining *why* states cooperated in the EC. They built upon the established schools of thought in international relations: liberalism and realism. Whereas liberalist thinkers dealt mainly with economic interdependence and domestic actors (low politics), realists looked primarily at security and material power (high politics). The longstanding debate between neofunctionalism and intergovernmentalism continued in the context of European integration, without coming much closer to being resolved. After the period of presumed Eurosclerosis, the 1980s saw the European Community acquire new momentum under the successive Delors Commissions (CHAPTER 4). This brought the EC back onto the radar of political scientists, who looked beyond the binary opposition between neofunctionalism and intergovernmentalism, finding merit in both theories.

The most ambitious attempt at proposing an integrated explanatory model for European integration came to be known as **liberal intergovernmentalism** (LIG). As the title of its most prominent book *The Choice for Europe: Social Purpose and State Power from Messina to Maastricht* (1998) suggests, the EC was a project of member states that deliberately chose to integrate, as intergovernmentalism held. In order to understand *why* they did so, however, its author Andrew Moravcsik, based at Harvard University, questioned the *who* of European integration. In addition to the usual suspects of European integration, he argued that it was necessary to look beyond ministries of foreign affairs and political elites. What member states understood to be their economic self-interest, after all, was part of a domestic political process Moravcsik called 'preference formation', in which economic, political, and policy elites played a role. The 'liberal' interplay between these elite interests aggregated into national positions vis-à-vis European integration. At the European level, too, a 'liberal' dynamic arose between member states, in which they bargained for or against plans and proposals, formed coalitions, sought to shape agendas, and made compromises.

In Moravcsik's conception, European integration thus progressed through these continuous and layered liberal interactions. Whereas classical inter-governmentalist thought revolved almost exclusively around member states and the extent to which they facilitated further integration or not, Moravcsik also had eye for the shared institutions. The European Commission, after all, was part of the same liberal dynamic: it made proposals that reflected the preferences of member states. This meant that it generally sided with what the largest member states preferred, or that it sought to reflect the lowest common denominator between states.

What Moravcsik added to the intergovernmental perspective, then, was the sense that European integration did have a dynamic that was sometimes beyond the control of national governments, something neofunctionalists also argued with the concept of spillover. Moravcsik's analysis showed that the answer to the question as to *who* drives European integration forward is not unequivocal and can include various players. His answer to the question about the prime driver behind European integration remained more intergovernmentalist than neofunctionalist, however. The cover of *The Choice for Europe* illustrates this. Displaying a windjammer with sails in the form of national flags, it suggests that the socio-economic momentum of integration made the individual member states become aligned and billow, thus driving integration forward. By the late 1990s, this sense of momentum was justified, given the progress that had been made with the single market programme and the subsequent creation of the EU in Maastricht. This had begun with the Single European Act (SEA) which, according to Moravcsik, was predominantly the product of converging West German, French, and British economic interests (CHAPTER 5).

Moravcsik also differed from preceding theorists in his method. Rather than building his explanatory model on very current and recent events and extrapolating from there, Moravcsik built his theory on historical source material, by evaluating five key historical turning points from the Treaty of Rome to the Treaty of Maastricht. In that sense, his book was indebted to the work of Alan Milward, who had demonstrated the importance of economic actors as drivers of European integration in history (CHAPTER 8). Rather than seeing the grand theories of neofunctionalism and intergovernmentalism as mutually exclusive, scholars such as Moravcsik identified where they were complementary. LIG is therefore not so much a grand theory itself, but more an offshoot of intergovernmentalism. Contributions like that of Moravcsik have helped the theoretical debate about European integration move away from its isolationist beginnings and become more embedded in general scholarly debates on international relations, international organizations, and government systems.

Post-Maastricht: the diversification and professionalization of EU studies

The 1990s marked a shift in the study of European integration. The end of the Cold War and the signing of the Maastricht Treaty heralded a phase of unprecedented optimism about European integration. Indeed, the EU embodied many of the values that seemed to be emerging victorious: liberal democracy, capitalism, and the technocratic pursuit of peace and prosperity. To a large extent, these developments vindicated the progressive and rational character that classical grand theories ascribed to European integration. To critical observers, however, there were also clear signs that these progressive theories of European integration had their blind spots and shortcomings. As European integration permeated ever more areas of society and governance, its complexity grew and societal attitudes toward European integration changed. Theories of European integration gradually came to reflect this complexity and diversity, and offered alternatives and additions to the grand theories.

This growing intricacy was a feature of European integration itself as well as of scholarship on European integration. Whereas US-based scholars had led the way in theorizing European integration in the first three decades, now European scholars, often based at European universities, became increasingly prominent. Key to this development was the establishment of programmes for European studies, often highly subsidized by the EU itself. Having originated in the US, such programmes were often interdisciplinary, and so the political science-dominated field of European studies started to benefit from other fields, such as public administration, sociology, law, economics, and history as well. This growing interest of other disciplines also reflected the fact that the EU increasingly resembled a fully-fledged state system. It was no longer the exclusive domain of international relations scholars and legal scholars, but a subject of interest to scholars of comparative politics and sociologists, who started taking an interest in its societal impact.

What the alternatives to the grand theories had in common was that they generally abandoned the idea that European integration was of a progressive nature, that the state, non-state, and institutional actors within it behaved rationally, and that its course could therefore be predicted. Rather than extrapolating from past experiences, these new theories focused on making sense of contemporary developments. First of all, they directed their attention toward the institutions of the EU, their inner workings, and their interactions with other public authorities and non-state actors. Second, as European integration came to affect more areas of life, scholars observed that public attitudes toward the EU became more politicized and were affecting European integration itself. Third and finally, the EU's position in the world became of interest to scholars who, following the EU's new competences in that field, started studying the EU as a geopolitical actor.

Amid all these new theoretical developments, the classical grand theories of neofunctionalism and (liberal) intergovernmentalism continued to inspire new scholarly work. After all, the EU developed in new and unexpected ways in response to internal and external challenges, such as the 2005 Referendum on the Treaty establishing a Constitution for Europe, the eurozone crisis, Brexit, or the Russian invasion of Ukraine, and this called for theoretical explanations. In seeking such explanations, scholars often turned to the established grand theories and developed new theories of how European integration progressed and developed. In that sense, the 1990s did not mark a break with established theoretical foundations, but a branching out from the theoretical groundwork of preceding decades.

Multilevel governance and the rediscovery of institutions

Intergovernmentalist scholars tended to see European integration first and foremost as a matter of high politics, where national interests, as determined by government leaders, shaped the EU. They were less interested in the low politics of European integration, which involved the mechanisms and processes of the day-to-day running of EU institutions, or what was increasingly referred to in the 1990s as 'governance'. The concept of governance gained traction in distinction to the static and state-centric concept of government, to highlight the processes and mechanisms of governing. It reflected the notion that neat and static organization charts hardly sufficed to capture the intricacies and dynamics of European integration. As the Maastricht Treaty saw the EU move into monetary, foreign, and judicial affairs, officials and scholars alike came to use this concept. As a result, the question *how* the EU functioned in practice became increasingly prominent in scholarship.

What became especially clear by the 1990s was how the world had become thoroughly interwoven as a consequence of economic globalization. International norms, standards and procedures had permeated deep into all layers of the world economy and public administration. By the same token, the EU was becoming increasingly involved in lower levels of decision-making, raising the question where competences and authority in the EU resided. The 1992 Maastricht Treaty established the principle of **subsidiarity**, which determined that decisions should be taken at the European level only when necessary, and as closely to citizens as possible. The Treaty also set up the Committee of the Regions, which had the express goal of safeguarding this subsidiarity principle. This preoccupation with the question of hierarchy and authority reflected a growing concern on the part of EU institutions with their relation to citizens, in response to the popular image of EU legislation as decrees imposed by a meddlesome Brussels bureaucracy.

In the wake of these developments, scholars also became increasingly preoccupied with the question of the dispersion of authority in the EU. When the political scientist Gary Marks paid a research visit to the Directorate-General (DG) for Regional Policy and Cohesion in the early 1990s, he was struck by these interdependencies of different layers of government. The Maastricht Treaty had created a so-called Cohesion Fund, which served the public development of less developed regions in the Union. With more funds to distribute, the European Commission had become more active in engaging with so-called sub-national levels of government and cultivated a continuous relationship with them. Together with Liesbet Hooghe, Marks became interested in this question of interdependence. They observed the emergence of so-called policy networks, new modes of policymaking and other interactions that connected the European level of governance with lower ones. Characteristics of these interactions varied between member states and even regions, because of diverging institutional structures and administrative traditions. This was a dynamic that none of the grand theories accounted for, yet it was an integral part of the administrative reality of both Brussels and (sub-)national authorities across the EU.

In seeking to capture their observations, Hooghe and Marks coined the concept **multilevel governance**. There is some debate as to whether multilevel governance is actually a theory, since it has a strongly descriptive character. There is no doubt, however, that the concept has encouraged scholars to study European integration from hitherto unexplored angles and with new questions. How do interdependencies between layers of governance come about? What explains the behaviour of actors operating in multilevel systems and variances between them? In this sense, multilevel governance has offered a perspective that scholars in political science and beyond can adopt. It has also allowed scholars to focus on a variety of different actors, including Non-Governmental Organizations (NGOs) and their campaigns, government officials responsible for implementing European policies, or national courts interpreting European law.

In some respects, multilevel governance constituted a move away from international relations perspectives and a return to neofunctionalism, with its focus on technocrats and non-state actors. It fundamentally differs from neofunctionalism, however, in that it makes no predictive claims of any kind about the trajectory of European integration. Rather than seeking to explain European integration as a process, multilevel governance is a way of looking at the EU – encouraging scholars to look at networks, interactions, actors, and the institutional settings they operate in. Hooghe and Marks' approach inspired scholarship on a variety of subjects, such as the national implementation of EU legislation, the emergence of new forms of governance, the question of accountability in EU governance, and the study of public opinion.

Multilevel governance was part of a broader development in the social sciences to study the functioning of state and EU institutions from a decen-tralized perspective, and to see how the development of these institutional structures incentivized, pressured, or conditioned the various actors within and surrounding them. Moravcsik's notion of preference formation by economic and policy elites suited this development, for example. Looking more at the internal functioning of institutions, the school of **historical institutionalism**, like Moravcsik, built on historical evidence to explain the behaviour of institutional actors. A key concept in historical institutionalism is **path dependency**, which means that choices made in the past may limit the scope of possibilities for subsequent decisions, and sometimes even necessitate one specific decision. As a consequence, actors may find themselves advocating standpoints that they never would have taken beforehand. Decisions taken in the past may therefore set policies on paths that produce so-called unintended consequences.

One example of such an unintended consequence in the EU is policy on human rights and minorities. The accession of central and eastern European states in 2004 demanded the formulation of European norms in this area. The inevitable result has been that, very gradually, even the founding member states are being called to account in that regard, and that human rights policy has also entered foreign policy.

The American political scientist Paul Pierson has been the most prominent scholar of historical institutionalism in EU studies. He developed his theory as a response to intergovernmentalist theories of European integration, including Moravcsik's. In arguing that member states were in control of European integration only to a limited extent, Pierson sided with the neofunctionalists in this ongoing debate. Indeed, the unintended consequence of EU enlargement described above is a clear example of neofunctionalist spillover. Historical institutionalists such as Pierson explained *how* the EU could acquire new competences in spite of initial resistance from member states: the weight of historical decisions ultimately compelled them to accept this.

A people's project? Democracy, politics, and identity post-Maastricht

On the back of theories that emphasized the institutional dimension and the *how* of European integration, the 1990s also saw the rise of studies of the *who* of European integration. Up to then, that had largely been a question of states, institutions, and elites, with the popular dimension receiving little scholarly attention. The ratification process of the Maastricht Treaty in 1992 was one event that demonstrated the power of ordinary Europeans, in their capacity as voters. The narrow approval of the Treaty in France and Ireland and the initial 'no' in Denmark showed that broad, albeit tacit, public support for European integration was no longer a given (CHAPTER 5). The Irish 'no' in a referendum on the Treaty of Nice in 2001, and especially the

Dutch and French rejection of the 2005 Treaty establishing a Constitution for Europe further underlined the importance of studying popular attitudes to European integration.

In this line of research, too, Liesbet Hooghe and Gary Marks rose to prominence. Building on their theory of multilevel governance, they inquired how elections and referendums worked in a multilevel environment, and what role identity and public opinion played in shaping the EU. None of the traditional grand theories of European integration accounted for the emergence of public opposition to European integration, such as had become manifest across the EU in the 1990s – even though this development had deeper historical roots. Hooghe and Marks therefore proposed a new theory of European integration that acknowledged the importance of public opinion and identity. Tellingly, they named this theory **postfunctionalism**, implicitly heralding the end the progressive nature of European integration. According to Hooghe and Marks, the permissive consensus that European integration had thrived on for decades had come to an end around the time of the Maastricht Treaty. In its place came a so-called constraining dissensus: fundamental popular disagreement about European integration that might impede European integration and even lead to disintegration.

It is a legitimate historical question to ask whether the Maastricht Treaty was really such a turning point in the politicization of European integration. What is clear, nonetheless, is that public opposition to European integration or specific European policies presented a new kind of pressure on decision-making in European integration. Postfunctionalism constituted a break with neofunctionalist and intergovernmentalist perspectives, because these theories presented European integration as a rational process based on economic interests. While acknowledging that there were functional pressures such as spillovers and constructive interstate bargaining, Hooghe and Marks argued that domestic pressures from public opinion could uproot the progressive impetus to European integration. In their eyes, the EU had become an inextricable part of domestic politics, and therefore the politicization of the EU in national contexts was a new kind of pressure on European integration that political scientists had to take into account.

Hooghe and Marks drew scholarly attention to the ways in which political parties engaged in strategic competition on the issue of the EU. They observed that roughly until the 1980s, European political parties largely steered clear of the issue of European integration. As the EU's powers, policies, and membership expanded, however, Euroscepticism became a viable political strategy – on the political left in opposition to the capitalist overtones of market integration, and on the political right in defence of the national community. Postfunctionalism was part and parcel of a broader trend in EU studies to turn to opinion polls, surveys, and other quantitative data, as well as non-quantitative data such as focus groups. The aim was to understand how the politicization of the EU in national contexts shaped popular attitudes and influenced party strategies and European integration at large. Hooghe and Marks stressed that postfunctionalism did not have any predictive quality. That being said, the politicization of the EU as a subject in domestic politics became a very prescient theme in the run-up to and in the wake of the 2016 Brexit referendum in the United Kingdom. To some observers, Brexit demonstrated that this politicization could become a force for disintegration in the EU.

In addition to attempts to describe the turbulent developments since the 1990s, the question of the relationship between the EU and the public has also become the subject of normative scholarly debates. The question to what extent the EU can be considered democratic has stood at the heart of these debates. One school of thought points towards what has been called the no demos-problem. It holds that democracy presupposes a demos, a people that shares a sense of community. This is conspicuously absent in the EU, with its many official languages and citizens who primarily identify with their national or regional background rather than their Europeanness. This is not just a question of identity, but of political communication as well. Unlike its member states, the EU lacks what is known as a public sphere – a shared communicative space with European media outlets, where European political figureheads debate European political themes, which would allow citizens to identify and engage with, to form their own views on, pan-European issues.

This absence of a European public sphere is in fact one of the points of departure of postfunctionalist theory. After all, it encourages scholars to look at the **politicization** of the EU in national contexts, not on a European scale. Part of the reason why such a European public sphere is lacking is because the European Parliament is not the central political arena that national parliaments are. As much as the European Parliament has gained in power since its creation, it has not acquired the power, prerogatives, and profile to become the heart of public debate on European integration in Europe. Emblematic of this fact is that, in the absence of a uniform European electoral law, European elections are based on national electoral systems. National political parties run the campaigns, and citizens can vote only for candidates who stand for election in their resident country.

Such institutional perspectives on the question of democracy in the EU have become pervasive in the decades since Maastricht. Since then, a debate has been raging on the legitimacy of the EU. In this debate, some have argued that the EU suffers from a so-called **democratic deficit**. This debate is in fact as old as the EU itself, and the term dates back to the early 1970s. By the 1990s, however, it became apparent to many observers that the progressive accumulation of powers in Brussels had not been accompanied by the necessary growth of countervailing parliamentary power, democratic control, and accountability. This debate revolves primarily around the question whether or not the EU suffers from a democratic deficit, and if so, where it can be pinpointed and how it can be resolved. It is a normative debate that inevitably invokes the question what we mean by democracy and what democratic standards we should use to assess the EU by. This debate therefore touches upon the question *who* rules the EU, but also *what* the EU actually is. Can the EU be compared with a nation state, the largest scale at which we know democracy works? Or is the EU *sui generis* and must it be assessed on its own terms?

The EU as a world power?

Even though the founding theories of European integration were offshoots of international relations, much theorizing of European integration has actually occurred in relative isolation. Neofunctionalism in particular cast the EC as a polity that developed on its own terms. The reality is, of course, that the EC developed in the context of the bipolar world order of the Cold War, and that it was always tied up with questions of international trade, diplomacy, and European defence. The end of the Cold War and the Maastricht Treaty were a clear sign that the question of the EU's place in the world could no longer be ignored. The creation of the Common Foreign and Security Policy (CFSP), with the High Representative as its figurehead, was a manifestation of the EU's ambition to become more of a unitary actor on the global stage. The question was, of course, *how* the EU operated in this post-Cold War, multipolar world. Neofunctionalists and intergovernmentalists had argued that the EU excelled at achieving unitary positions on matters of low politics, but how it would function in the face of high politics remained to be seen.

Multilevel governance offered a way to think through the question of the EU's place in the world. The EU, after all, is but a regional top layer in a larger system of global governance. The EU participates as an observer in organizations such as the UN. It is a party to some 50 international UN agreements and a full participant at UN summits on climate change. As such, the European Green Deal is in line with the 2015 Paris Agreement and the UN's Sustainable Development Goals.

The EU thus acts as a node in a network of global governance. When it comes to geopolitics and projecting European power on the world stage, the EU operates notably less as a bloc. This became painfully apparent shortly after the establishment of the CFSP, when the Croatian War of Independence (1991–1995) and the Bosnian War (1992–1995) put the EU's capacity to act as a unitary actor for peace and security to the test – a test it failed, by most accounts (CHAPTER 5). The weakness in forming a unitary position on matters of foreign policy and security continued to be a problem, as became apparent in the EU's positioning vis-à-vis Russia when it annexed Crimea in 2014. Since CFSP was still a matter that required unanimous decisions in the Council, it was easy for member states to veto proposals. As a result of this dynamic, the EU was often divided internally, rather than asserting its geopolitical power (CHAPTER 6).

For all intents and purposes, the EU does not operate in foreign affairs as its member states do. Then again, the urgency to do so was not really felt in the period of relative geopolitical calm on Europe's borders following the wars in former Yugoslavia. This led scholars to hypothesize that there might be other ways in which the EU projected its power on the world stage. In the early 2000s, the political scientist Ian Manners proposed the notion that the EU was not a military or geopolitical power in the traditional realist sense, but a **normative power**. According to Manners, the EU influenced global norms through its diplomatic and trade relations, for example in the field of human rights. Having been founded on a normative basis of democratic principles, rule of law, liberty, respect for human rights, and fundamental freedoms, the EU could propagate and embody these principles and set them as standards for third states to follow.

Studying the EU's role in the abolition of the death penalty, Manners found that the EU had made a positive difference in the world. In so doing, he showed that the EU's internal market and trade agreements were not mere technical rules regarding trade, but a powerful instrument through which the EU could pursue foreign policy goals and project its benign power. Manners' argument reflected a positivism that existed ahead of the 2004–2007 'big bang' enlargement. In the run-up to their accession, the ten new member states had been in a continuous dialogue with the EU to implement reforms in accordance with the Copenhagen criteria, in their economies, public administration, and rule of law (CHAPTER 5). This, too, could be seen as a more direct and purposeful manifestation of the EU's soft power.

The example of the 2004–2007 enlargement also illustrated, however, that soft power amounts to little if there is no mechanism to uphold and enforce norms of democracy, liberty, and the rule of law. As the examples of Poland

and Hungary have shown in recent years, the EU struggles to muster the sanctioning power to defend these principles among its own membership, let alone outside its borders. The idea of normative power therefore reflects a conception of the EU at a specific point in time, and a strong belief in the universal character and progressive dissemination of liberal values. In that sense, Manners cast the EU as a *sui generis* organization, because it could project its power without having a military of its own or other coercive powers to enforce its position.

As the 2010s saw the increase of instability and insecurity in the world, the EU's weaknesses as a geopolitical actor again came to light. This inspired theoretical work along various established schools of thought. Yet theories that emphasized the strengths of the EU as a global actor sparked more scholarly debate. In line with Manners' theory, it was clear that the EU played to its strengths when engaging in low rather than high politics. Its strength as a **regulatory power** was particularly pronounced, meaning that the EU projected its power through the rules and regulations that governed the internal market. Over the decades, the internal market had become a body of rules, standards, and norms on products, services, and trade – rules that the EU also actively exported as a signatory party in international trade agreements. Although these rules were often technical and seemingly far removed from high politics, there was a longstanding idea in law, economics, and international relations that the rules of international trade were also a feature of geopolitics. Its forums were international trade organizations such as the General Agreement on Tariffs and Trade (GATT) and the World Trade Organization (WTO). Although theorists did not always recognize it at the time, the ability to shape international rules for trade was a sign of economic power, as well as a way to exert power and influence in other areas.

This struggle for regulatory power is also known as regulatory competition. Up until the 1970s, this competition primarily played out in the areas of raw materials and product standards. From then on, however, new areas of regulation emerged, such as the protection of consumers and the environment. This development showed that regulatory competition did not have to incentivize a so-called race to the bottom, in which the progressive liberalization of trade regimes would come at the expense of workers, producers, consumers, or the environment. Regulatory competition could also result in a race to the top, in which trading powers would compete to set the highest standards and strictest rules, thus compelling others to comply with its standards. During the 1990s, the EU became the world's most ambitious and dominant regulatory power, overtaking the

US. It reflected the fact that the EU internal market had become the largest internal market in the world.

The most influential recent account of the EU's rise to becoming a dominant global regulatory power was written by Anu Bradford from Columbia Law School. In her 2020 book *The Brussels Effect: How the European Union Rules the World*, she provides a survey of the areas in which the EU sets global standards, in rules for market competition, the digital economy, consumer health and safety, and the environment. She distinguished two ways in which the EU acted as a global regulatory power through what she called the Brussels effect: *de facto* and *de jure*. The former describes how multinational corporations are often inclined to take the EU's rules on product safety, digital privacy, and environmental protection as the global standard, simply because the EU's standards are often the strictest and most widespread, and therefore tend to comply with the rules in third markets as well. This means that acting through multinational corporations, such as big tech firms from Silicon Valley, the EU indirectly manages to determine global standards. Following from this, the *de jure* effect means that these multinational corporations, having adopted EU standards, have a vested interest in lobbying their national governments to formally adopt EU standards. Complying with EU rules, after all, gives these corporations a competitive edge over competitors that do not.

Bradford's book was especially timely because its appearance marked a change in global trading relations. Whereas global free trade, with the EU as one of its main protagonists, had ventured towards increasing free trade for decades, this started shifting in the 2010s. The rise of the Chinese state capitalist economy with its many powerful state-owned firms, and the US' desire to shield its economy from the influx of goods from its economic rival, ushered in an era of protectionism. When the COVID-19 pandemic subsequently demonstrated how vulnerable global supply chains were, this inspired economic thinking to move beyond liberalization. In the EU, as in many other countries, these developments intersected with a burgeoning climate policy. In this constellation, the EU started to impose stricter regulations on access to the internal market – on carbon-intensive products, for example. It shows that, in addition to the Brussels effect, the EU has become much more assertive in imposing its standards on global trade.

Failing forward and differentiated integration

In recent years, the EU has faced a series of external challenges. In addition to changes in global trade and the COVID-19 pandemic, there was the eurozone debt crisis, the migrant 'crisis', Brexit, and the Russian invasion of Ukraine (CHAPTER 6). Each of these crises sparked political debate and reinforced dissensus over the EU, leading some observers to predict disintegration or even the demise of the EU. Not only has the EU survived these crises, however, it arguably emerged from them with renewed vigour and competences. Clearly, neither grand theory can provide a comprehensive explanation for how the EU dealt with these crises. Neofunctionalism and intergovernmentalism posited that progress in European integration would be achieved especially through low politics, but these crises were very much a matter of high politics, characterized by frequent Council summits, dramatic media coverage, and heated national political debates.

The EU's recent crises have therefore sparked much debate among political scientists on how to theorize the way the EU has coping with these crises. Some have sought explanations in these grand theories. Others have sought to theorize disintegration, while yet another group, by contrast, has put forward a model of integration through crisis. The latter idea is far from new. Already in his 1978 memoirs, Jean Monnet argued that 'Europe will be forged in crises, and will be the sum of the solutions adopted for those crises.' The political scientists Erik Jones, Daniel Kelemen, and Sophie Meunier argued against this famous adage in a 2021 article. Introducing the theory of **failing forward**, the authors argued against Monnet's idea of progress through crisis by pointing out that it was not external events alone that propelled European integration forward. They also drew attention to the EU's flawed institutional architecture.

The idea behind failing forward was that the nature of intergovernmental decision-making in the EU necessarily resulted in flawed institutions and policies, simply because states had to reach agreement on the lowest common denominator. These inadequacies could go unnoticed as long as they were not confronted with challenges, in which case they could become fundamental crises for the EU, requiring urgent strengthening of these hitherto flawed institutions and policies.

The clearest example of this dynamic is the eurozone debt crisis. Even at the time of the negotiations on the Maastricht Treaty, ideas were being proposed to shore up the nascent monetary union with a political union, a banking union and/or a stability mechanism. There was insufficient political support for these plans, however, and so ways to ensure the resilience of the monetary union were left undecided. The vulnerability of this system became all too clear in the wake of the 2008 financial crisis. Suddenly, under pressure, measures that had proven too controversial during the Maastricht negotiations seemed necessary. In quick succession, the member states agreed on the European Financial Stability Facility, the European Stability Mechanism, and the European Banking Union, while the European Central Bank significantly increased its mandate to intervene in financial markets (CHAPTER 6).

Whereas the theory of failing forward presents a more erratic notion of progress in European integration, there is a distinct neofunctionalist slant to it. It supposes that flawed integration in some areas may lead to spillovers, i.e. to a deepening or widening of integration, as a consequence of decisions taken under the pressure of crises. There is also an intergovernmentalist dimension to the theory, however, specifically a liberal intergovernmentalist one. In these moments of crisis, after all, a liberal dynamic of interstate bargaining emerges, in which coalitions are formed for different kinds of reforms and solutions, and the politics between these coalitions determine which reforms will actually be pursued. The theory of failing forward thus presents a synthesis of neofunctionalism and liberal intergovernmentalism. The added value of this synthesis is that it nuances the often-presumed opposition between supranationalism and intergovernmentalism, where the latter acts as a damper or restraint on the former. The theory of failing forward shows, however, how interstate bargaining can produce unintended consequences that create room for states to seek supranational solutions rather than resisting such reforms.

It is important to emphasize that Jones, Kelemen, and Meunier did not present their theory of failing forward as yet another grand theory, with the ambition of explaining European integration in its entirety. Rather, they acknowledged that the EU was the product of a complex interplay of dynamics, including crisis pressures, 'business as usual', disintegration, and failing forward.

Encompassing 27 member states and a decades-long history, the EU and its member states themselves acknowledge this complexity and diversity in moving the project forward. The idea, originally envisaged by Monnet and theorized by Haas, that European integration is a linear process toward uniformity clearly no longer holds. This has in fact been true at least since the 1980s, when five of the then ten EC member states negotiated the Schengen Agreement, which subsequently became integrated into the EU Treaty in Amsterdam in 1997. While Schengen was open to states outside the EU, the UK chose to opt out of the Schengen Agreement (CHAPTER 5). This prime example of what came to be known as **differentiated integration** was also visible in other areas, such as the euro. This differentiation has also opened up opportunities for smaller groups of member states to pursue integration in other areas, but initiatives in this respect remain limited. This idea of an

EU *à la carte* has altered the way scholars look at the EU, and created new opportunities for thinking about future enlargement rounds.

Conclusion

After decades of theorizing about European integration, our theoretical understanding of *why* and *how* European integration occurs has become increasingly intricate, as the EU has become an increasingly large and complex polity. As much as the classical grand theories of neofunctionalism and intergovernmentalism are reflective of contemporary developments and of the ideals of the 1950s and 1960s, they have inspired thinking that still carries weight in the 2020s. What was a rather binary scholarly debate then, however, has become integrated into a much broader and interdisciplinary field, which encompasses political science, law, public administration, economics, history, and many other disciplines. As such, the study of European integration has gone from seeking to predict its course to acknowledging its contingent nature and the ways in which internal and external pressures shape it.

Likewise, answers to the question *what* the EU is have gone from seeking to capture its essence to exploring its fringes, external and internal effects, as well as interactions with the outside world. The Maastricht Treaty has been a pivotal moment in this respect, as it greatly expanded the reach of the EU's capacities and marked the beginning of a dramatic expansion of its membership. Scholars have long tried to capture the 'nature of the beast', often concluding that the EU was really *sui generis*. Today, however, there are also debates that signal the fact that the EU is increasingly accruing core state powers, which means that the question whether the EU is moving toward a federal system is far from settled.

The question *who* drives European integration, meanwhile, has become more democratic in nature. What was originally seen by neofunctionalists and intergovernmentalists as a matter for economic and political elites, together with the EC institutions and ministries for foreign affairs, is now also an integral part of the political life of its citizens. The dynamic that the pioneers of postfunctionalism observed has only become more pronounced as the EU has faced a series of crises in recent years that have made the EU a divisive issue in domestic politics. At the same time, events such as Brexit and the Russian invasion of Ukraine have seemingly harnessed support for EU membership, and made it a more salient subject for substantive political debate. Whereas these moments of crisis have shown that understanding European integration is an endeavour riddled with uncertainty, this understanding is also grounded in theoretical work that has, to varying degrees, stood the test of time.

Further reading

- Bradford, Anu. *The Brussels Effect: How the European Union Rules the World.* Oxford: Oxford University Press, 2020.
- Eilstrup-Sangiovanni, Mette, ed. *Debates on European Integration: A Reader.* Basingstoke: Palgrave Macmillan, 2006.
- Føllesdal, Andreas, and Simon Hix. 'Why is There a Democratic Deficit in the EU? A Response to Majone and Moravcsik.' *Journal of Common Market Studies* 44, no. 3 (2006): 533–62.
- Haas, Ernst B. *The Uniting of Europe: Political Social and Economic Forces 1950–1957.* London: Stevens, 1958.
- Hoffmann, Stanley. *The European Sisyphus: Essays on Europe 1964–1994.* Boulder, CO: Westview, 1995.
- Hooghe, Liesbet, and Gary Marks. 'A Postfunctionalist Theory of European Integration: From Permissive Consensus to Constraining Dissensus.' *British Journal of Political Science* 39, no. 1 (2009): 1–23.
- Hooghe, Liesbet, and Gary Marks. *Multi-Level Governance and European Integration.* Lanham, MD: Rowman & Littlefield, 2001.
- Jones, Erik, R. Daniel Kelemen, and Sophie Meunier. 'Failing Forward? Crises and Patterns of European Integration.' *Journal of European Public Policy* 28, no. 10 (2021): 1519–36.
- Lindberg, Leon N., and Stuart A. Scheingold. *Europe's Would-Be Polity: Patterns of Change in the European Community.* Englewood Cliffs, NJ: Prentice-Hall, 1970.
- Manners, Ian. 'Normative Power Europe: A Contradiction in Terms?' *Journal of Common Market Studies* 40, no. 2 (2021): 235–58.
- Mitrany, David. *A Working Peace System: An Argument for the Functional Development of International Organization.* Oxford: Oxford University Press, 1943.
- Moravcsik, Andrew. *The Choice for Europe: Social Purpose and State Power from Messina to Maastricht.* Ithaca, NY: Cornell University Press, 1998.
- Pierson, Paul. 'The Path to European Integration: A Historical Institutionalist Analysis.' *Comparative Political Studies* 29, no. 2 (1996): 123–63.
- Wiener, Antje, Tanja Börzel, and Thomas Risse, eds. *European Integration Theory.* 3rd ed. Oxford: Oxford University Press: 2019.

8. Historical perspectives on European integration

The story of European integration has been written in many ways. Through a multitude of narratives, perspectives, and sources, historians have attempted to make sense of European integration: its character, its development, and direction, and its protagonists. At the same time, European integration has always been about more than the narrow EC/EU: it is embedded in longer and wider histories of Europe in the world. Histories of European integration in recent years have increasingly reflected this temporal, geographical, and thematic widening. An understanding of the ways in which the history of European integration has been written also reveals a lot about the current European Union. Learning about its history prompts considerations of founding narratives and myths, trials and errors, breaks and continuities – and how the story has transformed over time.

The EC/EU has also, throughout its existence, produced its own history. The process of European integration unfolded in interrelation with the writing of its narratives, and the availability of sources and perspectives which support it. The early history of the EC/EU was often written on the basis of the memoirs of its protagonists, yielding a narrative of the 'founding fathers'. The perspective of the nation states and the role of national interests has been represented through the inclusion of sources from the national archives of the member states. The European institutions that were created from the 1950s onwards have generated their own body of archival material, broadening the scope of historical research in consequence. The EC/EU has also incentivized scholarship by setting up research services and promoting research into its own history.

The traditional narrative of European integration history can be divided into two main strands: the federalist narrative and the nation state narrative. At its core, the debate between these two sets of scholarship was concerned with the question of *why* the Six chose to integrate in the first place. Crucial points in this debate were to what extent the European nation states actually transferred or ceded essential power to European institutions in the 1950s and 1960s; why they did so; and to what extent the outcome of the integration process was based on rational choices by the responsible political leaders. Subsequently, the question as to whether the process of European integration was to be interpreted as weakening the power of the nation state, or instead, as a deliberate attempt by the nation states to slow down the restriction of their sovereignty as a consequence of processes of globalization by partially transferring that power, is a point of contention.

In the **federalist narrative**, European integration was hailed as the spiritual legacy of the democratic resistance to the Nazis. The historian Walter Lipgens was particularly influential in this school, specifically a 1968 work of his, in which he discussed wartime plans for European integration in resistance movements. In this tradition, the unity of Europe was an idea for the self-preservation and self-protection of western Europe, rooted in the experiences of the first half of the twentieth century. According to Lipgens and his followers, the perception of the necessity for European integration was fuelled by the conviction that an economically and politically fragmented Europe would be pushed aside by the two new major powers after the Second World War. The decreasing power of the western European nation states in the world, which became ever clearer during decolonization, was to be halted by the political and economic integration of Europe, culminating in a federalist super state. Although Lipgens and his disciples regarded European unification as an inevitable and progressive process, key individuals such as Jean Monnet, were able to bring the goal of federation nearer. In this view, the political integration of Europe was the end goal for Monnet, while economic integration was a means in this process for him.

The **nation state narrative**, by contrast, emphasized the national interests of states as the main impetus behind European integration. Alan Milward's 1992 work *The European Rescue of the Nation State* was highly influential in challenging the federalist narrative. Milward denied that there was any contradiction between European and national interests, thus emphasizing the primacy of domestic politics. On the basis of government archives released for research in the 1980s, Milward found that the pursuit of European integration by nation states was the consequence of a hidden agenda of nationally minded politicians and policymakers, who did not see European integration as an end but, rather, as a means to further their domestic economic and political interests, as well as to obtain legitimacy. Milward posited that the desire of national government to create socioeconomic security for its individual citizens was the driving force behind European integration. Therefore, the driving force behind European integration was not the 'miraculous doings' of the 'European saints' or any neofunctionalist spillover effect but, rather, the European 'rescue' of the nation state and the legitimacy of national politics. European integration created the prosperity and employment opportunities that constituted the conditions for the construction of national welfare states, which connected citizens more strongly to their own nation states and in consequence strengthened the nation state.

In recent years, research into the history of European integration has developed in multiple directions, moving beyond the binary opposition between the federalist and the nation state narrative. Although extremely varied, recent scholarship can be characterized as less teleological, less concerned with motivations and driving forces, and less focused on the narrow EC/EU. Instead, recent work emphasizes the history of European integration as embedded in a wider set of historical developments in the twentieth century. A key work which exemplifies the changes in orientation of the history of European integration is Kiran Klaus Patel's *Project Europe: A History*, published in 2020. It both summarizes and proposes crucial innovations to European integration scholarship. First, there is the importance of understanding the impact and consequences of European integration on the citizens and societies of the member states. Second, there is the importance of regarding European integration in interaction with other organizations, as well as processes of global economic and political change.

This chapter serves as a guide to recent developments in and contributions to the historiography of European integration. It does so in three parts, guided by the overarching questions of this book: *what* is Europe and *what* is the EC/EU; *why* is there the EC/EU; and *who* has made the EC/EU. It also offers suggestions for further reading in the form of historiographical review articles, to further delve into the themes and debates which have characterized the writing of the EC/EU's history. And as scholarly contributions are referred to in this chapter only by the names of their authors or editors, the full bibliography can be consulted for further research.

What is the EC/EU?

In 1985, Jacques Delors famously referred to the EC as an 'unidentified political object'. Indeed, the complex nature of EC/EU makes it difficult to define, stimulating debates among political scientists. For instance, the question whether it is an international organization or a federation remains a matter for debate (CHAPTER 7). In contrast, historians rarely formulate their research questions as *what* is the EC/EU? Nevertheless, this question remains important for the discipline as a long-term perspective offered by history enables us to grasp the dynamic nature of EC/EU geography and identity. By looking at the EC/EU's relations with its 'others', historians have helped to understand *what* the EC was. By focusing on specific competences of the EC/EU's institutions, they underscored the EC/EU's different roles, thus helping to define it by its function.

Changing geography and fluid identity

The debate on *what* Europe is predates European integration itself. The fact that the continent lacks clear geographic borders makes it a product of imagination. Its definitions varied greatly depending on who formulated them, when, and for what purpose. For instance, during the Renaissance, when Italy was an intellectual centre, Europe's northern boundaries were questionable. Later, during the Enlightenment, once the intellectual centre shifted to France and Britain, its eastern borders sparked more controversies. Similarly, during the Crusades, Europe was crucially defined as Christendom, namely lands dominated by Roman Catholics as opposed to those dominated by Orthodox Christians and Muslims. With secularization, however, Europe came to be understood as a region shaped by the ideas of the Enlightenment. During the nineteenth-century era of high imperialism, Europe supposedly embodies reason and civilization, in contrast to the rest of the world. Scholars such as Anthony Pagden, Patrick Pasture, and Michael Wintle examined how the 'idea of Europe' evolved over the centuries. While these debates might seem confined to academic lecture halls, they often surface in the politics of European integration. For instance, in 2004, the question of whether to include the 'Christian roots of Europe' in the preamble to the European Constitution sparked controversies among EU member states and parties.

In contrast to Europe, the EC/EU geographical boundaries could be defined by membership. However, since the Treaty of Rome was signed in 1957 by six founding states, the EC/EU acquired 22 new members. The increase in size became a permanent feature of European integration history. Scholars have scrutinized all seven rounds of enlargement as well as negotiations with each member state. An edited volume by Haakon A. Ikonomou, Aurélie Andry, and Rebekka Byberg, as well as one by Jürgen Elvert and Wolfram Kaiser, presented contributions exploring enlargement history.

Enlargements have not only altered the borders of the EC/EU, but have also significantly influenced *what* the EC/EU was. For instance, research by Emma De Angelis and Eirini Karamouzi demonstrated that the southern enlargements played a crucial role in shaping the EC's democratic identity. It was only when confronted with the membership interest of authoritarian regimes that the EC began to emphasize democratic values (CHAPTER 4). From the creation of the European Coal and Steel Community (ECSC), initially focused on cooperation within a limited economic sector, European integration has progressively come to encompass economic, political, and cultural dimensions. Comprehensive works spanning the entire history of the EC/EU, such as Patel's *Project Europe*, capture the evolution of the organization's identity particularly well.

Historians have not only reminded us of the EC/EU's dynamic geography and identity but have also looked critically at the EC/EU's attempts to define itself. Jacob Krumrey offered an account of the EC's symbolic policies, which since the 1950s aimed to present it as a unique organization predestined to become a European government. A vast political science literature also exists on symbolic politics in the context of attempts to create a European identity (CHAPTER 7). Wolfram Kaiser's studies also investigated EC/EU's attempts to define itself. A collective volume he edited with Richard McMahon presented papers that reconstructed clashing narratives of European integration. In doing so, the volume emphasized the idea that there is not just one way of narrating and defining the EC/EU.

The EC/EU's 'others'

Accepting the EC's geography as changeable, and its identity as fluid complicates the task of defining it. Historical studies examining the EC/EU's relations with other actors might be able to facilitate this task. Like every identity, the EC/EU's identity was defined through its relations with 'others'.

The list of the EC/EU's 'others' starts with Europe's own **past**. In this understanding, the EC/EU is, above all, not what its member states used to be before and during the Second World War. Such an approach was proposed by Tony Judt in *The Past is Another Country*, in which he presented postwar Europe as a project of collective forgetting painful and clashing memories of the Second World War. The booming field of memory studies merged with European integration scholarship in the works of authors such as Aline Sierp. Her research showed how European memory politics mattered for European integration and how they were often carefully crafted to foster European identity.

Scholars such as Patrick Pasture revealed that European forgetting concerned not only continental but also imperial history. The federalist narrative of European integration long ignored the fact that at the time of the EC formation, three out of six members were still **colonial empires**. However, recent scholarship on European integration and decolonization has reversed this perspective. Scholars such as Peo Hansen and Stefan Jonsson have highlighted attempts to reconcile empires with integration and the painful divorces from colonies that followed. Giuliano Garavini has offered an account of the EC's efforts to maintain its advantageous position vis-à-vis the Global South. Some scholars even framed European integration as a neo-colonial project aimed at safeguarding European superiority. In *Eurowhiteness*, Hans Kundnani argued that this sentiment is essential to the EU's identity (CHAPTER 2 and 3).

The **European socialist regimes** were also the EC's 'others'. Although the EC originated during the Cold War, the histories of European integration and the Cold War functioned separately for many years. Only recently, have the histories of the Cold War and European integration started to align, thanks to scholars such as Piers Ludlow, Angela Romano, and Federico Romero. On one hand, these historians showed how the existence of socialist regimes in close proximity shaped the economic model championed by the EC and its member states and encouraged their unity. On the other hand, this scholarship evidenced the influence the EC had on the European socialist regimes, the majority of which are now EU members. For instance, Benedetto Zaccaria looked at the relationship between the EC and socialist Yugoslavia, while Aleksandra Komornicka demonstrated the EC's effects on socialist Poland. A subfield of literature, represented by authors such as Suvi Kansikas, also exists on relations between the EC and the Council for Mutual Economic Assistance (CMEA). These two models of economic cooperation in Europe functioned in parallel and influenced each other. When looking at European integration history through the prism of the Cold War, the EC stood first and foremost for the capitalist economy and the alliance with the United States.

At the same time, however, the EC/EU is not identical to the **United States**, a centre of global capitalism. The transatlantic relationship played a pivotal role in European integration. Most importantly, the United States provided Europe with the Marshall Plan, encouraging its integration, and maintained, and still maintains, its security through NATO. However, US involvement not only encouraged the process of European integration but also allowed the EC to define itself in relation to its closest ally. Aurélie Elisa Gfeller and Daniel Möckli demonstrated that divergences between the United States and EC member states during the crisis of 1970s, facilitated the EC's cooperation in new policy areas. Once defined in contrast to the United States, the EC is sometimes characterized by its 'third way-ism'. Mary Nolan showed that despite the United States' superpower status, the implementation of its economic model in the postwar years needed to be negotiated within the European context. This negotiation was one of the factors that resulted in a European welfare system that is significantly more developed than in the United States. Regarding foreign policy, Angela Romano revealed the EC's attempt to seek a 'third way' in bilateral Cold War politics through active engagement in the Conference on Security and Cooperation in Europe (CSCE).

Since the end of the Cold War, the list of European 'others' has evolved. The inclusion of post-socialist states in the EU has complicated its memory politics. As Ivan Krastev has explored, differences in memories concerning the postwar period continue to hinder European integration and explain persistent East-West differences. While the EC 'othered' its pre-1945 past, post-socialist states also insist on 'othering' the Cold War experience. Moreover, the transformation of European socialist regimes and their subsequent integration into the EU marked the final reorientation of the EC/EU from postcolonial to pan-European, a process that began with southern enlargement. While socialist regimes were no longer considered 'others', the 'otherness' of post-colonial states increased. James Mark has discussed this phenomenon in his studies.

Functional definitions

Historical research on the EC/EU's relationships with external actors is a relatively new phenomenon that has developed alongside growing interest in the EC/EU's international role. Studies of enlargements, decolonization, East-West contacts during the Cold War, transatlantic relations, as well as the EC's relations with other countries and organizations all portray the EC as an **international actor.** Ulrich Krotz, Patel, and Federico Romero gathered such perspectives in their edited volume on Europe's Cold War relations. By doing so, they also bridged often-separated fields of history and international relations.

While the EC/EU's role as an international actor may seem central from today's perspective, it was not until the 1970s that member states began cooperation in foreign affairs, and it was not until the Single European Act (SEA) that this cooperation became institutionalized. Initially, the EC was primarily a **market.** This perspective on the EC stems from the Milward school of European integration history, which emphasized the economic logic of integration. Patel's scholarship followed Milward in this regard. From the perspective of these scholars, the EC's success lies in its exclusive focus on economic integration and in the fact that it initially set aside integration in fields that were critical for national sovereignty.

This approach inspires studies exploring the economic dimension of integration. For instance, authors such as Patel and Ann-Christina Knudsen examined the Common Agricultural Policy (CAP). Works by Laurent Warlouzet and Katja Seidel shed light on the history of competition policy. More recently, the EC's environmental policies have also come under scrutiny in studies by Jan-Henrik Meyer, Wim van Meurs, and Liesbeth van de Grift.

Within this field, the Economic and Monetary Union (EMU) has received special attention. Works such as Harold James' on the Committee of Central Bank Governors, and Emmanuel Mourlon-Druol's on the European Monetary System, scrutinize the long-term bargaining and debates preceding the introduction of the EMU. From the perspective of these studies, the EC crucially aspired to become a **monetary union** (CHAPTER 4 and 5).

The 2008 global financial crisis further increased historians' interest in the economic dimension of the EC/EU. Older approaches, such as that of John Gillingham, who saw European integration as a neoliberal project from the onset, came under revision. For instance, Markus K. Brunnermeier, Harold James, and Jean-Pierre Landau proposed examining the making of EMU as a battle of ideas, exploring the clash between German ordoliberalism and the French *dirigiste* tradition. Similarly, Laurent Warlouzet offered a typology of economic traditions that underlined European policymaking. In his scholarship, he distinguished social, neo-mercantilist, and neoliberal approaches and explains why the latter eventually prevailed. Building on this typology, Aurélie Andry explored the 1970s idea of 'social Europe' and its demise. Other scholars, such as Quinn Slobodian and Roberto Ventresca, also saw neoliberalism as an approach which came to define the EC/EU policies only in the 1980s (CHAPTER 4).

Historians have also looked at the EC/EU in terms of its **legal entity** in close relation to economic policymaking. Particularly, studies of competition policy have brought together scholars interested in economics and those interested in law. This can be illustrated by the contributions to a volume on the historical foundation of competition law edited by Patel and Heike Schweitzer. Scholars examining European integration from a legal perspective also investigated the gradual emergence of the EC's 'constitutional practice', recognizing it as critical for fostering European integration. Works by authors such as Morten Rasmussen, Brigitte Leucht, and Karin van Leeuwen explore this phenomenon.

The historiography on European integration also looked at the EC/EU as a **democracy**. In doing so, the discipline contributed to explaining the origins of the EU's democratic deficit (CHAPTER 7). As historians such as Martin Conway or Jan-Werner Müller remind us, the EC was shaped by the character of postwar democracy. In contrast to the interwar years, after the Second World War, western European states aimed to provide effective governance rather than to reflect popular will. Created in this spirit, the

EC was, at its origin, a technocratic institution and its democratic deficit stems from this particular postwar context.

Why the EC/EU?

The question *why* countries sought to integrate lies at the heart of the theory and historiography of European integration. The federalist narrative presents integration as a natural process, which, although troubled, continuously leads to increased supranational cooperation. Such an approach unsurprisingly focuses on milestones of European integration, such as the signing of the Treaty of Rome or the creation of the SEA. As noted by Laurent Warlouzet, portraying European integration as a history of 'crises' and 'relaunches' limits our understanding of the phenomenon. In recent years, historians have significantly contributed to undermining this understanding of European integration. In addition to broadening the timeframe and geographical scope of studies on European integration, they also raised previously unexplored questions. Patel's famous postulate to 'provincialize the EU' has encouraged historians not only to contemplate *why* European states chose to integrate but also *why* they chose to integrate within the EC/EU? Moreover, Brexit and the increasing influence of Eurosceptic forces have sparked academic interest in the phenomenon of disintegration.

Explaining integration

In contrast to the federalist narrative, which focused on the role of states and individuals, newer perspectives on the European integration history link the phenomenon with larger processes. When attempting to explain *why* European countries sought integration, historians have pointed to the role of internationalization and Europeanization, as well as key processes marking the end of European global domination, such as the Cold War, decolonization, and globalization.

The increase in cooperation among European states was part of a broader phenomenon of increasing cooperation among states in general, known as **internationalization**. While European countries had waged wars against each other for centuries and later concluded peace agreements, these events were neither officially regulated nor institutionalized. Similarly, trade agreements were bilateral and were made according to current needs. Even the 'Congress System', a European governance system between the 1815 Congress of Vienna and the beginning of the First World War in 1914, was based only on ad hoc conferences. However, these nineteenth-century conferences laid the groundwork for a more elaborate form of global governance, fostering internationalization, and leading to early forms of institutionalization (CHAPTER 1). Scholars such as Mark Mazower and Glenda Sluga explore the importance of these nineteenth-century ideas and forms of international cooperation.

The creation of the League of Nations in 1919 marked the first institutionalized attempt at forming global governance. The federalist narrative often dismisses the organization as an ineffective project that failed to prevent the Second World War. However, as the works of Patricia Clavin show, the League was much more than just a peace project. Its creation stemmed from earlier attempts at internationalization and the proliferation of transnational problems resulting from the war and its aftermath. Challenges such as migration, minority rights, pandemics, and economic matters were all areas of interest for the League, and it proved much more successful there than in maintaining peace. These experiences were significant for postwar European integration. Because the League provided a template for organizational structure and a learning curve, and because it trained civil servants, the history of the League cannot be separated from the history of the EC/EU (CHAPTER 1).

The process of internationalization went hand in hand with **Europeanization.** While political scientists understand Europeanization as an increase in the number and influence of European political structures, historians assign a much broader meaning to the term. An edited volume by Patel and Martin Conway explored the various forms of strengthening European interconnectedness and practices labelled as European in the twentieth century. Other authors have taken a similar approach. The book series *Making Europe: Technology and Transformation, 1850–2000*, edited by Johan Scott and Philip Scranton, explored how experts, industries, and institutions fostered Europeanization. Within this field, some authors looked at early and unrealized projects for European integration (CHAPTER 1). For instance, Peo Hansen and Stefan Jonsson examined Richard Coudenhove-Kalergi's *Pan-Europa* vision. Mathieu Segers, Matthew D'Auria, and Trineke Palm also researched this project, as well as other interwar visions of an integrated Europe.

While long-term processes of internationalization and Europeanization began when European states still held a dominant global position, actual integration started only once this position began to decline. The 'European century', as the nineteenth century is sometimes referred to due to the dominance of European empires over the rest of the world, came to a decisive end after the Second World War. Indeed, European states emerged from the conflict economically exhausted and politically diminished. The importance of this postwar situation is central to Milward's thesis. In his view, integration and the limited transfer of national sovereignty to supranational institutions were necessary to safeguard weak European nation states.

Similarly, studies linking European integration with the **Cold War** and **decolonization** propose viewing European integration as resulting from the weakness rather than the strength of European states. During the Cold War, Europe became a playground for the superpowers, and the process of European integration was part of their bipolar world division. Such a perspective is particularly present in studies that emphasize the importance of the United States for European integration, including Geir Lundestad, who famously referred to the United States approach to Europe as an 'empire by invitation'. In similar vein, scholars of European integration and decoloniza- tion, including Giuliano Garavini, pointed out how the decline of empires shaped integration in Europe. Besides the central role of economics and reconstruction, from the perspective of the Cold War and decolonization, integration was also an attempt at safeguarding Europe's role in the world.

Finally, European integration is often portrayed as a response to **globaliza- tion**. In such interpretations, the increasing cooperation among European states is only one of many forms of regional cooperation necessitated by the increasingly globalized economy and political structures. A special volume edited by Claudia Hiepel and studies by Laurent Warlouzet and Emmanuel Mourlon-Druol proposed seeing major developments in European integration since the 1970s as responses to globalization (CHAPTER 4). This approach is also present in studies on business and European integration. Authors such as Bastiaan van Apeldoorn, Grace Ballor, or Sigfrido M. Ramírez Pérez interpreted the increasing engagement of business actors in European integration by pointing to rising global competition, particularly from US and Japanese companies.

The choice for the EC/EU

In 2000, Dipesh Chakrabarty famously called for historians to 'provincialize Europe', arguing that the idea of Europe and its uniqueness is entrenched in social sciences. Paraphrasing this formulation, Patel in 2013 proposed to 'provincialize the EU'. Like Chakrabarty, who criticized the dominance of Eurocentric thinking in the entire discipline of history, Patel argued that historians of European integration often assume the EC's uniqueness and its predestined success. Instead, he encouraged scholars to examine the

EC within the context of various forms of integration. In his view, the EC developed within a broader landscape of European, transatlantic, and global organizations. The EC could draw from the experiences and personnel of these other bodies and was stimulated by the competition they created.

A volume edited by Matthew Broad and Suvi Kansikas has presented contributions that explore European integration 'beyond Brussels'. The EC's main competitors in the postwar period have also received independent scholarly attention. Works by Birte Wassenberg delved into the history of the Council of Europe, while Sally Rohan examined the history of the Western European Union. A substantial body of literature, including works by Milward, Daniel Speich Chassé, and Martin Schain, also exists on the Marshall Plan. The subsequent creation of the Organization for European Economic Cooperation (OEEC) and its functioning was scrutinized in the works by Matthieu Leimgruber and Matthias Schmelzer, as well as in an edited volume by Richard T. Griffiths. Jorrit Steehouder studied the European Payments Union created under OEEC auspices. Daniel Stinsky explored the history of the United Nations Economic Commission for Europe, while Matthew Broad and Richard T. Griffiths looked at the history of the European Free Trade Association (EFTA). All these works provide insights into the limitations of the abovementioned organizations, thus explaining *why* none of them emerged as a principal organization in Europe (CHAPTER 2).

Apart from the proliferation of forums for European cooperation after the Second World War, significant integration also occurred on transatlantic and global levels. Timothy Andrews Sayle offered an account of NATO's history. The International Monetary Fund (IMF) and the Bretton Woods System were analysed by Harold James. Works by Douglas Irwin, Petros Mavroidis, and Alan O. Sykes, as well as studies by Francine McKenzie shed light on the history of the General Agreement on Tariffs and Trade (GATT). Lucia Coppolaro examined the GATT specifically in the context of European integration.

As Patel's argument suggested, transatlantic and global organizations played an essential role in the EC's success, enabling it to focus on limited economic integration. For instance, NATO gave western European states security, which meant the EC members did not have to worry about complex security cooperation. In explaining *why* the EC prevailed over other forms of cooperation, Patel also highlights the spillover effect from the common market, the influence of European law on national regulations, and the EC's financial resources, which were larger than those of other organizations and, since the 1970s, no longer relied on member states' contributions but on the EC's own revenues.

Laurent Warlouzet also explores *why* the EC outperformed other forms of international cooperation. His focus on the 1970s crisis illustrates how the EC became a primary forum for regulating globalization. Warlouzet argues that while the EC was not the initial solution for European states, it was reinstated when both national and global approaches proved ineffective. Like Patel, he underscores the significance of the EC's legal framework. Moreover, he notes that, unlike other organizations, the EC comprised only liberal democracies sharing common geopolitical objectives. The EC's small size and the similarities between its members substantially facilitated cooperation.

Patel and Warlouzet agree that it was not until the 1970s that the EC emerged as the primary forum for European cooperation. Their contributions, alongside other scholars' research on this period, have significantly revised the understanding of European integration in the 1970s, previously labelled Eurosclerosis. Michele Di Donato provided a review of this new historiography of the 1970s, which now sees the decade as critical for understanding the EU as we know it today (CHAPTER 4).

The question *why* states chose to integrate within the EC/EU has also been explored by historians applying national perspectives. All member states' rationales behind participating in European integration have been explored by scholars publishing in English, and even more developed scholarship on this topic exists in national languages.

Disintegration

Brexit and the rise of Eurosceptic forces have strongly undermined the federalist narrative of European integration and posed a challenge to scholars studying this phenomenon. In contrast to political scientists, who seek to adapt their theories to the circumstances of disintegration, historians have turned their attention to examining the long-term presence of Euroscepticism and its conceptualization within the broader context of European integration (CHAPTER 7).

A volume edited by Mark Gilbert and Daniele Pasquinucci shed light on various challenges to European integration that existed long before Brexit. Similarly, a special issue edited by Richard McMahon and Wolfram Kaiser explored counter-narratives of European integration developed throughout the twentieth and twenty-first centuries. Both contributions nuanced the federalist narrative by recognizing that Eurosceptic forces often played a role in European integration. They did so, for instance, by mobilizing pro-European forces or by proposing alternative European projects that, while not based on supranational cooperation, implied Europeanization.

While the United Kingdom, known as an 'awkward partner', had long held the interest of historians of European integration, this interest has only intensified since Brexit. Authors including Piers Ludlow, Martin Conway, and Thorsten Borring Olesen have offered historical accounts of British Euroscepticism. Lindsay Aqui, in her monograph, examined the first British membership referendum in 1975 (CHAPTER 4).

The threat of disintegration has also prompted scholars to revisit precedents of European disintegration. Patel questioned whether Brexit was indeed 'something new under the sun?' and reminded readers of the cases of Algeria and Greenland, which joined the EC as part of France and Denmark respectively. Later, after becoming independent, they both opted to leave the organization. The case of Algeria was also explored in detail by Megan Brown (CHAPTER 3 and 4).

Who has made the EC/EU?

Although the EC/EU was structured to a great extent by external developments and its relations with its 'others', and although its faceless, technocratic character has been criticized, the EC/EU was also very much made by a range of actors: individuals, institutions, and non-state actors. The way in which this history has been written is closely connected to the availability and development of source material, ranging from individual actors' memoirs and national archives to a growing body of sources from the institutions and non-state actors' archives. The next section discusses a selection of recent contributions to scholarship on the actors in European integration, divided into three parts: individuals, institutions, and non-state actors.

Individuals

In traditional accounts of European integration, in particular concerning the early period of European integration, approaches from **diplomatic history** have held a fairly dominant position. Once the diplomatic archives of the nation states from the 1950s were opened in the 1980s, this historiographical orientation acquired new impetus, too. Just like Milward's work, this branch of historiography – which concentrates above all on the negotiations among diplomats and other representatives of nation states – explained the stance of foreign ministers and their civil service apparatuses regarding

European integration rather than the position of, for instance, national party politics. In this strand of historiography, the actors were the nation states and their government leaders, acting under international pressure. From this perspective, the EC/EU was regarded as a special form of international interaction between member states, but nothing more.

The focus on the importance of nation states in European integration history has yielded a strong emphasis on the role of great men (and a few women): the **government leaders** who shaped Europe. In this view, a distinction was often made between the 'good' Europeans (Konrad Adenauer, Alcide De Gasperi) and the critics (Charles de Gaulle, Margaret Thatcher), and the history of European integration tends to be written as a struggle between these opposing forces. Several scholars have criticized this view for being overly simplistic and ignorant of the fact that pro-European politicians also pursued national interests, while Thatcher and de Gaulle in certain regards greatly contributed to the EC. Laurent Warlouzet, for instance, argued that de Gaulle was so influential in the development of the EEC that he could well be described as a new 'Father of Europe'.

The focus on the role of individuals in the making of Europe is nowhere clearer than with regard to the '**European saints**'. A wealth of scholarship is dedicated to the efforts of the 'founding fathers', including Robert Schuman, Jean Monnet, Paul-Henri Spaak, Alcide De Gasperi, and Jacques Delors. In recent years, approaches to writing the history of these key actors in the history of European integration have evolved. Piers Ludlow's work on Roy Jenkins and his presidency of the European Commission from 1977 to 1980 was a methodologically innovative contribution. He combined a biographical-institutional approach and situated this in the broader framework of the Commission as an institution at the heart of Europe, while also combining multiple national perspectives.

The actor-oriented approach to writing the history of European integration is now no longer limited to the 'founding fathers' or political leaders. Scholars have shown how other individuals, such as **intellectuals, experts, and bureaucrats,** often embedded in transnational networks, provided the crucial technical and bureaucratic scaffolding of European cooperation. This scholarship is also closely connected to the broader historical concept of Europeanization as elaborated by Patel and Martin Conway. The Europe before the 'Europe of integration' comes into view here too: many of these actors were key figures in international organizations that pre-date the creation of the EC/EU. Patel and Wolfram Kaiser identified these actors as 'carriers of continuity', who often acted as bridge-builders between the interwar and postwar era in European cooperation. The role of experts as drivers of the 'hidden integration' of Europe through the transnational circulation of knowledge has been explored by Johan Schot and Wolfram Kaiser. Building on histories of science and technology, they showed how many cross-border issues in Europe required technical expertise, which subsequently became embedded in European governing structures.

Institutions

The creation of supranational institutions has been a key element of European integration since its inception. However, the institutions of the EC/EU only became objects of historical inquiry over the course of the 1990s. A major reason for this was the availability of **archival material**. In the 1970s, efforts commenced to organize the records of the EC institutions, a complicated division of labour between the archival services of the Community institutions in Brussels and the actual archives. These would go on to become the Historical Archives of the European Union, housed at the European University Institute in Florence. An additional difficulty for historians was the thirty-year embargo on official papers and records. As a consequence, detailed work on the actual workings of the Community institutions in the 1960s only became possible in the 1990s.

Since then, scholarly work on the institutions of the EC/EU has proliferated, although an imbalance exists in terms of scholarly attention to the various European institutions. The **European Commission** in particular has been studied extensively, perhaps prompted by the tendency to regard the Commission as the most dynamic and original of the EC institutions, and as the 'driver of integration' in the formative years of European integration in particular. In recent years, the European Commission has also positioned itself as a driver of research into its own history, leading to a series titled *History and Memories of an Institution*, written by a consortium of historians. Three volumes in this series have been published, all of which are based not only on archival research but also on an oral history programme featuring interviews with officials who worked in the European Commission in the period under discussion. Volume I covers the years from 1958 to 1972; Volume II the years 1973 to 1986; and Volume III the period of 1986 to 2000.

The **European Council** has for a long time remained somewhat understudied in comparison with other institutions, and due to its intergovernmental character, it is often assessed in contrast with the supranational Commission. In this narrative, the debate between intergovernmental and supranational practices of integration, the European Council is often portrayed as the villain. Seeking to overcome this reductive vision, Emmanuel Mourlon-Druol argued that the institution of the European Council in 1974 represented one of the most significant institutional developments in the history of the EC, and that the Council was in fact a key contributor to the strengthening of the Community method (the decision-making processes in the EC/EU in which the supranational institutions take the lead). Instead of adhering to the traditional intergovernmental vs. supranational dichotomy, the European Council was able to establish itself as a hybrid institution, characterized by both intergovernmental and supranational elements. Luuk van Middelaar has referred to the increasing interconnection between the Community and intergovernmental realms in the history of European integration as the 'intermediate sphere', in which the states act collectively with European institutions, as opposed to the 'internal sphere', where administrative rules and procedures of the Treaties and Commission take precedence, and the 'outer sphere' of sovereign states and their interests. The European Council also became embedded in an evolving system of international summits, as Emmanuel Mourlon-Druol and Federico Romero have shown. They proposed that the emergence of the European Council, as well as other forums for summits such as the G7, were part of deliberate attempts at global governance, and represented a major transformation of the European and international institutional systems.

Scholarly work on the history of the **European Parliament** has also been subject to new perspectives and focal points. The majority of scholarship on the European Parliament focuses on the watershed moment of 1979 and the first direct elections, as well as on the post-1979 period with its changes in the EP's formal institutional powers. By contrast, more recent work offers a key innovation by de-emphasizing '1979' in the longer history of the European Parliament and its predecessor, the Common Assembly of the ECSC. In this line of work, scholars analyse the ways in which the European Parliament was able to establish itself as a representative institution in spite of its limited powers; its role in policymaking and institution-building; and its role as a discursive power and agenda-setter. Mechthild Roos has shown how the European Parliament, before its formal empowerment, gained informal power and influence through the supranational activism of the members of the European Parliament (MEPs). In doing so, the EP was able to carve out an agenda-setting role for itself, in particular in policy areas with strong ideational dimensions such as social policy. In the field of environmental policy, the European Parliament also established itself as an influential actor, as Jan-Henrik Meyer has researched. The European Parliament also became an important site for processes of socialization and Europeanization, as demonstrated by Ann-Christina Knudsen, demonstrating that MEPs conceived of their role as being Euro-parliamentarians, rather than members of a technocratic control institution. Furthermore, Koen van Zon has shown that to MEPs, democratization was primarily an institutional question and a matter of acquiring supranational power, rather than a question of politicizing internal and external relations and seeking to establish the EP as a political arena.

Scholarship on the **Court of Justice** has seen an upsurge in recent years, through two connected developments. First, the archives of the Court of Justice were finally opened only in 2015, a decision which quickly generated a range of research projects into the institution's history. Second, as a consequence, a thriving 'integration through law' research agenda has developed, often interdisciplinary in nature, in which the EC/EU is explored as a legal actor. One remarkable work is Fernanda Nicola and Bill Davies' interdisciplinary analysis of Court of Justice rulings, which emphasized its contingent and non-linear character. Dorte Sindbjerg Martinsen has explored the role of the ECJ through the lens of its famed (and often criticized) political power and role as 'master of integration'.

The process of European institution-building unfolded in interrelation with the emergence of a European **supranational bureaucracy**. The political dynamics between the EC/EU institutions and their personnel gave way to a particular administrative culture, with new European rules and norms. Scholarly contributions in this line of work aimed to combine both the institutional and actorial dimensions of the history of European integration, generating a trans- and supranational perspective on the role and influence of these networks of European civil servants. Katja Seidel has demonstrated how these European administrative elites had a vital influence on the European integration process, by devising and administering key European policies. Ann-Christina Knudsen and Morten Rasmussen have shown how the establishment of a range of committee structures was influential in the workings of the European political system, especially as the EC/EU's policy areas expanded throughout its history.

Non-state actors

Influenced by the post-Cold War globalization of the 1990s, the early 2000s saw a resurgence of scholarly interest in the concept of transnationalism, which greatly influenced historical writing on European integration. **Transnational perspectives** have diminished the weight of state-centric approaches in European integration history, giving way to an increased focus on the role and influence of non-state actors. A major contribution by Wolfram Kaiser,

Brigitte Leucht, and Morten Rasmussen aimed to recast the history of the European Union as the gradual emergence of a trans- and supranational polity at the European level. Drawing heavily on social science methodologies, the authors show the emergence, growth, and character of a transnational European political system. Crucially, this includes the 'formative phase of core Europe integration', which established the foundations for institutional and policy options that still influence the EU today. The role of transnational networks in European integration governance has been explored by Wolfram Kaiser, Brigitte Leucht, and Michael Gehler. While traditional political science scholarship on networks and governance locates its emergence in contemporary politics, the authors extend its temporal scope to the history and even pre-history of European integration. During the negotiations for the Schuman Plan, for instance, transnational policy networks made up of academics and other experts, civil servants, and non-state actors were crucial in shaping budding supranational institutional frameworks.

Historical scholarship into the role and influence of non-state actors in the European Community to a certain extent reflects the political and institutional priorities of the EC during that time. For instance, **agricultural organizations** were among the first organizations to create a 'European' presence for themselves in Brussels. Consequently, and also because of the prominence of agricultural politics in the history of European integration, the role and influence of agricultural organizations in the European Community is well-researched. The work of Carine Germond in particular has demonstrated the ways in which European farmers' groups have lobbied the European institutions as well as mobilized their constituencies in protest actions, thereby engaging in transnational societal mobilization (CHAPTER 3).

Similarly, European **trade unions** strengthened their presence at the EC level since the early 1950s. It has received ample scholarly attention as another example of an established societal interest, in particular from French historians. Christophe Degryse and Pierre Tilly wrote a history of the European Trade Union Confederation (ETUC), illuminating the European trade union movement in its political, economic, and social contexts. Francesco Petrini has shown how ETUC lobbied the European institutions for the regulation of workers' rights in multinational corporations. Others have directed their gaze at wider dimensions of trade union participation in European integration. As Matthew Broad has demonstrated, for instance, in the 1950s transnational trade unions were key players in the negotiations for the establishment of both the EEC and the European Free Trade Association (EFTA).

The prominence of market integration and economic policies in the EC/ EU has drawn **business groups** to Brussels but has also drawn scholars to the study of the role and influence of these business groups in the history of European integration. Maria Green Cowles was the first to demonstrate the involvement of the European Round Table of Industrialists (ERT) in the making of the SEA. Authors including Bastiaan van Apeldoorn and Anjo Har- ryvan followed in her footsteps, providing further insights into this group's role in the EC. Other business clubs have also been investigated by authors including Alexis Drach, Anne-Myriam Dutrieue, Michel Dumoulin, and Sigfrido Ramírez Perez. The European peak organization for national busi- ness associations, the Union des Industries de la Communauté Européenne (Union of Industrial and Employers' Confederations of Europe, UNICE) is also topic of inquiry, in particular its influence on European competition policy as it was negotiated in the 1950s, as Werner Bührer and Laurent Warlouzet have investigated. The role of business in European integration has also been studied at a national level. For instance, Neil Rolling looked at British business, while Yohann Morival examined the case of France in this context.

The role of non-state actors in European integration history is further being explored by scholars working on the emergence and influence of interest groups in European polity-building and policymaking. The period of the 1970s has in recent years received particular scholarly attention, as this was a period when the European Community expanded its work to other policy areas beyond economic integration, while at the same time interest groups were seeking access to the EC (CHAPTER 4). Furthermore, many of these groups represented 'newer' societal interests that had emerged on the political agenda, such as the environment and consumer protection. As Wolfram Kaiser and Jan-Henrik Meyer have demonstrated, the actual involvement and influence of these non-state actors varied considerably: interest groups concerned with more traditional policies such as agriculture were less challenging, whereas non-state actors in the newly developing fields of development policy and environmental policy were eager for change. Focussing on the relationship between the EC and European citizens, Liesbeth van de Grift has shown how in the 1970s the presence of consumer and environmental groups was strengthened in 'Brussels' with the aim of making the European institutions more representative of modern society and responsive to citizens' demands.

Conclusion

Since Milward's challenge to the federalist narrative of European integration, its historiography has grown larger and become more diversified. These studies contributed significantly to our understanding of *what* the EC/EU has been, *why* it came to be, and *who* made it. This has been achieved through bridging the historiography of European integration with other fields of historical inquiry. The history of capitalism, the Cold War, decolonization, globalization, democracy, memory, technology, institutions, and business are nowadays all entangled with inquiry into the history of the EC/EU. This broadening also enabled closer dialogue between history and other disciplines, including political science, international relations, law, and economy. Historians currently often join forces with scholars representing these disciplines to study particular dimensions of the EC/EU. The history of European integration is not confined to museums but remains closely linked with the current European Union.

Moreover, the dynamic character of the historiography on European integration mirrors the dynamic character of European integration itself. Historians quickly respond to new challenges facing the EU. For example, the 2008 financial crisis spurred increased research on the EC/EU's economic policies, while Brexit drew attention to the phenomenon of disintegration and the study of Euroscepticism. Similarly, historians have recently begun examining EC/EU environmental policies. Future developments will undoubtedly prompt historians to define new research agendas.

The state of the art in the historiography of European integration sets the bar for future research high. Many topics have already been covered and the field often requires multi-lingual and multi-archival research. It would nowadays be hard to imagine a comprehensive study on one of EC/EU's policies without including perspectives of its multiple institutions, member states, and non-state actors. However, this abundance of policies and actors, and the many processes that European integration formed part of, should also encourage anyone interested in pursuing research on the history of European integration. Rather than providing an exhaustive review of the entire historiography of European integration, this chapter has aimed to facilitate such endeavours by offering a starting point and inspiration for new research projects.

Further reading

-   Di Donato, Michele. 'Landslides, Shocks, and New Global Rules: The US and Western Europe in the New International History of the 1970s.' *Journal of Contemporary History* 55, no. 1 (2020): 182–205.
-   Gilbert, Mark. 'Historicising European Integration History.' *European Review of International Studies* 8, no. 2 (2021): 221–40.

– Gilbert, Mark. 'Narrating the Process: Questioning the Progressive Story of European Integration.' *Journal of Common Market Studies* 46, no. 3 (2008): 641–62.

– Kaiser, Wolfram, and Antonio Varsori, eds. *European Union History: Themes and Debates*. Basingstoke: Palgrave Macmillan, 2010.

– Patel, Kiran Klaus. 'Widening and Deepening? Recent Advances in European Integration History.' *Neue Politische Literatur* 64, no. 2 (2019): 327–57.

– Warlouzet, Laurent. 'Dépasser la crise de l'histoire de l'intégration Européenne.' *Politique Européenne* 44, no. 2 (2014): 98–122.

About the authors

Koen van Zon is a postdoctoral researcher at Studio Europa Maastricht. His research revolves around the historical relation and tensions between the institutions of the European Community and European citizens. He is the author of *Heralds of European Democracy: Representation without Politicization in the European Community 1948–68* (Agenda Publishing, 2024).

Matthew Broad is an Assistant Professor in History and International Studies in the Institute for History, Leiden University. His research examines the history and politics of European integration since 1945, including non-EU integration, enlargement, Euroscepticism, and Anglo-Nordic relations. His publications include *Britain, the Division of Western Europe and the Creation of EFTA, 1955–63* (Palgrave Macmillan, 2022 – with Richard T. Griffiths).

Aleksandra Komornicka is an Assistant Professor at the Faculty of Arts and Social Sciences at Maastricht University. She specializes in the international history of the 20th century, in particular in the history of European integration, business, and the Cold War. She is the author of *Poland and European East-West Cooperation in the 1970s The Opening Up* (Routledge, 2023).

Paul Reef is PhD Candidate and Lecturer in International and Political History at Radboud University, Nijmegen. His PhD research explores the transnational history of protest around the Olympic Games and Football World Cup, on which he has published in the *Routledge Handbook on Mega-Sporting Events and Human Rights* (Routledge, 2023).

Alessandra Schimmel is Lecturer in International and Political History at Radboud University, Nijmegen. Her PhD research at Utrecht University examines the history of consumer representation and activism in the European Community.

Jorrit Steehouder is Assistant Professor History of International Relations at Utrecht University. Currently, his research revolves around the economic aspects of European security in the first half of the twentieth century, with special attention to dynamics between East, West and Central Europe.

Abbreviations

The list below contains all acronyms and abbreviations used in this book. An English abbreviation is provided for nearly all institutions. In some exceptional cases, the French or German original name is added in brackets. For official translations of EU terminology and abbreviations in all EU languages, see: IATE (https://iate.europa.eu/).

ACC	Allied Control Council
AFD	Alternative für Deutschland (Alternative for Germany)
AI	Artificial Intelligence
BEUC	Bureau Européen des Unions de Consommateurs (European Bureau of Consumers' Unions)
CAP	Common Agricultural Policy
CBAM	Carbon Border Adjustment Mechanism
CEE	Central and Eastern Europe
CEEC	Conference for European Economic Cooperation
CFSP	Common Foreign and Security Policy
CMEA	Council for Mutual Economic Assistance
COPA	Comité des Organisations Professionelles Agricoles (Committee of Professional Agricultural Organisations)
COREPER	Comité des représentants permanents (Committee of Permanent Representatives)
CSCE	Conference of Security and Cooperation in Europe
DG	Directorate-General
EAEC	European Atomic Energy Community
EBU	European Banking Union
EC	European Community/European Communities
ECB	European Central Bank
ECHR	European Convention for the Protection of Human Rights and Fundamental Freedoms
ECJ	European Court of Justice
ECMT	European Conference of Ministers of Transport
ECSC	European Coal and Steel Community
ECU	European Currency Unit
EDC	European Defence Community
EDF	European Development Fund
EEA	European Economic Area
EEAS	European External Action Service

EESC	European Economic and Social Committee
EEC	European Economic Community
EFO	Economic and Financial Organization
EFRD	European Fund for Regional Development
EFSF	European Financial Stability Facility
EFTA	European Free Trade Association
EGD	European Green Deal
EIB	European Investment Bank
ELEC	European League for Economic Cooperation
EM	European Movement
EMS	European Monetary System
EMU	Economic and Monetary Union
EMU	European Monetary Union
ENP	European Neighbourhood Policy
EP	European Parliament
EPC	European Political Community
EPC	European Political Cooperation
EPPO	European Public Prosecutor's Office
EPU	European Payments Union
ERT	European Round Table of Industrialists
ESF	European Social Fund
ESM	European Stability Mechanism
ETS	Emissions Trading System
ETUC	European Trade Union Confederation
EU	European Union
FDI	Fratelli d'Italia (Brothers of Italy)
FRG	Federal Republic of Germany
FTA	Free Trade Area
GATT	General Agreement on Tariffs and Trade
GDP	gross domestic product
GDPR	General Data Protection Regulation
GDR	German Democratic Republic
IAR	International Authority for the Ruhr
IGC	Intergovernmental Conference
ILO	International Labour Organization
IMF	International Monetary Fund
JHA	Justice and Home Affairs
LIG	Liberal intergovernmentalism
M5S	Movimento 5 Stelle (Five Star Movement)
MEP	Member of the European Parliament

MPF	Mouvement pour la France (Movement for France)
NATO	North Atlantic Treaty Organization
NGEU	Next Generation European Union
NGOS	Non-Governmental Organizations
OEEC	Organization for European Economic Cooperation
OPEC	Organization of the Petroleum Exporting Countries
OSCE	Organization for Security and Cooperation in Europe
PHARE	Poland and Hungary Assistance for Reconstruction of Economy
PIS	Prawo i Sprawiedliwość (Law and Justice Party)
PVV	Partij voor de Vrijheid (Dutch Freedom Party)
QMV	qualified majority voting
SALT	Strategic Arms Limitation Talks
SEA	Single European Act
SGP	Stability and Growth Pact
TCE	Treaty Establishing a Constitution for Europe
TEU	Treaty on European Union
TFEU	Treaty on the Functioning of the European Union
UEF	Union of European Federalists
UK	United Kingdom
UKIP	United Kingdom Independence Party
UN	United Nations
UNECE	United Nations Economic Commission for Europe
UNICE	Union des confédérations de l'industrie et des employeurs d'Europe (Union of Industrial and Employers' Confederations of Europe)
UNRRA	United Nations Relief and Rehabilitation Administration
US	United States
WEU	Western European Union
WTO	World Trade Organization

Bibliography

Albors-Llorens, Albertina, Catherine Barnard, and Briggite Leucht, eds. *Cassis de Dijon: 40 Years On*. Oxford: Hart Publishing, 2021.

Andry, Aurélie Dianara. *Social Europe, the Road Not Taken: The Left and European Integration in the Long 1970s*. Oxford Studies in Modern European History. Oxford: Oxford University Press, 2022.

Apeldoorn, Bastiaan van. *Transnational Capitalism and the Struggle Over European Integration*. London: Routledge, 2002.

Apeldoorn, Bastiaan van. 'Transnational Class Agency and European Governance: The Case of the European Round Table of Industrialists.' *New Political Economy* 5, no. 2 (2000): 157–81.

Aqui, Lindsay. *The First Referendum: Reassessing Britain's Entry to Europe, 1973–75*. Manchester: Manchester University Press, 2020.

Ballor, Grace. *Enterprise and Integration: Big Business and the Making of the Single European Market*. Cambridge: Cambridge University Press, forthcoming.

Ballor, Grace. 'Liberal Environmentalism: The Public-Private Production of European Emissions Standards.' *Business History Review* 97, no. 3 (2023): 575–601.

Bicchi, Federica, and Daniel Schade. 'Whither European Diplomacy? Long-Term Trends and the Impact of the Lisbon Treaty.' *Cooperation and Conflict* 57, no. 1 (2022): 3–24.

Bickerton, Christopher J., Dermot Hodson, and Uwe Puetter, eds. *The New Intergovernmentalism: States and Supranational Actors in the Post-Maastricht Era*. Oxford: Oxford University Press, 2015.

Börzel, Tanja A. 'European Integration and the War in Ukraine: Just Another Crisis?' *JCMS: Journal of Common Market Studies* vol 61, no. 1 (2023): 14–30

Bradford, Anu. *The Brussels Effect: How the European Union Rules the World*. Oxford: Oxford University Press, 2020.

Broad, Matthew, and Richard T. Griffiths. *Britain, the Division of Western Europe and the Creation of EFTA, 1955–1963*. Cham: Palgrave Macmillan, 2022.

Broad, Matthew, and Suvi Kansikas, eds. *European Integration Beyond Brussels: Unity in East and West Europe Since 1945*. Cham: Springer International Publishing, 2020.

Brown, Megan. *The Seventh Member State. Algeria, France, and the European Community*. Cambridge, MA: Harvard University Press, 2022.

Brunnermeier, Markus K., Harold James, and Jean-Pierre Landau. *The Euro and the Battle of Ideas*. Princeton: Princeton University Press, 2016.

Bührer, Werner, and Laurent Warlouzet. 'Regulating Markets: Peak Business Associations and the Origins of European Competition Policy.' *In Societal Actors in European Integration*, edited by Wolfram Kaiser and Jan-Henrik Meyer, 59–83. Palgrave Studies in European Union Politics. London: Palgrave Macmillan, 2013.

Bussière, Éric, Vincent Dujardin, Michel Dumoulin, N. Piers Ludlow, Jan Willem Brouwer, and Pierre Tilly, eds. *The European Commission, 1973–86: History and Memories of an Institution*. Luxembourg: Office for Official Publications of the European Communities, 2014.

Chakrabarty, Dipesh. 'Provincializing Europe: Postcoloniality and the Critique of History.' *Cultural Studies* 6, no. 3 (1992): 337–57.

Chassé, Daniel Speich. 'Towards a Global History of the Marshall Plan: European Post-War Reconstruction and the Rise of Development Economic Expertise.' In *Industrial Policy in Europe after 1945*, edited by Christian Grabas and Alexander Nützenadel, 187–212. London: Palgrave Macmillan, 2014.

Cianetti, Licia, James Dawson, and Seán Hanley. 'Rethinking "Democratic Backsliding" in Central and Eastern Europe – Looking Beyond Hungary and Poland.' *East European Politics* 34, no. 3 (2018): 243–56.

Clavin, Patricia. *Securing the World Economy: The Reinvention of the League of Nations, 1920–1946.* Oxford: Oxford University Press, 2013.

Conway, Martin. 'Brexit: 100 Years in the Making.' *Contemporary European History* 28, no. 1 (2019): 6–9.

Conway, Martin. *Western Europe's Democratic Age, 1945–1968.* Princeton: Princeton University Press, 2020.

Conway, Martin, and Kiran Klaus Patel, eds. *Europeanization in the Twentieth Century.* London: Palgrave Macmillan, 2010.

Coppolaro, Lucia. *The Making of a World Trading Power: The European Economic Community (EEC) in the GATT Kennedy Round Negotiations (1963–67).* London: Routledge, 2013.

Cowles, Maria Green. 'Setting the Agenda for a New Europe: The ERT and EC 1992.' *JCMS: Journal of Common Market Studies* 33, no. 4 (1995): 501–26.

Crump, Laurien, and Angela Romano. 'Challenging the Superpower Straitjacket (1965–1975): Multilateralism as an Instrument of Smaller Powers.' In *Margins for Manoeuvre in Cold War Europe: The Influence of Smaller Powers*, edited by Laurien Crump and Susanna Erlandsson, 13–31. London: Routledge, 2018.

D'Auria, Matthew, and Jan Vermeiren, eds. *Visions and Ideas of Europe during the First World War: Ideas beyond Borders.* London: Routledge, 2020.

De Angelis, Emma, and Eirini Karamouzi. 'Enlargement and the Historical Origins of the European Community's Democratic Identity.' *Contemporary European History* 25, no. 3 (2016): 439–58.

Degryse, Christophe, and Pierre Tilly. *1973–2013: 40 Years of History of the European Trade Union Confederation.* Brussels: ETUI, 2013.

Di Donato, Michele. 'Landslides, Shocks, and New Global Rules: The US and Western Europe in the New International History of the 1970s.' *Journal of Contemporary History* 55, no. 1 (2020): 182–205.

Diefendorf, Jeffrey M., Axel Frohn, and Hermann-Josef Rupieper, eds. *American Policy and the Reconstruction of West Germany, 1945–1955.* Cambridge: Cambridge University Press, 1994.

Dinan, Desmond, Neill Nugent, and William E. Paterson, eds. *The European Union in Crisis.* London: Palgrave, 2017.

Diogo, Maria Paula, and Dirk van Laak. *Europeans Globalizing: Mapping, Exploiting, Exchanging.* Making Europe: Technology and Transformations, 1850–2000. London: Palgrave Macmillan, 2016.

Drach, Alexis. 'Reluctant Europeans? British and French Commercial Banks and the Common Market in Banking (1977–1992).' *Enterprise & Society* 21, no. 3 (2020): 768–98.

Dujardin, Vincent, Éric Bussière, N. Piers Ludlow, Federico Romano, Dieter Schlenker, and Antonio Varsori, eds. *The European Commission 1986–2000: History and Memories of an Institution.* Luxembourg: Publications Office of the European Union, 2019.

Dumoulin, Michel, ed. *The European Commission, 1958–72: History and Memories of an Institution.* Luxembourg: Office for Official Publications of the European Communities, 2007.

Dumoulin, Michel, and Anne-Myriam Dutrieue. *La Ligue européenne de coopération économique, 1946–1981: un groupe d'étude et de pression dans la construction européenne.* Bern: Peter Lang, 1993.

Dyson, Kenneth, and Ivo Maes, eds. *Architects of the Euro: Intellectuals in the Making of the European Union.* Oxford: Oxford University Press, 2016.

Dyson, Kenneth, and Kevin Featherstone. *The Road to Maastricht: Negotiating Economic and Monetary Union.* Oxford: Oxford University Press, 1999.

Eichengreen, Barry. *The European Economy since 1945: Coordinated Capitalism and Beyond.* Cambridge: Cambridge University Press, 2007.

Eilstrup-Sangiovanni, Mette, ed. *Debates on European Integration: A Reader.* Basingstoke: Palgrave Macmillan, 2006.

Elvert, Jürgen, and Wolfram Kaiser, eds. *European Union Enlargement.* Routledge Advances in European Politics. Abingdon: Routledge, 2004.

Fickers, Andreas, and Pascal Griset. *Communicating Europe: Technologies, Information, Events.* Making Europe: Technology and Transformations, 1850–2000. London: Palgrave Macmillan. 2019.

Fischer, Conan. *A Vision of Europe: Franco-German Relations during the Great Depression, 1929–1932.* Oxford: Oxford University Press, 2017.

Føllesdal, Andreas, and Simon Hix. 'Why is There a Democratic Deficit in the EU? A Response to Majone and Moravcsik.' *JCMS: Journal of Common Market Studies* 44, no. 3 (2006): 533–62

Garavini, Giuliano. *After Empires: European Integration, Decolonization, and the Challenge from the Global South 1957–1986.* Translated by Richard R. Nybakken. Oxford Studies in Modern European History. Oxford: Oxford University Press, 2012.

Geddes, Andrew Peter. *Britain and the European Union.* The European Union Series. Basingstoke: Palgrave Macmillan, 2013.

Germond, Carine. 'An Emerging Anti-Reform Green Front? Farm Interest Groups Fighting the 'Agriculture 1980' Project, 1968–72.' *European Review of History: Revue Européenne d'histoire* 22, no. 3 (2015): 433–50.

Germond, Carine. 'Defending the Status Quo: Agricultural Interest Groups and the Challenges of Overproduction.' *Comparativ. Zeitschrift für Globalgeschichte und vergleichende Gesellschaftsforschung* 20, no. 3 (2010): 62–82.

Gfeller, Aurélie Elisa. *Building a European Identity: France, the United States, and the Oil Shock, 1973–1974.* Berghahn Monographs in French Studies, vol. 12. New York: Berghahn, 2012.

Gilbert, Mark. 'Historicising European Integration History.' *European Review of International Studies* 8, no. 2 (2021): 221–40.

Gilbert, Mark. 'Narrating the Process: Questioning the Progressive Story of European Integration.' *JCMS: Journal of Common Market Studies* 46, no. 3 (2008): 641–62.

Gilbert, Mark, and Daniele Pasquinucci. *Euroscepticisms: The Historical Roots of a Political Challenge.* Leiden: Brill, 2020.

Gillingham, John. *Coal, Steel, and the Rebirth of Europe, 1945–1955: The Germans and French from Ruhr Conflict to Economic Community.* Cambridge: Cambridge University Press, 1991.

Godard, Simon. *Le laboratoire de l'internationalisme. Le CAEM et la construction du bloc socialiste.* Paris: Presses de Sciences Po, 2021.

Gray, Mark, and Alexander Stubb. 'The Treaty of Nice: Negotiating a Poisoned Chalice?' *JCMS: Journal of Common Market Studies* 392, vol. 1 (2001): 5–23.

Griffiths, Richard T. *Explorations in OEEC History.* OECD Historical Series. Paris: Organisation for Economic Co-operation and Development, 1997.

Grift, Liesbeth van de. 'Representing European Society: The Rise of New Representative Claims in 1970s European Politics.' *Archiv für Sozialgeschichte* 58 (2018): 263–278.

Grift, Liesbeth van de, and Wim van Meurs. 'Europeanizing Biodiversity: International Organizations as Environmental Actors.' In *Greening Europe: Environmental Protection in the Long Twentieth Century – A Handbook,* edited by Anna-Katharina Wöbse and Patrick Kupper, 419–446. Contemporary European History, vol. 1. Berlin: De Gruyter, 2022.

Grob-Fitzgibbon, Benjamin. *Continental Drift: Britain and Europe from the End of Empire to the Rise of Euroscepticism*. Cambridge: Cambridge University Press, 2016.

Haas, Ernst B. *The Uniting of Europe: Political Social and Economic Forces 1950–1957*. London: Stevens, 1958.

Hansen, Peo, and Stefan Jonsson. *Eurafrica: The Untold History of European Integration and Colonialism*. London: Bloomsbury, 2014.

Hetherington, Philippa, and Glenda Sluga. 'Liberal and Illiberal Internationalisms.' *Journal of World History* 31, no. 1 (2020): 1–9.

Hewitson, Mark, and Matthew D'Auria, eds. *Europe in Crisis: Intellectuals and the European Idea, 1917–1957*. New York: Berghahn, 2012.

Hiepel, Claudia, ed. *Europe in a Globalising World: Global Challenges and European Responses in the 'Long' 1970s*. Veröffentlichungen der Historiker-Verbindungsgruppe bei der Kommission der EG, vol. 15. Baden-Baden: Nomos, 2014.

Hodson, Dermot. *Circle of Stars: A History of the EU and the People Who Made It*. New Haven: Yale University Press, 2023.

Hoffmann, Stanley. *The European Sisyphus: Essays on Europe 1964–1994*. Boulder, CO: Westview, 1995.

Högselius, Per, Arne Kaijser, and Erik van der Vleuten. *Europe's Infrastructure Transition: Economy, War, Nature*. Making Europe: Technology and Transformations, 1850–2000. Basingstoke, 2015.

Hooghe, Liesbet, and Gary Marks. 'A Postfunctionalist Theory of European Integration: From Permissive Consensus to Constraining Dissensus.' *British Journal of Political Science* 39, no. 1 (2009): 1–23.

Hooghe, Liesbet, and Gary Marks. *Multi-Level Governance and European Integration*. Lanham, MD: Rowman & Littlefield, 2001.

Ikonomou, Haakon A., Aurélie Andry, and Rebekka Byberg, eds. *European Enlargement across Rounds and beyond Borders*. Routledge Advances in European Politics, vol 132. London: Routledge, 2017.

Irwin, Douglas A., Petros C. Mavroidis, and Alan O. Sykes. *The Genesis of GATT*. Cambridge: Cambridge University Press, 2008.

James, Harold. *International Monetary Cooperation since Bretton Woods*. Oxford: Oxford University Press, 1996.

James, Harold. *Making the European Monetary Union: The Role of the Committee of Central Bank Governors and the Origins of the European Central Bank*. Cambridge, MA: Belknap Press, 2012.

Jones, Erik, R. Daniel Kelemen, and Sophie Meunier. 'Failing Forward? Crises and Patterns of European Integration.' *Journal of European Public Policy* 28, no. 10 (2021): 1519–36

Judt, Tony. *Postwar: A History of Europe since 1945*. New York, NY: Penguin Books, 2006.

Judt, Tony. 'The Past is Another Country: Myth and Memory in Postwar Europe.' *Daedalus* 121, no. 4 (1992): 83–118.

Kaiser, Wolfram. *Christian Democracy and the Origins of European Union*. Cambridge: Cambridge University Press, 2007.

Kaiser, Wolfram. 'Clash of Cultures: Two Milieus in the European Union's "A New Narrative for Europe" Project.' *Journal of Contemporary European Studies* 23, no. 3 (2015): 364–77.

Kaiser, Wolfram. 'Limits of Cultural Engineering: Actors and Narratives in the European Parliament's House of European History Project.' *JCMS: Journal of Common Market Studies* 55, no. 3 (2017): 518–34.

Kaiser, Wolfram. 'One Narrative or Several? Politics, Cultural Elites, and Citizens in Constructing a "New Narrative for Europe."' *National Identities* 19, no. 2 (2017): 215–30.

Kaiser, Wolfram, and Antonio Varsori, eds. *European Union History: Themes and Debates*. Basingstoke: Palgrave Macmillan, 2010.

Kaiser, Wolfram, Brigitte Leucht, and Michael Gehler, eds. *Transnational Networks in Regional Integration: Governing Europe 1945–83*. Palgrave Studies in European Union Politics. Basingstoke, Palgrave Macmillan, 2014.

Kaiser, Wolfram, Brigitte Leucht, and Morten Rasmussen, eds. *The History of the European Union: Origins of a Trans- and Supranational Polity*. London: Routledge, 2008.

Kaiser, Wolfram, and Jan-Henrik Meyer. 'Non-State Actors in European Integration in the 1970s: Towards a Polity of Transnational Contestation.' *Comparativ. Zeitschrift für Globalgeschichte und vergleichende Gesellschaftsforschung* 20, no. 3 (2010): 7–24.

Kaiser, Wolfram, and Johan Schot. *Making Europe: Experts, Cartels, and International Organizations*. Making Europe: Technology and Transformations, 1850–2000. Basingstoke: Palgrave Macmillan, 2014.

Kaiser, Wolfram, and Richard McMahon, eds. *Transnational Actors and Stories of European Integration: Clash of Narratives*. London: Routledge, 2019.

Kansikas, Suvi. *Socialist Countries Face the European Community: Soviet-Bloc Controversies over East-West Trade*. Frankfurt am Main: Peter Lang, 2014.

Karamouzi, Eirini. *Greece, the EEC and the Cold War, 1974–1979*. London: Palgrave Macmillan UK, 2014.

Kelemen, R. Daniel. 'Will the European Union Escape its Autocracy Trap?' *Journal of European Public Policy*. Advance online publication (2024).

Knudsen, Ann-Christina. *Farmers on Welfare: The Making of Europe's Common Agricultural Policy*. Ithaca: Cornell University Press, 2009.

Knudsen, Ann-Christina, and Morten Rasmussen. 'A European System in the Making 1958–1970: The Relevance of Emerging Committee Structures.' *Journal of European Integration History*, 14, no. 1 (2008): 51–68.

Komornicka, Aleksandra. 'Stable Support, Scant Initiative: European Business Associations and Economic and Monetary Union, 1946–1992.' *Business History*. Advance online publication (2024).

Komornicka, Aleksandra. '"The Unity of Europe Is Inevitable": Poland and the European Economic Community in the 1970s.' *Cold War History* 20, no. 4 (2020): 483–501.

Krastev, Ivan. *After Europe*. Updated edition. Philadelphia: University of Pennsylvania Press, 2020.

Krotz, Ulrich, Kiran Klaus Patel, and Federico Romero. *Europe's Cold War Relations: The EC towards a Global Role*. New Approaches to International History. London: Bloomsbury, 2020.

Krumrey, Jacob. *The Symbolic Politics of European Integration: Staging Europe*. Cham: Springer International Publishing, 2018.

Kundnani, Hans. *Eurowhiteness: Culture, Empire and Race in the European Project*. London: Hurst & Company, 2023.

Laczó, Ferenc. 'Moderately Failing Forward: The EU in the Years 2004–2019.' In *European Integration Outside-In*, edited by Mathieu Segers and Steven Van Hecke. Vol. 1 of *The Cambridge History of the European Union*. Cambridge: Cambridge University Press, 2023. 163–186.

Laursen, Johnny, ed. *The Institutions and Dynamics of the European Community, 1973–83*. Baden-Baden: Nomos, 2014.

Leeuwen, Karin van. 'On Democratic Concerns and Legal Traditions: The Dutch 1953 and 1956 Constitutional Reforms "Towards" Europe.' *Contemporary European History* 21, no. 3 (2012): 357–74.

Leimgruber, Matthieu, and Matthias Schmelzer, eds. *The OECD and the International Political Economy since 1948*. Cham: Palgrave Macmillan, 2017.

Leucht, Brigitte. 'The Policy Origins of the European Economic Constitution.' *European Law Journal* 24, no. 2–3 (2018): 191–205.

Lindberg, Leon N., and Stuart A. Scheingold. *Europe's Would-Be Polity: Patterns of Change in the European Community*. Englewood Cliffs, NJ: Prentice-Hall, 1970.

Loth, Wilfried, ed. *Crises and Compromises: The European Project 1963–1969*. Baden-Baden: Nomos, 2001.

Ludlow, N. Piers. 'European Integration and the Cold War.' In *Crises and Détente*, edited by Melvyn P. Leffler and Odd Arne Westad, 179–97. Vol. 2 of *The Cambridge History of the Cold War*. Cambridge: Cambridge University Press, 2010.

Ludlow, N. Piers, ed. *European Integration and the Cold War: Ostpolitik-Westpolitik, 1965–1973*. Cold War History Series, vol. 16. London: Routledge, 2007.

Ludlow, N. Piers. 'European Integration in the 1980s: On the Way to Maastricht?' *Journal of European Integration History* 19, no. 1 (2013): 11–22.

Ludlow, N. Piers. 'From Deadlock to Dynamism: The European Community in the 1980s.' In *The Origins and Evolution of the EU*, edited by Desmond Dinan, 218–32. Oxford: Oxford University Press.

Ludlow, N. Piers. *Roy Jenkins and the European Commission Presidency, 1976–1980: At the Heart of Europe*. Basingstoke: Palgrave Macmillan, 2016.

Ludlow, N. Piers. 'The British Are Coming: The Arrival and Impact of the First Cohorts of British Fonctionnaires in the European Commission.' In *Teilungen Überwinden. Europäische und Internationale Geschichte im 19. und 20. Jahrhundert. Festschrift für Wilfried Loth*, edited by Michaela Bachem-Rehm, Claudia Hiepel, and Henning Türk, 517–30. München: Oldenbourg Verlag, 2014.

Ludlow, N. Piers. *The European Community and the Crises of the 1960s: Negotiating the Gaullist Challenge*. London: Routledge, 2006.

Ludlow, N. Piers. 'The Historical Roots of the "Awkward Partner" Narrative.' *Contemporary European History* 28, no. 1 (2019): 35–38.

Ludlow, Peter. *The Making of the European Monetary System: A Case Study of the Politics of the European Community. Butterworths European Studies*. London: Butterworth Scientific, 1982.

Lundestad, Geir. 'Empire by Invitation? The United States and Western Europe, 1945–1952.' *Journal of Peace Research* 23, no. 3 (1986): 263–77.

Maes, Ivo, and Ilaria Pasotti. *Robert Triffin: A Life. Oxford Studies in the History of Economics*. Oxford: Oxford University Press, 2021.

Manners, Ian. 'Normative Power Europe: A Contradiction in Terms?' *JCMS: Journal of Common Market Studies*, 40, no. 2 (2021): 235–58

Mark, James, Bogdan C. Iacob, Tobias Rupprecht, and Ljubica Spaskovska. *1989: A Global History of Eastern Europe: New Approaches to European History*. Cambridge: Cambridge University Press, 2019.

Mark, James, and Quinn Slobodian. 'Eastern Europe in the Global History of Decolonization.' In *The Oxford Handbook of the Ends of Empire*, edited by Martin Thomas and Andrew S. Thompson, 352–373. Oxford: Oxford University Press, 2018.

Martinsen, Dorte Sindbjerg. *An Ever More Powerful Court? The Political Constraints of Legal Integration   in the European Union*. Oxford: Oxford University Press, 2015.

Mazower, Mark. *Governing the World: The History of an Idea*. London: Penguin Books, 2013.

McKenzie, Francine. *GATT and Global Order in the Postwar Era*. Cambridge: Cambridge University Press, 2020.

McMahon, Richard, and Wolfram Kaiser. 'Narrative Ju-Jitsu: Counter-Narratives to European Union.' Journal of Contemporary European Studies 30, no. 1 (2022): 1–9.

Meyer, Jan-Henrik. 'Greening Europe? Environmental Interest Groups and the Europeanization of a New Policy Field.' *Comparativ. Zeitschrift für Globalgeschichte und vergleichende Gesellschaftsforschung*, 20, no. 3 (2010): 83–104.

Meyer, Jan-Henrik. 'Pushing for a Greener Europe: The European Parliament and Environmental Policy in the 1970s and 1980s.' *Journal of European Integration History* 27, no. (2021): 57–78.

Middelaar, Luuk van. *Alarums and Excursions: Improvising Politics on the European Stage*. Newcastle upon Tyne: Agenda Publishing, 2019.

Middelaar, Luuk van. *The Passage to Europe: How a Continent Became a Union*. New Haven: Yale University Press, 2013.

Milward, Alan. *The European Rescue of the Nation-State*. Second Edition. London: Routledge, 2000.

Milward, Alan. *The Reconstruction of Western Europe, 1945–51*. London: Methuen & Co., 1984.

Mitrany, David. *A Working Peace System: An Argument for the Functional Development of International Organization*. Oxford: Oxford University Press, 1943.

Möckli, Daniel. *European Foreign Policy during the Cold War: Heath, Brandt, Pompidou and the Dream of Political Unity*. London: I.B. Tauris, 2009.

Monnet, Jean. *Memoirs*. Garden City, NY: Doubleday & Company, 1978.

Moravcsik, Andrew. *The Choice for Europe: Social Purpose and State Power from Messina to Maastricht*. Ithaca, NY: Cornell University Press, 1998.

Moravcsik, Andrew, and Kalypso Nicolaïdis. 'Explaining the Treaty of Amsterdam: Interests, Influence, Institutions.' *JCMS: Journal of Common Market Studies* 37, no. 1 (1999): 59–85.

Morival, Yohann. 'Reassessing the Historical Dynamics of European Business Associations: The Genesis of UNICE, Late 1940s to 1970s.' *Business History* (2022).

Mourlon-Druol, Emmanuel. *A Europe Made of Money: The Emergence of the European Monetary System*. Cornell Studies in Money. Ithaca: Cornell University Press, 2012.

Mourlon-Druol, Emmanuel. 'Steering Europe: Explaining the Rise of the European Council, 1975–1986.' *Contemporary European History* 25, no. 3 (2016): 409–37.

Mourlon-Druol, Emmanuel, and Federico Romero, eds. *International Summitry and Global Governance: The Rise of the G7 and the European Council, 1974–1991*. Abingdon: Routledge, 2014.

Müller, Jan-Werner. *Contesting Democracy: Political Thought in Twentieth-Century Europe*. New Haven, CT: Yale University Press, 2011.

Müller, Uwe, and Dagmara Jajeśniak-Quast, eds. 'Comecon Revisited. Integration in the Eastern Bloc and Entanglements with the Global Economy.' Special issue, *Comparativ. Zeitschrift für Globalgeschichte und vergleichende Gesellschaftsforschung* 27, no. 5–6 (2017).

Nicola, Fernanda, and Bill Davies, eds. *EU Law Stories: Contextual and Critical Histories of European Jurisprudence*. Cambridge: Cambridge University Press 2017.

Nolan, Mary. *The Transatlantic Century: Europe and America, 1890–2010. New Approaches to European History*. Cambridge: Cambridge University Press, 2012.

Oldenziel, Ruth, and Mikael Hård. *Consumers, Tinkerers, Rebels: The People Who Shaped Europe*. Making Europe: Technology and Transformations, 1850–2000. Basingstoke: Palgrave Macmillan, 2018.

Olesen, Thorsten Borring. 'Back to the 1960s or Further Back? Brexit as a European Dilemma between Past and Future.' *Contemporary European History* 28, no. 1 (2019): 39–41.

Pagden, Anthony, ed. *The Idea of Europe: From Antiquity to the European Union*. Cambridge: Woodrow Wilson Center Press/Cambridge University Press, 2002.

Palm, Trineke. 'Interwar Blueprints of Europe: Emotions, Experience and Expectation.' *Politics and Governance* 6, no. 4 (2018): 135–143.

Pasture, Patrick. *Imagining European Unity since 1000 AD*. London: Palgrave Macmillan, 2015.

Pasture, Patrick. 'The EC/EU between the Art of Forgetting and the Palimpsest of Empire.'
    European Review 26, no. 3 (2018): 545–81.

Patel, Kiran Klaus, ed. *Fertile Ground for Europe? The History of European Integration and the
    Common Agricultural Policy since 1945.* Baden-Baden: Nomos, 2009.

Patel, Kiran Klaus. *Project Europe: A History.* Cambridge: Cambridge University Press, 2020.

Patel, Kiran Klaus. 'Provincialising European Union: Co-Operation and Integration in Europe
    in a Historical Perspective.' *Contemporary European History* 22, no. 4 (2013): 649–73.

Patel, Kiran Klaus. 'Something New under the Sun? The Lessons of Algeria and Greenland.'
    Brexit and Beyond: Rethinking the Futures of Europe, edited by Benjamin Martill and Uta
    Staiger, 114–20. London: UCL Press, 2018.

Patel, Kiran Klaus. *The New Deal: A Global History.* Princeton: Princeton University Press, 2016.

Patel, Kiran Klaus. 'Widening and Deepening? Recent Advances in European Integration History.'
    Neue Politische Literatur 64, no. 2 (2019): 327–57.

Patel, Kiran Klaus, and Heike Schweitzer, eds. *The Historical Foundations of EU Competition Law.*
    Oxford, Oxford University Press, 2013.

Petrini, Francesco. 'Demanding Democracy in the Workplace: The European Trade Union
    Confederation and the Struggle to Regulate Multinationals.' In *Societal Actors in European
    Integration*, edited by Wolfram Kaiser and Jan-Henrik Meyer, 151–72. Palgrave Studies in
    European Union Politics. London: Palgrave Macmillan, 2013.

Pierson, Paul. 'The Path to European Integration: A Historical Institutionalist Analysis.' *Compara-
    tive Political Studies* 29, no. 2 (1996): 123–63.

Popova, Maria, and Oxana Shevel. *Russia and Ukraine. Entangled Histories, Diverging States.*
    Cambridge: Polity Press, 2024.

Ramírez Pérez, Sigfrido. 'Crises and Transformations of European Integration: European Business
    Circles during the Long 1970s.' *European Review of History: Revue Européenne d'histoire*
    26, no. 4 (2019): 618–35.

Ramírez Pérez, Sigfrido. 'The Strange Non-Death of Federalism in the Historiography of European
    Integration.' *Politique européenne* 53, no. 3 (2016): 110–29.

Rasmussen, Morten. 'The Legal History of the European Union: Building a European Constitution.'
    In *Oxford Research Encyclopedia of Politics*, edited by Finn Laursen. Online publication.
    Oxford: Oxford University Press, 2019.

Rasmussen, Morten. 'Towards a Legal History of European Law.' *European Papers* 6, no. 2 (2021):
    923–32.

Rohan, Sally. *The Western European Union: International Politics between Alliance and Integration.*
    British Politics and Society, vol 30. London: Routledge, 2020.

Rollings, Neil. *British Business in the Formative Years of European Integration, 1945–1973.* Cambridge
    Studies in the Emergence of Global Enterprise. Cambridge: Cambridge University Press, 2007.

Romano, Angela. *From Détente in Europe to European Détente: How the West Shaped the Helsinki
    CSCE.* Brussels: Peter Lang, 2009.

Romano, Angela. 'Untying Cold War Knots: The EEC and Eastern Europe in the Long 1970s.' *Cold
    War History* 14, no. 2 (2014): 153–73.

Romano, Angela, and Federico Romero, eds. *European Socialist Regimes' Fateful Engagement
    with the West: National Strategies in the Long 1970s.* London: Routledge, 2021.

Romero, Federico, and Silvio Pons. 'Europe Between the Superpowers, 1968–1981.' In *Europe in
    the International Arena During the 1970s: Entering a Different World*, edited by Antonio
    Varsori and Guia Migani, 85–97. Brussels: Peter Lang, 2011.

Roos, Mechthild. *The Parliamentary Roots of European Social Policy: Turning Talk into Power.*
    Palgrave Studies in European Union Politics. Cham: Springer International Publishing, 2021.

Ruggie, John G. 'International Regimes, Transactions, and Change: Embedded Liberalism in the Postwar Economic Order.' *International Organization* 36, no. 2 (1982): 379–415.

Sayle, Timothy A. *Enduring Alliance: A History of NATO and the Postwar Global Order.* Ithaca, NY: Cornell University Press, 2019.

Schain, Martin, ed. *The Marshall Plan: Fifty Years After.* Europe in Transition: The NYU European Studies Series. New York: Palgrave, 2001.

Segers, Mathieu. *The Netherlands and European Integration, 1950 to Present.* Amsterdam: Amsterdam University Press, 2020.

Segers, Mathieu. *The Origins of European Integration: The Pre-History of Today's European Union, 1937–1951.* Cambridge: Cambridge University Press, 2023.

Seidel, Katja. 'DG IV and the Origins of a Supranational Competition Policy: Establishing an Economic Constitution for Europe.' In *The History of the European Union: Origins of a Trans- and Supranational Polity, 1950–1972*, edited by Wolfram Kaiser, Brigitte Leucht and Morten Rasmussen, 129–147. London: Routledge, 2008.

Seidel, Katja. *The Process of Politics in Europe: The Rise of European Elites and Supranational Institutions.* Library of European Studies 14. London: Tauris Academic Studies, 2010.

Sierp, Aline. 'EU Memory Politics and Europe's Forgotten Colonial Past.' *Interventions* 22, no. 6 (2020): 686–702.

Sierp, Aline. 'Europeanising Memory: The European Union's Politics of Memory.' In *Handbook on the Politics of Memory*, edited by Maria Mälksoo, 81–94. Cheltenham, Edward Elgar Publishing, 2023.

Sierp, Aline. *History, Memory, and Trans-European Identity: Unifying Divisions.* Routledge Studies in Modern European History, vol. 23. New York: Routledge, 2014.

Slobodian, Quinn. *Globalists: The End of Empire and the Birth of Neoliberalism.* Cambridge, MA: Harvard University Press, 2018.

Sluga, Glenda. *The Invention of International Order: Remaking Europe after Napoleon.* Princeton: Princeton University Press, 2021.

Sluga, Glenda, and Patricia Clavin, eds. *Internationalisms: A Twentieth-Century History.* Cambridge: Cambridge University Press, 2016.

Smith, Karen. *The Making of EU Foreign Policy: The Case of Eastern Europe.* Basingstoke: Palgrave Macmillan, 1999.

Steehouder, Jorrit. 'In the Name of Social Stability: The European Payments Union.' In *European Integration Outside-In*, edited by Mathieu Segers and Steven Van Hecke, 209–33. Vol. 1 of *The Cambridge History of the European Union.* Cambridge University Press, 2023.

Stevenson, David. 'The First World War and European Integration.' *The International History Review* 34, no. 4 (2012): 841–63.

Stinsky, Daniel. *International Cooperation in Cold War Europe: The United Nations Economic Commission for Europe, 1947–64.* London: Bloomsbury Academic, 2021.

Ther, Philipp. *Europe since 1989: A History.* Translated by Charlotte Hughes-Kreutzmüller. Princeton: Princeton University Press, 2016.

Tooze, Adam. *Crashed: How a Decade of Financial Crises Changed the World.* New York: Viking, 2018.

Trischler, Helmuth, and Martin Kohlrausch. *Building Europe on Expertise: Innovators, Organizers, Networkers.* Making Europe: Technology and Transformations, 1850–2000. Basingstoke: Palgrave Macmillan, 2014.

Usherwood, Simon. 'Realists, Sceptics and Opponents: Opposition to the EU's Constitutional Treaty.' *Journal of Contemporary European Research* 1, no. 2 (2005): 4–12.

Ventresca, Roberto. 'Neoliberal Thinkers and European Integration in the 1980s and the Early 1990s.' *Contemporary European History* 31, no. 1 (2022): 31–47.

Warlouzet, Laurent. 'A Flanking European Welfare State: The European Community's Social Dimension, from Brandt to Delors (1969–1993).' *Contemporary European History* 33, no. 1 (2024): 23–36.

Warlouzet, Laurent. 'Competition versus Planning: A Battle that Shaped European Integration.' In *European Integration Inside-Out*, edited by Mathieu Segers and Steven Van Hecke, 234–60. Vol 2 of *The Cambridge History of the European Union*. Cambridge: Cambridge University Press, 2023.

Warlouzet, Laurent. 'De Gaulle as a Father of Europe: The Unpredictability of the FTA's Failure and the EEC's Success (1956–58).' *Contemporary European History* 20, no. 4 (2011): 419–34.

Warlouzet, Laurent. 'Dépasser la crise de l'histoire de l'intégration Européenne.' *Politique Européenne* 44, no. 2 (2014): 98–122.

Warlouzet, Laurent. *Governing Europe in a Globalizing World: Neoliberalism and Its Alternatives Following the 1973 Oil Crisis*. London: Routledge, 2017.

Warlouzet, Laurent, and Tobias Witschke. 'The Difficult Path to an Economic Rule of Law: European Competition Policy, 1950–91.' *Contemporary European History* 21, no. 3 (2012): 437–55.

Wassenberg, Birte. *History of the Council of Europe*. Strasbourg: Council of Europe Publishing, 2013.

Weller, Shane. *The Idea of Europe: A Critical History*. Cambridge: Cambridge University Press, 2021.

Wiener, Antje, Tanja Börzel, and Thomas Risse, eds. *European Integration Theory*. 3rd ed. Oxford: Oxford University Press: 2019.

Wintle, Michael J. *The Image of Europe: Visualizing Europe in Cartography and Iconography*. Cambridge Studies in Historical Geography, vol. 44. Cambridge: Cambridge University Press, 2009.

Zaccaria, Benedetto. *The EEC's Yugoslav Policy in Cold War Europe, 1968–1980*. London: Palgrave Macmillan, 2016.

Zon, Koen van. *Heralds of a Democratic Europe: Representation without Politicization in the European Community, 1948–1968*. Newcastle upon Tyne: Agenda Publishing, 2024.

Index

For Product Safety Concerns and Information please contact our EU
representative GPSR@taylorandfrancis.com
Taylor & Francis Verlag GmbH, Kaufingerstraße 24, 80331 München, Germany

www.ingramcontent.com/pod-product-compliance
Lightning Source LLC
Chambersburg PA
CBHW050419280326
41932CB00013BA/1927